Lecture Notes in Computer Science 3134

Commenced Publication in 1973
Founding and Former Series Editors:
Gerhard Goos, Juris Hartmanis, and Jan van Leeuwen

Carmen Zannier   Hakan Erdogmus
Lowell Lindstrom (Eds.)

Extreme Programming and Agile Methods – XP/Agile Universe 2004

4th Conference on Extreme Programming and Agile Methods
Calgary, Canada, August 15-18, 2004
Proceedings

 Springer

Volume Editors

Carmen Zannier
University of Calgary, Department of Computer Science
2500 University Drive NW, Calgary, Alberta, Canada T2N 1N4
E-mail: zannierc@cpsc.ucalgary.ca

Hakan Erdogmus
National Research Council
Montreal Rd. M50, Ottawa, Ontario, Canada K1A 0R6
E-mail: hakan.erdogmus@nrc-cnrc.gc.ca

Lowell Lindstrom
Object Mentor, Inc.
501 North Riverside Drive, Suite 206, Gurnee, IL 60031, USA
E-mail: lindstrom@objectmentor.com

Library of Congress Control Number: 2004109934

CR Subject Classification (1998): D.1, D.2, D.3, F.3, K.4.3, K.6

ISSN 0302-9743
ISBN 3-540-22839-X Springer Berlin Heidelberg New York

Springer is a part of Springer Science+Business Media

springeronline.com

© Springer-Verlag Berlin Heidelberg 2004
Printed in Germany

Typesetting: Camera-ready by author, data conversion by Olgun Computergrafik
Printed on acid-free paper   SPIN: 11312239   06/3142   5 4 3 2 1 0

Preface

It was 1999 when *Extreme Programming Explained* was first published, making this year's event arguably the fifth anniversary of the birth of the XP/Agile movement in software development. Our fourth conference reflected the evolution and the learning that have occurred in these exciting five years as agile practices have become part of the mainstream in software development. These pages are the proceedings of XP Agile Universe 2004, held in beautiful Calgary, gateway to the Canadian Rockies, in Alberta, Canada.

Evident in the conference is the fact that our learning is still in its early stages. While at times overlooked, *adaptation* has been a core principle of agile software development since the earliest literature on the subject. The conference and these proceedings reinforce that principle. Although some organizations are able to practice agile methods in the near-pure form, most are not, reflecting just how radically innovative these methods are to this day. Any innovation must coexist with an existing environment and agile software development is no different. There are numerous challenges confronting IT and software development organizations today, with many solutions pitched by a cadre of advocates. Be it CMM, offshoring, outsourcing, security, or one of many other current topics in the industry, teams using or transitioning to Extreme Programming and other agile practices must integrate with the rest of the organization in order to succeed. The papers here offer some of the latest experiences that teams are having in those efforts.

XP Agile Universe 2004 consisted of workshops, tutorials, papers, panels, the Open Space session, the Educators' Symposium, keynotes, educational games and industry presentations. This wide range of activities was intended to provide an engaging experience for industry practitioners, leading consultants, researchers, academics, and students. Feedback from the 2003 conference was used to adjust the content to better suit the needs of the attendees. The sessions at the conference were selected through the dedicated work of the Track Chairs and the Program Committee, to whom we are extremely grateful. Their names are listed in the pages that follow and the contributions of these individuals to the experience of the attendees of the conference cannot be overstated. Over 100 submissions were received to the various activities, with roughly half accepted into the conference. Each submission was reviewed by at least 3 members of the Program Committee, with an average of just under 5 reviewers per submission. The accepted papers are presented in their entirety in these proceedings. Summaries of the workshops and tutorials are presented as a reference for those who attended the conference. The results of the Open Space session can be accessed via the conference website at xpuniverse.com or agileuniverse.com.

The invited speakers to the conference were Christopher Avery, Robert Biddle, Eric Evans, Alejandro Goyen, Craig Larman, Brian Marick, Robert C. Martin, Mary Poppendieck, and Herb Sutter. These speakers represent the breadth and depth of the conference in terms of three main threads: technical practices; business and project management; and teamwork.

The tutorials and workshops continued the trend beyond the programming trenches, focusing primarily on requirements, project management, and acceptance-testing techniques, with some introductory sessions for attendees new to extreme programming and agile practices. The conference also continued its history with hands-on programming events which allowed attendees to join projects that ran throughout the conference using the tools and practices common on agile teams.

In these proceedings, one can find a rich set of papers reflective of the experiences of leading practitioners. Eighteen technical and research papers, experience reports, and educators' symposium papers were accepted out of a total of 45 submissions, representing an acceptance rate of 40%. A number of papers provide advanced discussion on tools and techniques for testing and the trend towards combining the requirements, testing, and specification activities. Three papers discuss methods for better understanding and expressing the customer or user needs in an agile way. For readers who are confronted with many of the challenges faced by today's environment, such as security concerns, CMM auditing, and offshore development teams, there are representative papers describing the use of agile development techniques in those environments.

We are deeply indebted to the organizing committee and the conference sponsors for providing the infrastructure for making the conference happen. The content of the conference and these proceedings would not have been possible without the submissions and all of the effort that goes into them. For those courageous enough to submit their work to the conference, we thank and salute you. But mostly, we thank the attendees, for supporting the conference, giving it its positive energy, and making it the magical gathering that it has become.

August 2004   Lowell Lindstrom and Hakan Erdogmus

Program Chairs

Hakan Erdogmus National Research Council Canada
Lowell Lindstrom Object Mentor

Track Chairs

Tutorials Brian Button, Agile Solutions Group
Workshops Dave Astels, ThoughtWorks, Inc.
Grigori Melnik, University of Calgary
Panels, Short Activities Mike Cohn, Mountain Goat Software
Educators' Symposium Rick Mercer, University of Arizona
Open Space, Birds-of-a-Feather Ann Anderson, First Data Corporation
William Wake, Independent Consultant

Organizing Committee

General Chair Lance Welter, Object Mentor
Conference Coordinator Jennifer Goodsen, RADsoft
Calgary Coordinator Janet Gregory, Wireless Matrix
Social Fun Committee John Goodsen, RADsoft
Sponsorship and Exhibits Lance Welter, Object Mentor
Web Master Micah Martin, Object Mentor
Community Liaisons US – Alex Viggio
Canada – Shaun Smith
Academic Liaison Frank Maurer, University of Calgary
Proceedings Coordinator Carmen Zannier, University of Calgary
On-site Logistics Janet Gregory, Wireless Matrix
Information Coordinators Talisha Jefferson, Object Mentor
Susan Rosso, Object Mentor

Educators' Symposium Committee

Rick Mercer University of Arizona
Joe Bergin Pace University
Robert Biddle Carleton University
Jim Caristi Valparaiso University
Jutta Eckstein Independent Consultant
James Grenning Object Mentor
Diana Larsen Industrial Logic
Grigori Melnik University of Calgary
Rick Mugridge University of Auckland
Daniel Steinberg O'Reilly Networks
Eugene Wallingford University of Northern Iowa

Open Space and Birds-of-a-Feather Committee

Ann Anderson	First Data Corporation
Lisa Crispin	Fast401k
J.B. Rainsberger	Diaspar Software Services
William Wake	Independent Consultant

Program Committee

Ann Anderson	First Data Corporation
Jennitta Andrea	Clearstream Consulting
Ken Auer	Role Model Software
Mike Beedle	e-Architects Inc.
Robert Biddle	Carleton University
Jim Coplien	Vrije Universiteit Brussel
Alain Desilets	National Research Council Canada
Dwight Deugo	Carleton University
Armin Eberlein	American University of Sharjah
Jutta Eckstein	Independent Consultant
Alejandro Goyen	Microsoft
John Favaro	Consulenza Informatica
Steve Fraser	Independent Consultant
John Grundy	University of Auckland
John Goodsen	RADSoft
Philip Johnson	University of Hawaii
Brian Hanks	University of California
Chet Hendrickson	HendricksonXP
Michael Hill	Independent Consultant
Paul Hodgetts	Agile Logic
Andy Hunt	The Pragmatic Programmers
Ron Jeffries	XPProgramming
Bil Kleb	NASA
Jykri Kontio	Helsinki University of Technology
Philippe Kruchten	University of British Columbia
Tom Kubit	Gene Codes Forensics
Manfred Lange	Independent Consultant
Diana Larsen	Industrial Logic
Jim Leask	Sybase
Tim Mackinnon	Connextra
Brian Marick	Testing Foundations
Robert C. Martin	Object Mentor
Frank Maurer	University of Calgary
Pete McBreen	Software Craftsmanship
Todd Medlin	SAS Institute

Grigori Melnik	University of Calgary
Steve Mellor	Project Technology
Granville Miller	Borland
Maurizio Morisio	Politecnico di Torino
Rick Mugridge	University of Auckland
Gary Pollice	Worcester Polytechnic Institute
Linda Rising	Independent Consultant
Ken Schwaber	Agile Alliance
David Stotts	University of North Carolina
Shaun Smith	Sandbox Systems
Oryal Tanir	Bell Canada
Dave Thomas	The Pragmatic Programmer
Dave Thomas	Bedarra Research Labs
Jim Tomayko	Carnegie Mellon University
Marco Torchiano	Politecnico di Torino
David Trowdridge	Microsoft
Jay Turpin	Intel
William Wake	Independent Consultant
Don Wells	ExtremeProgramming.org
Frank Westphal	Independent Consultant
Laurie Williams	North Carolina State University
William Wood	NASA

Sponsoring Institutions

Galaxy Class	Object Mentor
	Microsoft
	ThoughtWorks, Inc.
	Valtech Technologies, Inc.
Star Class	ClearStream Consulting, Inc.
	Rally Software Development
	BrightSpot Consulting
Satellite Class	VersionOne
	RADSoft
Media Partners	Software Development Magazine
	DevTown Station
	Integration Developer News
	Java Developer's Journal
	Better Software Magazine
	Linux Journal
	Cutter Consortium

Table of Contents

Process Adaptations

Educators' Symposium

Workshop Summaries

Panels

Tutorials

Combining Formal Specifications
with Test Driven Development*

Hubert Baumeister

Institut für Informatik
Ludwig-Maximilians-Universität München
Oettingenstr. 67, D-80538 München, Germany
baumeist@informatik.uni-muenchen.de

Abstract. In the context of test driven development, tests specify the behavior of a program before the code that implements it, is actually written. In addition, they are used as main source of documentation in XP projects, together with the program code. However, tests alone describe the properties of a program only in terms of examples and thus are not sufficient to completely describe the behavior of a program. In contrast, formal specifications allow to generalize these example properties to more general properties, which leads to a more complete description of the behavior of a program. Specifications add another main artifact to XP in addition to the already existent ones, i.e. code and tests. The interaction between these three artifacts further improves the quality of both software and documentation. The goal of this paper is to show that it is possible, with appropriate tool support, to combine formal specifications with test driven development without loosing the agility of test driven development.

1   Introduction

Extreme Programming advocates test driven development where tests are used to specify the behavior of a program before the program code is actually written. Together with using the simplest design possible and intention revealing program code, tests are additionally used as a documentation of the program. However, tests are not sufficient to completely define the behavior of a program because they are only able to test properties of a program by example and do not allow to state general properties. The latter can be achieved using formal specifications, e.g. using Meyer's design by contract [21].

As an example we consider the function primes, that computes for a given natural number n a list containing all prime numbers up to and including n. Tests can only be written for special arguments of the primes function, e.g. that primes(2) should produce the list with the number 2 as its only element, and that primes(1553) is supposed to yield the list of prime numbers from 2 up to 1533. Actually, a program that behaves correctly w.r.t. these tests could have the set of prime numbers hard coded for these particular inputs and return arbitrary lists for all other arguments. One solution is to move from tests to specifications, which allow to generalize the tested properties. For example, the behavior of primes would be expressed by a formal specification stating that the result of the function primes(n) contains exactly the prime numbers from 2 up to n, for all natural numbers n.

---

* This research has been partially sponsored by the EC 5th Framework project AGILE: Architectures for Mobility (IST-2001-32747)

C. Zannier et al. (Eds.): XP/Agile Universe 2004, LNCS 3134, pp. 1–12, 2004.

This example shows that formal specifications provide a more complete view on the behavior of programs than tests alone. However, while it is easy to run tests to check that a program complies with the tests, the task of showing that a program satisfies a given specification is in general more complex. To at least validate a program w.r.t. a specification, one can use the specification to generate run-time assertions and use these to check that the program behaves correctly.

The study of formal methods for program specification and verification has a long history. Hoare and Floyd pioneered the development of formal methods in the 1960s by introducing the Hoare calculus for proving program correctness as well as the notions of pre-/postconditions, invariants, and assertions [13, 10]. Their ideas were gradually developed into fully fledged formal methods geared towards industrial software engineering, e.g. the Vienna Development Method (VDM) developed at IBM [17], Z [23], the Java Modeling Language (JML) [19] and, more recently, the Object Constraint Language (OCL) [25] – which again originated at IBM – used to specify contraints on objects in UML diagrams. For an overview of formal methods and their applications refer to the WWW virtual library on formal methods [5].

An important use of formal specifications is the documentation of program behavior without making reference to an implementation. This is often needed for frameworks and libraries, where the source code is not available in most cases and the behavior is only informally described. In general, the documentation provided by a formal specification is both more precise and more concise compared to the implementation code because the implementation only describes the algorithm used by a method and not what it achieves. Not only the literature on formals methods, but also in the literature on the pragmatics of programming, e.g. [15, 20], recommends to make explicit the assumptions on the code using specifications because this improves the software quality.

The goal of this paper is to show that it is possible, with appropriate tool support, to combine formal specifications with test driven development without loosing the agility of the latter. This is done by using the tests, that drive the development of the code, also to drive the development of the formal specification. By generating runtime assertions from the specification it is possible to check for inconsistencies between code, specifications, and tests. Each of the three artifacts improves the quality of the other two, yielding better code quality and better program documentation in the form of a validated formal specification of the program.

Our method is exemplified by using the primes example with Java as the programming language, JUnit[1] as the testing framework, and the Java Modeling Language (JML) [19] for the formulation of class invariants and pre- and postconditions for methods. We use JML since JML specifications are easily understood by programmers, and because it comes with a runtime assertion checker, [6], which allows to check invariants and pre- and postconditions of methods at runtime.

2   Formal Specifications and Tests

As with test driven development, in our proposed methodology, tests are written before the code. Either now or after several iterations of test and code development, the prop-

---

[1] www.junit.org

erties that underly the tests are generalized into formal JML-specifications. We then generate assertions from these specifications using the JML runtime assertion checker. The invariants and pre- and postconditions are finally validated during test runs. Any inconsistency between code, tests, and formal specification will result in an exception. This leads to additional confidence in the code, the tests, and the specification. Making the specification underlying a set of tests explicit may reveal that some tests are still missing. On the other hand, an exception thrown by the assertion checker is the result of an error either in the code or in the specification. The method we propose has 5 steps:

1. Write the test
2. Implement the code
3. Refactor the code
4. Generalize the tests to a specification, and
5. Refactor the specification

Each of the steps is performed as needed, therefore not all the steps need to appear in each iteration of our method.

2.1 Example

We continue the primes examples, introduced in Section 1, with Java as implementation language and the JUnit test framework. The goal is to implement a static member function `primes(int n)` in class `Primes` that returns a list containing an integer object if, and only if it is a prime number in the range from 2 up to and including n. The sequence of tests used in this paper follows closely that of Beck and Newkirk [3], which uses the `primes` function as an example for refactoring.

Step 1: Write the test. A first test for the primes function is to assert that `primes(0)` returns the empty list.

```
public void testZero() {
    List primes = Primes.primes(0);
    assertTrue(primes.isEmpty());
}
```

Step 2: Implement the code. The obvious implementation just returns the empty list.

```
public static List primes(int n) {
    return new LinkedList();
}
```

Step 3: Refactor the code. Since the above code does not suggest any refactorings, we omit the code refactoring step.

Step 4: Generalize the tests to a specification. The following JML specification states that if n is 0 then the result should be the empty list.

```
public behavior
  requires n == 0;
  ensures \result.isEmpty();
```

The precondition is n == 0 and is given by the `requires` clause, and the postcondition is \result.isEmpty() and is given by the `ensures` clause. The keyword \result represents the result of the method. The keywords `public behavior` indicate that the following is a public specification for the method `primes(int n)`. Note that the precondition n == 0 makes it obvious that we are not yet done with specifying and implementing the primes method as we want our method to work also with other inputs than 0.

Using the JML assertion generator, assertions for the pre- and postconditions of the JML specification are generated and integrated in the class file of class Primes. Now the tests are run again and a JML exception is thrown if a precondition or a postcondition is violated.

Step 5: Refactor the specification. In the next step we generalize the precondition to $n \leq 1$.

```
public behavior
  requires n <= 1;
  ensures \result.isEmpty();
```

This generalization step shows that a test is missing, i.e., primes(1).isEmpty(). However, we choose not to add a new test because this new test would not fail and thus does not force us to change existing code [2].

This finishes the first iteration of our method. Since we are not done with the implementation of the primes method, we proceed with the next iteration of writing tests, code, and specifications.

Step 1: Write the test. The next test case tests that `primes(2)` returns the list that contains as its only element an integer object with value 2.

```
public void testTwo() {
   List primes = Primes.primes(2);
   assertEquals(1, primes.size());
   assertTrue(primes.contains(new Integer(2)));
}
```

Step 2: Implement the code. The following implementation validates this test:

```
public static List primes(int n) {
   List primes = new LinkedList();
   if (n == 2) primes.add(new Integer(2));
   return primes;
}
```

Step 4: Generalize the tests to a specification. The corresponding specification looks as follows.

```
public behavior
    requires n <= 1;
    ensures \result.isEmpty();
  also
```

```
requires n == 2;
ensures \result.size() == 1 &&
        \result.contains(new Integer(2));
```

We use the `also` keyword to add a new pre- and postcondition specification to an existent one. In this case, either n `<= 1` is true, then `\result.isEmpty()` has to be true, or n `== 2` is true and then

```
\result.size() == 1 && \result.contains(newInteger(2))
```

has to hold. In the above case, both preconditions are disjoint; however, if both preconditions are satisfied, then both postconditions also have to hold. As in the first iteration, running the tests with generated assertions for the JML specification yields no error.

Step 1: Write the test. After having dealt with the simple cases, we now deal with more complex situations: we write a test that ensures that all the prime numbers from 2 to 1000 are contained in the result of `primes(1000)`.

```java
public void testLots1() {
    int n = 1000;
    List primes = Primes.primes(n);
    for (int i = 1; i <= n; i++) {
        if (isPrime(i))
            assertTrue(primes.contains(new Integer(i)));
    }
}
```

The boolean function `isPrime(int i)` is an auxiliary function that returns true if the argument is a prime number and false otherwise. It is given by the following specification, which directly reflects the definition of prime numbers.

```
public behavior
ensures
  \result <==> (n > 1 && (\forall int i; i > 1 && i < n; n % i != 0));
```

The expression `\forall var-decl; range-pred; pred;` asserts that for all values of the variables occurring in `var-decl` which satisfy `range-pred`, the predicate `pred` has to hold. The range predicate `range-pred` and the predicate `pred` may contain boolean expressions which in turn may contain Java methods of type boolean which do not modify the state (called *pure* methods in JML). Logical equivalence is written `<==>`.

An implementation satisfying the specification of `isPrime` is the following (validated using the method presented in this paper):

```java
public static boolean isPrime(int n) {
    if (n < 2) return false;
    for (int i = 2; i <= n/2; i++) {
        if (n % i == 0) return false;
    }
    return true;
};
```

Step 2: Implement the code. The simplest implementation that passes `testLots1` just returns a list with integer objects representing the integers from 2 to n.

```
public static List primes(int n) {
    List primes = new LinkedList();
    for (int i = 2; i <= n; i++) primes.add(new Integer(i));
    return primes;
}
```

Step 4: Generalize the tests to a specification. Instead of writing a specification for a fixed number (in our case 1000), we directly express the desired property for arbitrary integers n.

```
public behavior
    requires n <= 1;
    ensures \result.isEmpty();
also
    requires n == 2;
    ensures \result.size() == 1 &&
            \result.contains(new Integer(2));
also
    requires n > 2;
    ensures  (\forall int i; i >= 2 && i <= n;
                 isPrime(i) ==>
                      \result.contains(new Integer(i)));
```

In the above, the symbol `==>` denotes logical implication.

Looking at the specification we see that the implementation of the primes function is not yet complete. We have checked that all prime numbers occur in the result of `primes(n)`, but not that each number in the result of `primes(n)` is a prime number. Therefore, we need an additional test.

Step 1: Write the test.

```
public void testLots2() {
    int n = 1000;
    List primes = Primes.primes(n);
    for (Iterator e = primes.iterator(); e.hasNext();) {
        int prime = ((Integer) e.next()).intValue();
        assertTrue(isPrime(prime));
        assertTrue(prime <= n);
    }
}
```

Step 2: Implement the code. This test forces us to implement a more sophisticated primes function. In our example, we use the sieve of Eratosthenes to compute prime numbers. The idea is to remove all numbers k in the list from 2 to n which are dividable by some number occurring before k. The following is a possible implementation:

```
public static List primes(int n) {
    List primes = new LinkedList();
```

```
    for (int i = 2; i <= n; i++)
        primes.add(new Integer(i));
    for (int i = 0; i < primes.size(); i++) {
        int prime = ((Integer) primes.get(i)).intValue();
        for (int j = i + 1; j < primes.size(); j++) {
            int value = ((Integer) primes.get(j)).intValue();
            if (value % prime == 0)
                primes.remove(j);
        }
    }
    return primes;
}
```

Step 4: Generalize the tests to a specification. Again, the corresponding part of the specification allows to abstract from the number 1000 to an arbitrary integer n. Accordingly, our specification expresses that each element in the result is a prime number.

```
public behavior
    requires n <= 1;
    ensures \result.isEmpty();
also
    requires n == 2;
    ensures \result.size() == 1 &&
            \result.contains(new Integer(2));
also
    requires n > 2;
    ensures (\forall int i; i >= 2 && i <= n;
                isPrime(i) ==>
                    \result.contains(new Integer(i)));
also
    requires n > 2;
    ensures (\forall Integer i; \result.contains(i);
                        isPrime(i.intValue()));
```

After generating the assertions into the Primes class-file and running all the tests, we see that no pre-/postcondition pair is violated.

Step 5: Refactor the specification. In contrast to Beck [1], who argues that tests should not be refactored, we want to refactor specifications because we want to use specifications also as program documentation. The result of the refactoring yields a more concise specification as several pre- and postcondition pairs can be eliminated: We can delete all those pairs that are logical consequences of other, remaining pre/post pairs.

```
public behavior
    ensures
        (\forall int i; i >= 2 && i <= n;
            isPrime(i) ==>
                \result.contains(new Integer(i)));
        &&
        (\forall Integer i; \result.contains(i);
            isPrime(i.intValue()));
```

By running the JUnit tests instrumented with the corresponding run-time assertions generated from the JML specifications, we can be certain that we have not produced a specification that conflicts with the code. However, we have over-simplified the specification. This is not detectable by the tests. In this case the specification does not ensures that `primes(0).isEmpty()` holds, as the list containing new Integer(2) is in compliance with the specification. Considering this case reveals a missing assertion in the specification and the tests: `primes(n)` may contain prime numbers greater than n. It is questionable if we should modify the tests as with the above implementation the tests would not reveal a failure. Modifying the tests would therefore be in violation of the principle that test should only be written if they fail first [2]. On the other hand, it would make sense to include this condition in `testLot2` to document this condition. In any case, the condition needs to be added to the JML specification.

```
public behavior
    ensures
        (\forall int i; i >= 2 && i <= n;
            isPrime(i) ==>
            \result.contains(new Integer(i)))
        &&
        (\forall Integer i; \result.contains(i);
            isPrime(i.intValue()) && i.intValue() <= n);
```

The result of the presented process is a set of tests, code, and a specification which ensure that the code implements the desired behavior, which is documented by the specification. We can now use this specification of `primes` to describe its behavior without making reference to all the test cases and/or the code. Note that the resulting primes specification is both much shorter and much easier to understand than the tests and the code alone.

2.2   Advantages of Using Specifications

The advantage of specifications is that they provide an additional view on the software which complements the test and implementation view. While the test view describes the properties of a software in terms of examples, specifications distill specific examples into more general properties. The description of the behavior of a program using a formal specification is more abstract than the tests and the implementation (which, in addition, is not always available) and more precise than an informal textual description. A precise description of the behavior of a program which is given independently from its implementation is important, e.g., in the documentation of libraries or frameworks.

When the behavior of a program is given formally, that is, in computer understandable form, it is easy to derive properties of programs from the specification or to use the specification to generate black-box tests that can be used by a quality assurance team either automatically or at least semi-automatically. In contrast to tests written by the developer during test driven development, the generated tests are not biased by the programmer who has written the code. Furthermore, we can also use these specifications as input to tools which allow to verify that the code implements the specifications is actually correct, as we will demonstrate below.

One problem with test driven development is that it is possible to write non-tested code. This risk is minimized by the XP practices. With pair programming, four eyes are looking at the code, and a rule of thumb with test driven development is that each line of the production code has to be justified by tests. Our method poses a similar problem: it may happen that a specification, consisting of class invariants, pre- and postconditions, is not strong enough to logically imply the tests. That is, a specification might not express everything that is covered by the tests. The programmers who design the tests and the specification therefore have to make sure that the tests are actually implied by the specification. This is usually done by instantiating the abstract specification to concrete examples. E.g. the test that `primes(2)` returns the list with 2 as its only element can be obtained by instantiating n with 2 in our last specification of the primes method. On the other hand, the specification may be too strong, that is, it could impose stronger conditions than the tests. This case usually leads to failed assertions, i.e. a violated pre-/postconditions or invariant, in the present or a later iteration.

2.3   Validation vs. Verification

The basic idea of the presented method is to annotate code with assertions generated from a specification. During test runs, inconsistencies between tests, specification, and code are detected, in which case an exception is thrown. Note, that this method is only able to increase the confidence in the correctness of the code and the specification, but does not guarantee that the code satisfies the specification. As with tests, this method helps finding bugs but does not prove the absence of errors. Still, it leads to more complete specifications and more correct code compared to just separating the process of writing the specification and of implementing the code. In addition, our method can be accompanied with other tools, for example ESC/Java [9] for extended static type checking using a sublanguage of JML, and Krakatoa [7] and the LOOP tool [24] for verifying that the implementation meets its specification (cf. [16] for a more complete overview of available tools for Java). Of course the effort to prove code correct with these tools is considerably higher than the effort of validating the specification.

3   Conclusion

The method in this paper describes a practical way of combining formal specifications with test driven development which is geared towards XP. There are already several approaches (cf. [12, 8, 11]) combining XP and design by contract. These approaches try to replace tests by formal specifications by considering tests as special kinds of specifications. The problem with these approaches is that they need some means to either prove the code correct with respect to the specification (which requires a considerable effort), or to generate test cases from the specification. In our method, the test cases are designed in the usual way within test driven development. This accounts for the observation that it is easier to start with concrete examples and scenarios first and then generalize the examples into specifications in a second step. In addition, we get a third view, the specification view, on the software that complements the implementation and the test view. Our method hence improves the quality of all three views. A similar line of reasoning to the one presented here has been independently developed by Ostroff et al. in the context of Eiffel [22].

For applications where security is relevant the specification view helps, on the one hand, to develop more complete test suites than one usually gets with test driven development. For example, one can generate tests from the specification and the code (white-box and black-box tests), e.g. [4]. This is because the test generation strives for a complete set of tests while the goal of tests in test driven development is to drive the process of writing the program code. On the other hand, the specification view is a prerequisite for proving programs correct. This has been done, for example, in the context of smart cards using the JavaCard API and JML, e.g. [14].

The presented method was used in the EU-project AGILE[2] to develop a multi-user dungeon (MUD) game played by several players using their mobile phones. Players can interact with each other when they are in the same virtual room. They can, for example, trade objects, fight, or talk. Writing the specification revealed bugs in the code that were not detected by just using the tests alone and also helped to find new tests because the specification provides a more abstract view on the methods to be implemented. Vice versa, the use of tests showed that often the first attempt on writing a specification fails, usually because some specific cases are omitted.

The presentation of our method in this paper uses Java as the programming language and the Java Modeling Language (JML) as the specification language. However, the method is not restricted to the use of JML, Java, or even design by contract. In the MUD game, for example, the Hugo model-checker [18] was used in addition to JML to verify liveness and safety properties, e.g., that the protocol for trading objects among players is deadlock free and that both players agree on the outcome of a trade (i.e. successful or not successful).

Note that it does not always warrant the effort to maintain a specification view on the code. One has to balance the quality of the software with the work of maintaining the specification view. In situations where a concise and precise documentation of the behavior of a program independent from the code is needed, or where an improved software quality is needed, e.g. in applications where security is critical, the gain is worth the effort.

Acknowledgments

I would like to thank Hakan Erdogmus, Alexander Knapp, Dirk Pattinson, and the anonymous referees for helpful comments on earlier versions of this paper.

References

1. K. Beck. *Extreme Programming Explained: Embrace Change*. Addison-Wesley, 1999.
2. K. Beck. *Test Driven Development: By Example*. Addison-Wesley, 2002.
3. K. Beck and J. Newkirk. Baby steps, safely. article. PDF at groups.yahoo.com/group/testdrivendevelopment/files, February 2002.

---

[2] Architectures for Mobility; www.pst.ifi.lmu.de/projekte/agile

4. R. V. Binder. *Testing Object-Oriented Systems: Models, Patterns, and Tools*. Addison-Wesley, 2000.
5. J. Bowen. The World Wide Web virtual library: Formal methods. www.afm.sbu.ac.uk, 2004.
6. Y. Cheon and G. T. Leavens. A runtime assertion checker for the Java Modeling Language (JML). In H. R. Arabnia and Y. Mun, editors, *International Conference on Software Engineering Research and Practice (SERP'02)*, pages 322–328. CSREA Press, Las Vegas, 2002.
7. E. Contejean, J. Duprat, J.-C. Filiâtre, C. Marché, C. Paulin-Mohring, and X. Urbain. The Krakatoa tool for JML/Java program verification. Available at krakatoa.lri.fr, October 2002.
8. Y. A. Feldman. Extreme design by contract. In *Extreme Programming and Agile Processes in Software Engineering, 4th International Conference, XP 2003, Genova, Italy, May 2003*, volume 2675 of *LNCS*, pages 261–270. Springer, 2003.
9. C. Flanagan, K. R. M. Leino, M. Lillibridge, G. Nelson, J. B. Saxe, and R. Stata. Extended static checking for Java. In *Proceedings of the 2002 ACM SIGPLAN Conference on Programming Language Design and Implementation (PLDI)*, volume 37, pages 234–245. ACM, 2002.
10. R. W. Floyd. Toward interactive design of correct programs. In C. V. Freiman, J. E. Griffith, and J. L. Rosenfeld, editors, *Information Processing 71, Proceedings of IFIP Congress 71, Volume 1 - Foundations and Systems, Ljubljana, Yugoslavia, August 23-28*, pages 7–10. North-Holland, 1972.
11. H. Heinecke and C. Noack. Integrating extreme programming and contracts. In K. Beck, M. Marchesi, and G. Succi, editors, *2nd International Conference on Extreme Programming and Flexible Processes in Software Engineering, XP 2001, May 20–23, 2001, Villasimius, Sardinia, Italy*, pages 24–27, 2001.
12. A. Herranz and J. J. Moreno-Navarro. Formal extreme (and extremely formal) programming. In *Extreme Programming and Agile Processes in Software Engineering, 4th International Conference, XP 2003, Genova, Italy, May 2003*, volume 2675 of *LNCS*, pages 88–98. Springer, 2003.
13. C. A. R. Hoare. An axiomatic basis for computer programming. *Communications of the ACM*, 12(10):576–583, October 1969.
14. E. Hubbers, M. Oostdijk, and E. Poll. Implementing a formally verifiable security protocol in Java Card. In *Proc. of SPC'2003, 1st International Conference on Security in Pervasive Computing, Boppard, Germany, March 12-14, 2003*, 2003.
15. A. Hunt and D. Thomas. *The Pragmatic Programmer*. Addison–Wesley, 2000.
16. B. Jacobs, J. Kiniry, and M. Warnier. Java program verification challenges. In F. S. d. Boer, M. Bonsangue, S. Graf, and W.-P. de Roever, editors, *Formal Methods for Components and Objects, 1st International Symposium, FMCO 2002, The Netherlands, Novermber 5–8, 2002, Revised Lectures*, volume 2852 of *LNCS*, pages 202–219, 2003.
17. C. B. Jones. *Systematic Software Development Using VDM*. Prentice Hall international series in computer science. Prentice Hall, New York, 2nd edition, 1990.
18. A. Knapp, S. Merz, and C. Rauh. Model checking timed UML state machines and collaborations. In W. Damm and E. R. Olderog, editors, *Proc. 7th Inernational Symposium Formal Techniques in Real-Time and Fault Tolerant Systems*, volume 2469 of *LNCS*, pages 395–416. Springer, Berlin, 2002.
19. G. T. Leavens, A. L. Baker, and C. Ruby. JML: a notation for detailed design. In H. Kilov, B. Rumpe, and I. Simmonds, editors, *Behavioral Specifications for Businesses and Systems*, chapter 12, pages 175–188. Kluwer, 1999.
20. S. McConnell. *Code Complete*. Microsoft Press, 1993.
21. B. Meyer. *Object-Oriented Software Construction*. Prentice-Hall, Upper Saddle River, New Jersey, 1997.

22. J. Ostroff, D. Makalsky, and R. Paige. Agile specification-driven development. In *Extreme Programming and Agile Processes in Software Engineering, 5th International Conference, XP 2004, Garmisch-Partenkirchen, Germany, June 2004*, volume 3092 of *LNCS*. Springer, 2004.
23. J. M. Spivey. *The Z Notation: A Reference Manual*. International series in computer science. Prentice Hall, New York, 2nd edition, 1992.
24. J. van den Berg and B. Jacobs. The LOOP compiler for Java and JML. In T. Margaria and W. Yi, editors, *Tools and Algorithms for the Construction and Analysis of Systems*, volume 2031 of *LNCS*, pages 299–312. Springer, Berlin, 2001.
25. J. Warmer and A. Kleppe. *The Object Constraint Language: Precise Modeling with UML*. Addison-Wesley, 1st edition, 1998.

Long Build Trouble Shooting Guide

Jonathan Rasmusson

ThoughtWorks Canada Corporation, 805-10th Ave SW, 3rd floor
Calgary, Alberta, Canada T2R 0B4
jrasmusson@thoughtworks.com

Abstract. Excessively long build times severely reduce a team's ability to apply the XP practice of Continuous Integration. Long build times have a severe impact on team morale, productivity, and project ROI. With the application of techniques described in this Long Build Trouble Shooting Guide, teams will be able to keep their builds from exceeding 10 minutes in length. By keeping builds short, teams will be able to minimize the cost of integration, thereby freeing them to focus on other critical project areas.

1 Introduction

1.1 Why Long Builds Are Problematic

Feedback is a wonderful thing. There is a certain feeling of satisfaction and joy that comes in software development when we are able to make changes to a system and receive immediate feedback as to whether our change left the system in a better state than we found it. That's great feedback.

In fact, we are so addicted to feedback that anytime something increases the amount of time it takes us to receive feedback, we feel pain.

Long builds are painful because they decrease the speed at which we obtain feedback. We do not like the state of uncertainty - not knowing if our changes have been successfully integrated into the system.

Further, integration becomes more difficult the longer developers code without merging their changes. Integrating changes early and often, helps minimize the opportunity and impact of multiple parties working on a common code base.

Allowing the feedback duration to grow unchecked eventually impacts the team productivity. Instead of working on new features, a long build process forces developers to idly wait while the build runs. Or they go on and start adding new functionality to code that may not have yet already been checked in (thus further increasing the amount of integration to be done later).

One might suggest that there are many other things that developers could be doing while their build is running (helping others, catching up on email, surfing the web, or think about upcoming problems).

While this sounds good in theory, I find this does not happen in practice. Writing quality code is a thought intensive process. Every time a developer is distracted or pulled out of their problem domain, it takes a considerable period of time before they can return to their previous level of productivity. Anything that takes time away from coding and receiving rapid feedback from the system is counter productive.

C. Zannier et al. (Eds.): XP/Agile Universe 2004, LNCS 3134, pp. 13–21, 2004.

Another consequence of long builds is that developers may be tempted to take shortcuts. For instance, they may skip running the build locally before checking in – confident that their changes will not break the system. Or they may skip running all the tests and only check the compilation before checking in their changes.

Finally, the cumulative effect of long build times can have a negative effect on team morale. Nothing is more demoralizing then waiting an hour for your build to complete, only to find in the 59th minute that you forgot to uncomment a section of code critical to your bug fix. Fixing small incremental changes on long running builds can consume the better part of a team's day. Conversely, a solid, repeatable, fast build can give a team great confidence and speed.

All these negatives ultimately affect the project's bottom line and have a direct impact on the project's Return-On-Investment (ROI).

2   Background

2.1   Build/Continuous Integration Defined

Continuous Integration (CI) is the act of continuously integrating and merging people's code together into one common source repository. This is usually done with a fully automated build and test process that allows the team to test their software many times a day.

A core part of CI is compiling and executing of all the project code and their corresponding tests – or what we commonly refer to as the build. For the purposes of this article we will define a successful build as one whereby:

- All the latest sources are checked out of the configuration management system
- Every file is compiled from scratch
- The resulting object files are linked and appropriately packaged
- The system is started and a suite of tests are run against the system (all tests must pass 100%)
- All of these steps pass without error or human intervention

(http://www.martinfowler.com/articles/continuousIntegration.html)

The build is also the tools and artifacts used to actually do what we just described above. Because we are big fans of automated builds, we usually have an automated process running our builds (like CruiseControl) which execute our build scripts (Ant for J2EE or NAnt for .NET) and report back to us if there were any problems.

Before checking in any changes, developers are expected to run the build scripts against their local versions of the code. If the build passes, they are free to integrate their changes into the main repository.

2.2   How Long Is Long?

So what constitutes a long build? For my colleagues who build digital switches in the telecom industry, it is not unheard of for some builds to take days. Fortunately however, most applications we deal with at ThoughtWorks are not of this size. They are usually complex enterprise business applications – usually written in Sun Microsystem's J2EE or Micosoft .NET platform. Using these technologies, I have seen builds that run anywhere from a couple of minutes to a couple of hours.

Depending on the size of the project, teams will often have various stages of builds. A full system rebuild may include a complete re-building of the code base, execution of unit and acceptance tests, a database rebuild, and deployment to a remote server. A developer build may consist of rebuilding the code base, and execution of all unit tests.

When I say that all builds can be kept under 10 minutes in duration, I am referring to the build developers perform before checking in. This usually includes a complete recompile, and execution of all tests (unit tests at a minimum and potentially acceptance tests depending on how long they take to run). This would not include tasks that are not typically performed on a continuous basis (like a full system database rebuild).

Ten minutes is about all I can take before I begin to feel like I am being unproductive. In the early stages of the project, the build will often be much shorter (less than a minute). This is a real sweet spot because now team members can confidently make very small changes and check-in multiple times per hour.

2.3 About the Trouble Shooting Guide

The principle that drove much of the discovery of the long build issues could best be described as high level profiling. When we profile a build, we measure how long certain build tasks take, and then investigate why they take so long. For those sections that do take a long time we have two options: make the operations themselves faster or do them less often.

From my experience, the number one culprit of long running builds is the accumulation of long running automated tests. Working for a company that puts a strong emphasis on automated testing, projects with hundreds (sometimes thousands) of unit and acceptance tests are not uncommon. Initially I did not find this to be a great concern as I would much rather have too many automated tests then none at all. Over time however, the impact of long running builds became too great to ignore.

It is with this focus on automated tests that much of the trouble shooting guide content is directed.

3 The Long Build Trouble Shooting Guide

Below is the summarized form of the Long Build Trouble Shooting Guide. Root causes of long running builds are listed on the left, with one or more potential solutions listed on the right.

Table 1. Long Build Trouble Shooting Guide

Root Cause	Solution
Slow hardware	Acquire faster hardware
Poorly written test	Re-visit original intent of test
Testing at the wrong architectural layer	Write tests at proper architectural layer
Network Intensive Tests	Stubs and mocks
Large code base	All the above Break application into sub domains Run tests in parallel Serialize the check-in process

The following section summarizes the root causes of long running builds and their respective solutions.

Running a long build on slow hardware does not aid the team in achieving continuous integration nirvana. *Acquire faster hardware* explains how improving your computer hardware can deliver great bang for the buck.

Applying the 80/20 rule, we can greatly improve our build time by focusing on the longest running tests first. *Re-visit original intent of the test* looks at how tackling these few troublesome tests first can go a long way to rapidly lowering our build times.

Periodically when writing tests the team will inadvertently write them at the wrong architectural layer. *Write tests at the proper architectural layer* discusses the importance of ensuring tests are written at the appropriate architectural layer and the impact not following this rule can have on our builds.

A distributed remote call across the network to another computer can be several orders of magnitude greater than a local one. When we have many unit tests that make distributed calls, a large portion of our build time is spent communicating across the network to other machines. *Stubs and mocks* show us how, in some circumstances, it is desirable for us to make the network disappear and more directly focus on the original intent of our test.

Large code bases may be a fact of life, but that should not automatically translate into long running builds. *Break application into sub domains* describes how large code bases may be broken into smaller independent ones. *Run tests in parallel* describes how running groups of unit tests simultaneously can save build time. *Serialize the check-in process* does not actually reduce our build time, but it can prove handy when the consequences of breaking the build are too great to chance.

3.1 Acquire Faster Hardware

Taking advantage of Moore's Law can be the fastest way of reducing your build time. Because of the importance in getting rapid integration feedback, make the build box run on the fastest machine you can obtain. Newer computers with faster CPU's and disk IO can have drastically reduce your build time with little relative upfront investment. While this will not solve all your problems, minutes can be rapidly shaved off the build time with very little effort.

The other aspect of hardware to consider with long running builds is the network. Many projects have saved considerable build times by simply moving their build boxes closer to their source code repositories. This can have a particularly significant impact if you have a large code base as the time it takes to download the code from the repository will be much less.

3.2 Re-visit Original Intent of Test

When profiling long running tests, any test that consumed an abnormal amount of memory or network resources was one that garnered further investigation. Sometimes we found the test was simply poorly written in the first place. One test I remember in particular created a large collection of objects which were used in testing an overridden *equals* method on an object. When reviewing the intent of the test, it quickly became apparent that the test could be met with the same degree of confidence by using a much smaller collection. Re-writing this test alone shaved three minutes off of our one and a half hour build. A small but crucial first step was taken.

In other cases, the test itself had become redundant and obsolete. Two people were not pairing and wrote similar looking tests in different sections of the application. One could argue the root cause of this problem was more related to team communication and a longer build time was an indirect result. While true, redundant and non-essential tests still need to be removed.

Whatever the reason, the point is to revisit the test and determine how we can fix the problem that is causing the test to be long running in the first place.

3.3 Write Tests at Proper Architectural Layer

Unit tests play an invaluable role on all our projects. As developers, we unit test everything our software does. As the application grows, and more tested functionality is added, we begin to accumulate a large number of tests.

Because we also have demanding customers that want proof the system is working, we also write customer or acceptance tests. These tests are different from unit tests (which are at the class method level). Customer tests are written at a higher level. They test the system as a whole, and give our customers confidence that the system is doing what it needs to do in terms they understand.

What can sometimes occur when aggressively testing our applications is that the line between a unit test and a customer test can begin to blur. In other words, we will sometimes accidentally write customer tests where a unit test would have been more appropriate.

The consequence of writing tests at a higher level than necessary is two fold. First, we lose valuable feedback at the unit level when something in our code breaks. In other words, it takes longer for us to isolate the source of the problem because we have more code to search through. Second, the customer tests typically take longer to run than their unit test equivalent. This is due to the fact that there is more code to execute (often making use of expensive network resources unnecessarily).

I was once on a project that had the most wonderful GUI testing framework. You would start the application, hit the record button on the GUI tester, and it would proceed to record all the button clicks and mouse events the user performed while using the application. Further, the framework allowed testers to make assertions about things they would like to see on the screen – like the color of a given widget, or the visibility of a given dialog. This framework was easy to use and made writing customer tests very simple and convenient.

This testing framework's greatest asset (its ease of use) was also its greatest liability. Developers stopped writing unit tests for their code because it was easier to use the GUI tester and record what they wanted to see happen on screen.

After a couple months of this, the team started to notice the build time was steadily creeping upwards. It turns out that the accumulation of all these GUI tests was having a very significant impact on the build time (each GUI test required restarting the application in a clean state). Our once light quick build was now exceeding an hour in duration.

When we write customer tests where a unit test would have been more appropriate, we are not writing tests at the appropriate architectural layer. For instance, we should avoid writing persistence tests in the presentation and domain layer. Put persistence tests where they belong – in the persistence layer. This does not mean that we never write tests that span architectural layers. It just means that we do not want the bulk of these tests outside the level they are directed towards. Having a nicely layered architecture and writing focused tests at these layers goes a long way to producing a quality product while helping us keep our build time in check.

3.4 Network Intensive Tests

As Martin Fowler aptly reminds us, the first thing he recommends to clients who are building distributed applications is not to build distributed applications. Martin lists a variety of reasons for this, but the most important for the purposes of long build times is performance.

In the earlier stages of a project, when there are few tests that include network calls, the impact of calling a remote process on another machine (i.e. a database query) is relatively small. Indeed many small projects can quite regularly include network calls in their unit tests with impunity and not notice a significant impact on build times.

Large projects however, can not afford this luxury. There eventually comes a point on a large project where the impact of the unit tests chatting with remote services does begin to negatively affect the team's ability to continuously integrate.

If you are curious about how much of your build time is spent talking to network services fire up your favorite profiling tool and note which classes your build is spending most of its time in.

For those of you building J2EE applications, you may be surprised how much time is actually spent in java.io.Socket. On one project we discovered we spent as much as 94% of our unit test build time in this single class. This highlighted for us where most of our build time was being spent – chatting with the database across the network.

So what types of options do we have to minimize our network calls? Firstly, we can ensure that our tests are written at the appropriate architectural layer as discussed previously. Secondly, we can begin looking for ways to minimize the number of distributed network calls.

For example, a feature supported by platforms like .NET (and its respective database framework ADO.NET) is the ability to work with disconnected DataSets. ADO.NET allows us to store what looks like the result set from a database call locally on disk. This way when testing our code, we can load locally saved DataSets instead of making a remote call and fetching a new one.

With techniques like locally stored DataSets, we are avoiding the network by caching test data and results locally. Developers have been doing this for some time, although now it is nice to see the languages and frameworks providing native support for these features.

Other options include setting up databases locally on each developer's machine – thus eliminating the network call outright. If vendor specific database features are not included in the application, teams have also had success running fast in-memory databases locally and running the full production type database on their build boxes.

The rule of thumb with distributed network calls is to minimize them. I am not advocating not writing tests that communicate with databases and other remote services. When in doubt, write the test and worry about the build time later. For many smaller projects this will not even be an issue. For larger projects however, the importance of a layered architecture with properly focused tests minimizing network calls becomes critical in keeping the build time reasonable.

3.5 Stubs and Mocks

Periodically, we are forced to use objects not directly related to the things we want to test. If these objects are expensive to create, their accumulated use will have a negative impact on our build time. Stubs and mocks objects can help us keep our tests focused and not necessarily rely on these expensive objects.

For the purposes of this article, I will define a stub as an object that stands in place of the real object for testing convenience (i.e. a database connection stub or message queue stub). Mocks are often used in a similar context to stubs, and there is often confusion between the two terms. One definition of a mock object is one that records state as it is being used in place of the real domain object. Testers can then query the mock and make various assertions regarding its state [Freeman].

While I have used mocks in the past, I have found stubs are more useful when removing external dependencies from my tests (which is my primary motivation when tackling long builds) and will hence forth focus on stubs.

One useful place for a stub is when the application needs to remove a problematic dependency on a service during testing. My colleague David Rice gives a nice example of a pattern solving this problem called *Service Stub* [Fowler]. In this pattern, David describes the frustration developers feel when writing tests against enterprise systems that are slow, problematic and unreliable. To remove the dependency, David recommends creating a *Separated Interface* [Fowler] so developers can have one implementation that calls the real service and one that is only a stub. Developers can switch between the two declaratively using a pattern like *Plugin* [Fowler].

Once the tests are no longer dependent on the service, continuous integration can proceed much more reliably, and the build time is reduced. The advantage of a layered architecture is that inserting stubbed out interfaces like this is relatively easy. Developers are not sitting around waiting for the external services beyond their control to come back on-line and they can avoid putting short term hacks into the code to work as temporary work a rounds.

3.6 Break Application into Sub-domains

One way of turning long running builds into faster ones is to reduce the size of the code base. This can be done by trying to see if there are any sub-systems, or *shared kernels* as Eric Evans calls them, that can be extracted from the main code base and made their own [Evans].

Not only does breaking large code bases into smaller pieces promote component reuse and module design, it reduces the amount of code and tests that need to be executed for the module under change.

Before breaking up a code base into shared domains, teams must ensure their code base is receptive to this type of extraction. Basic OO practices like encapsulation, high cohesion and loose coupling come into play here. Classes must also be correctly packaged, and not have any unnecessary external dependencies. See Bob Martin's paper on how to apply the Dependency Inversion Principle (DIP) for advice on how to structure your class packing and namespaces [Martin].

Before attempting to break the code into sub-domains, teams must also ask themselves if a shared kernel in sub-domain even exists. If a kernel is forced where one does not exist, teams will find working with the code base cumbersome and awkward – largely because they will find themselves constantly needing to make changes to both code bases.

When faced with a large code base, consider breaking it into smaller pieces. If executed correctly, you may be able to reduce the build time and improve the design of your application simultaneously.

3.7 Run Tests in Parallel

If long running unit tests are the sole cause of a team's long running build, running the tests in parallel may save the team build time. This technique involves breaking the unit tests up and running them concurrently with other unit tests.

I have seen some teams modify their builds so that all the tests run concurrently in separate threads on the same build box (they were fortunate enough to have access to a Sun E10K). Those who have access to less powerful machines may opt to break up the tests and run them on multiple build boxes concurrently.

While breaking up the build along these lines is a reasonable start for reducing the build time, this technique will only take you so far. If you still have loads of development, and the project is not near completion, I strongly recommend teams look at the root cause of why their builds are taking so long, and apply solutions described within this paper and others.

3.8 Serialize the Check-in Process

Sometimes despite our best efforts, at the end of the day we still have builds that take longer than we would like. There is nothing worse than trying to make a high pressure deadline and not being able to check-in your code because the build is broken. Not only are you prevented from checking in your code, but everyone else on the team with changes is also held up.

One way of minimizing the chances of breaking the build and avoiding all integration conflicts, is to serialize the check-in process. By serialize I mean only one party checks in code at a time. This is different from the more normal free flowing practice whereby any developer can optimistically check-in as soon as they have run the build locally and all tests pass. By strictly controlling the manner in which team members can check-in code, we greatly reduce the possibility of the build breaking.

Note this technique does nothing to reduce our build time. Instead, it manages the impact of the long build time on the team by ensuring the build never breaks.

A list or queue is usually sufficient to keep track of who is next in line to check-in in. One team I worked with had a token they passed around indicating who had check-in in privileges. As soon as "Billy Bass" the singing fish broke into a rousing rendition of "Don't Worry Be Happy" you knew that someone had just successfully integrated their changes in to the system and the token was passed to the next in line.

While I am not a big fan of check-in serialization, it can serve as a stop gap until a more permanent solution can be applied to fixing the root cause - the long running build itself. Slowly applying some of the techniques described earlier can eventually bring long running builds down to more reasonable levels. Each team will have to ask themselves if the loss of time due to serializing the check-in in process, outweighs the loss of time spent fixing broken builds.

4 Summary

Long build times prevent teams from receiving the timely feedback and should be avoided at all costs. While projects with large code bases are usually more susceptible to long builds, small projects can be negatively affected if they are not vigilant. Builds exceeding ten minutes in length must be monitored closely. By focusing on those areas of the build that take the longest (usually automated tests) and applying techniques described herein, long builds can be brought down to more manageable times.

Acknowledgements

This article would not have been possible without the help and support of many people. I would like to thank Owen Rogers, Jason Yip, Brad Marlborough, Joe Walnes, Martin Fowler, Kerry Todyruik, and Tannis Rasmusson.

About the Author

Jonathan Rasmusson is a Computer Engineer with ThoughtWorks Canada. He enjoys building enterprise applications, and searching for better ways to write software. Areas of interest include Agile development methodologies and exploring the very human side of software development. He received a BS in Electrical Engineering and a MS in Computer Engineering from the University of Alberta, Canada. Jonathan Rasmusson can be reached at ThoughtWorks, 805-10th Ave SW, 3rd floor, Calgary, Alberta, Canada T2R 0B4; jrasmusson@thoughtworks.com

References

1. E. Evans, *Domain Driven Design*, Addison-Wesley, 2003.
2. M. Fowler, *Patterns of Enterprise Application Architecture*, Addison-Wesley, 2003.
3. S. Freeman, T. Mackinnon, P. Craig, *Endo-Testing : Unit Testing with Mock Objects*, Extreme Programming Examined, Addison-Wesley, 2001.
4. R. Martin, Agile *Software Development – Principles, Patterns and Practices*, Prentice Hall, 2003.
5. http://c2.com/cgi/wiki?MooresLaw

Acceptance Testing vs. Unit Testing:
A Developer's Perspective

R. Owen Rogers

ThoughtWorks Technologies (India) Pvt Ltd.
Diamond District, Airport Road
Bangalore, India
orogers@thoughtworks.com
http://www.thoughtworks.com

Abstract. Acceptance testing is one of the most important XP practices and yet it is often neglected or perceived as "too hard". But what if acceptance tests were like unit tests? This paper provides distilled practical advice in a context familiar to XP developers describing how you can start getting acceptance test-infected on your project.

1 Introduction

Extreme Programming is one of the few software development methodologies that speaks directly to the developer. It provides a comprehensive set of best development practices and a framework for implementing them. As a result, it is often developers that push for the introduction of XP into their workplace.

Many of the best practices advocated by Extreme Programming, such as test-driven development, refactoring, and continuous integration can be practiced by individual developers – even if the whole team or the team managers have not bought into the idea of XP. Because these practices bring direct, tangible benefit to the developers that apply them, they are often the first things to be implemented within a budding XP team.

However other XP practices, such as small releases, user stories, and acceptance testing are typically harder to get going because they require buy-in and participation from people in a variety of roles both inside and outside of the team. These practices tend to require team members to fundamentally change the way that they work, the roles they play and how they interact with the team. Acceptance testing is especially challenging because of the size and the scope of its impact on all members of the team (to say nothing of the technical challenges it presents).

As a result, acceptance testing is something that is often neglected on an XP project. It is perceived as just being too hard to get right. However, leaving it out is often to the detriment of the team. The goal of this paper therefore is to offer guidance on how to get acceptance testing going on your project. By drawing comparisons with unit testing, this paper seeks to provide a context that should be familiar to developers, the typical champions of XP on a project team. The differences between these two techniques are illuminating and the implications of those differences provide considerable insight into what acceptance tests are and how they can be implemented on your team.

C. Zannier et al. (Eds.): XP/Agile Universe 2004, LNCS 3134, pp. 22–31, 2004.

2   So, What Are Acceptance Tests?

Acceptance testing, although one of the core XP practices, is subject to a lot of confusion and there are a variety of different interpretations circulating as to exactly what acceptance tests are and are not[1]. So, to be clear on what I mean by acceptance tests, I will use the following simple definition:

> Acceptance tests are tests owned and defined by the customer to verify that a story is complete and correct.

To underscore the central role of the customer in defining these tests, acceptance tests are also known as **customer tests**[8]. As such, acceptance tests are a key mechanism for verifying that the system functions in accordance with the customer's expectations. They increase the overall confidence of the team that the system continues to operate correctly as it grows and evolves. If the acceptance tests are automated then they can be an excellent means of performing regression testing.

Although primarily perceived as a means of verification, acceptance tests are, equally, if not more importantly, an effective medium of communication. They play a central role in structuring conversation between the customer and the developers. The acceptance tests become a manifestation of the team's common domain language. As programmers are charged with the task of making the tests pass as the primary criterion for assessing a story's completion, acceptance tests ensure an ongoing dialog with the customer for clarification and refinement of the requirements. The acceptance tests become an absolute, indisputable metric for assessing a story's "done-ness".

With standard requirements documents, it is all too easy for the developer to give them a quick five-minute once-over and assume that the requirements are understood (despite the fact that the analyst may have spent hours writing them up). Acceptance tests, however, cannot be dismissed so easily. They ensure that holes in the programmer's tacit knowledge show up pretty quickly. Conversely, they tend to expose flaws in the customer's thinking as well. With a written document, it is easy for the customer to be vague around requirements that they have not fully thought through or do not have a clear design for. The process of designing the tests is can be instrumental in helping the customer think through the requirements. The acceptance tests also end up becoming documentation for the system being built[2]. However, unlike standard documentation, acceptance tests are always kept in sync with the system because as soon as a test no longer accurately reflects the system, the test will break and it is the priority of the team to fix it.

If the acceptance tests are written prior to the iteration planning game, they provide a host of additional benefits. For one, they simplify and improve the accuracy of estimation as the programmers have a clearer idea of what they are expected to implement (they can also more easily factor in the time spent getting the acceptance tests to pass). As the tests are more granular than the stories (there will typically be more than one test per story covering both positive and negative cases), they provide a good guide for determining how to split large stories. To ensure that negative test cases are considered, the customer can benefit from having assistance from QA in writing the tests; and the team as a whole benefits from having QA feedback early in the process.

3   Acceptance Tests Are Kind of Like Unit Tests, Right?

If you remove the customer from the equation and let the developers write the tests themselves, it is easy to make the inference that acceptance tests are just another type of functional test. After all, the customer could just dictate the requirements to the developer, and the developer could go off and write the tests on the customer's behalf[1].

As such, if the programmers are writing the tests, could they not be built using a xUnit framework? It is a tool that the programmers are already familiar with for writing unit tests. It's free and doesn't require the overhead of some heavyweight, regression testing tool. After all, like unit tests, acceptance tests need to be automated using encoded assertions to verify expected results. Acceptance tests need to set up and tear down the environment before and after every test, which is functionality that could be easily represented in a unit test fixture. And like unit tests, much of the power of acceptance tests derives from writing the tests first, prior to implementation. So, given these similarities, what's the difference anyway?

3.1   Difference: Customers Don't Code

First and foremost, acceptance tests are written by the customer. Acceptance tests are a key deliverable from the customer to the team. As such, they need to be written in a language that the customer can easily understand. So, what kind of language is appropriate for writing acceptance tests?

As developers, we are accustomed to writing tests directly using a pre-existing programming language. For unit tests, this is invariably the same programming language that we use to develop the software. However, programming languages are generally not well understood by the customer – nor are they necessarily the best means of expressing requirements. For the customer to feel comfortable writing and taking ownership of the tests (it is hard enough as it is just convincing the customer that writing tests is something that they should do in the first place), the testing language should not require much of a learning curve.

Natural language is typically the customer's default preference. In addition to being familiar to both the customer and the team, natural language is extremely flexible and expressive. However, the same shortcomings that make natural language inappropriate for software development also make it unsuitable for writing acceptance tests:

- Natural language is too vague – it lacks the precision and clarity required for defining tests.
- Natural language is too verbose – it requires a lot of words to express simple things.
- The complex grammar that structures written communication is largely unnecessary for testing.

What is required instead is a **requirements definition language** that combines the comfort and flexibility of natural language with the structure and precision of a context-free grammar[6]. This language should be developed collaboratively by the customer

---

[1] Incidentally, this is a common acceptance testing anti-pattern known as "Lunatics Running the Asylum" [9].

in concert with the rest of the team and should be a manifestation of the team's domain knowledge. Designing such a language sounds like a daunting task; however, it is not as hard as you might think.

The easiest thing to do is to let the language start simple and to allow the customer to grow and evolve it over time. However, it is essential that the language is not dictated to the customer[2]. For the customer to feel ownership over it, she should build it herself, with the consensus of the team. The basic considerations for the language are that it should be:

– Simple enough to be easily understood
– Generic enough to capture requirements
– Abstract enough to be maintainable

The last consideration regarding abstraction can be accomplished by ensuring that the language is couched in the vocabulary of the domain. It should be free of implementation details, focusing only on the business requirements. To demonstrate what such a requirements definition language could look like, here are two sample acceptance tests. The first test is a simple step-based acceptance test for the authentication pages in a web application:

– Open: Login Page
– Enter username: Owen
– Enter password:password
– Click: Login
– Verify page: Login Failed Page

Here is part of a more advanced table-based acceptance test for a back-end leasing application:

Action	Target	Value
Navigate	Create Quote	
Enter	Agreement	DFL-1
Check	Payoff Quote Date	01/04/2004
Check	Payoff Quote Income Method	Implicit
Check	Billto -Name	ORG1

There are a few things to note from these acceptance tests. First, they are easily readable and understandable by someone with no technical knowledge but with a reasonably good understanding of the domain and of the application being built. The grammar and structure of the tests is extremely simple. Each line corresponds to a single action or verification, and there are no looping constructs or conditionals or extra syntax for the customer to have to understand. Second, the tests are constructed from a set of simple,

---

[2] There is usually a temptation amongst QA and developers to use pre-existing scripting languages as the basis for the requirements definition language. However, this tends to be a mistake [9], as scripting languages are far more complex than is required. This complexity only serves to overwhelm the customer and undermine her sense of ownership of the testing language.

reusable keywords that can be recombined in different ways with different parameters to produce new tests. Third, the tests are largely abstracted from the implementation, so they aren't vulnerable to superficial changes in the user interface.

Customers are often accustomed to playing the role of an analyst and are familiar with writing detailed requirements documents. These documents are usually a good place to start identifying potential acceptance tests. Most requirements documents have a section that lists the success criteria for a story. For developers, these criteria are almost always the most useful part of the document because they clearly explain what needs to be done and how to know whether it has been done correctly. These criteria also come the closest to representing potential acceptance tests. Using existing artefacts as the basis for defining acceptance tests is a great way to reassure the customer that writing tests is not that different than what they currently do. In fact, the customer can do less work because the rest of the requirements document can be replaced by conversation.

While getting started with writing acceptance tests can be intimidating, presenting some example acceptance tests is a great way to demonstrate how simple it can be[3]. Get your customer excited about the idea, start small, try it out and evolve it as you go.

3.2 Difference: ATs Need an Implementation

As unit tests are implemented in the same programming language as the application under test, they can call directly into the code that they are testing. A unit test can instantiate the class under test, invoke methods on it and validate its responses. The compiler or interpreter that comes with the language implementation handles the task of converting your test code into a format that can be executed in your unit test runner.

Acceptance tests, on the other hand, don't do anything on their own. They are simply an abstract specification of what needs to be done. In order for the tests to interact with the system and verify its behaviour, some code needs to be written to handle this. Hence, there is a separation between the definition of an acceptance test and its implementation. The customer writes the acceptance test definition, but the implementation will need to be written by developers or by QA.

In the example acceptance tests shown above, each of the keywords in the tests needs to map onto some code that actually acts on the application. The simplest approach is to have each keyword map directly onto a method in an acceptance test fixture class. The parameters modifying the keyword in the test definition map onto the parameters passed into the fixture method. Figure 1 demonstrates how this mapping could work.

Notice that there needs to be some sort of interpreter in between the test definition and its implementation. This interpreter is responsible for parsing each line in the test definition and invoking the corresponding method in the test implementation using the specified parameters. Building a custom interpreter is not as difficult as it might seem. The Pragmatic Programmer provides some excellent examples showing just how simple this can be[10].

---

[3] For more sample acceptance tests, take a look at documentation for FIT[4] or at the C2 Wiki [1].

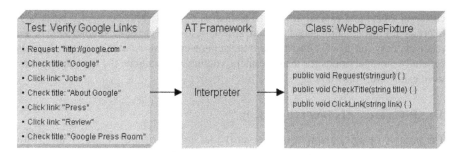

Fig. 1. Mapping an acceptance test definition onto its implementation.

There are also some generic acceptance testing frameworks, like FIT[4] or FAT[3], that can handle this mapping for you. FIT is designed to map generic table-based test definitions onto java classes, whereas FAT is designed more for procedural tests and supports .NET test implementations.

3.3   Difference: Customers Don't Use an IDE

As developers, we are generally accustomed to a specialised environment for developing software. This environment enables us to easily perform common programming tasks such as editing, compiling, and debugging source code. This same IDE can also be used for composing our unit tests.

Customers, however, don't use an IDE. Now while you can teach them to use an IDE, which is something that I have tried on a previous project[4], it is advisable to enable customers to use a tool that they are familiar with (such as Word or Excel or a text editor) or that is easily accessible to them (such as a Wiki or web application). Ideally it should be possible to not only write, but also save and execute tests from within this environment. The customer should be capable of going in and editing or executing any of the existing tests on her own at any point. As such, it may require developing a VBA plug-in for integration with Microsoft Office applications or some small form- or web-based application to help the customer out with these tasks.

As an alternative to using customer tools like Word or Excel, there are a few generic acceptance testing environments that provide this basic functionality. The best known frameworks are FIT and FitNesse[5] that both use a Wiki interface for the customer to enter and execute the tests. These tend to work well for most acceptance testing requirements, especially if the team is already using a Wiki as its information repository; however they provide relatively little assistance in helping the customer to write and manage their tests. JAccept[7] by RoleModel Software provides a Swing UI to help the

---

[4] After pairing with the customer for a few iterations to write acceptance test definitions directly in C#, the customer announced that it didn't look so hard and decided to start doing it herself. The problem, as we discovered, with this approach was that after defining the acceptance tests, the customer would never look at them again and wouldn't be able to edit them as they were in compiled code. The customer also had no direct way of running the tests.

customer create and execute tests. FAT, which is a bit like FIT, provides a basic web interface for test creation and execution. All of these tools are quite simple, so they are relatively easy for the customer to learn to use; however, this simplicity means that it is generally more laborious for the customer to define and maintain the tests than if they were using a full-blown IDE.

3.4   Difference: ATs Don't Go Quietly

The purpose of writing unit tests is to verify that the unit operates in accordance with the developer's expectations. As developers can see both the test and the code it is testing, it is easy for them to verify that the test and the code are doing the right thing. All verification of expected behaviour should be captured in code through assertions statements. As a result, unit tests should run silently; there should be no visible output when executing the tests, unless a test happens to fail. Including output from successfully executing tests is unnecessary and it distracts attention away from failing tests.

Acceptance tests, on the other hand, are a black box to the customer. The customer has no direct way of verifying that the acceptance test has been implemented in accordance with their expectations. The implementation could be doing nothing for all the customer knows. As the purpose of acceptance testing is to instil confidence in the customer that the system is implemented correctly, the acceptance testing framework needs to provide a way for the person running the test to see what is going on. This may involve displaying a browser window or the application user interface showing the test navigating through the test scenario. If the acceptance tests do not test at the level of the UI, then some form of log data is required for the customer to follow what is going on.

Another simpler approach for instilling confidence is to encourage the customer to regularly throw "spanners" into the works[9]. A spanner is deliberately erroneous test data. Recommend that the customer should periodically modify implemented acceptance tests with faulty data and verify that the system fails in the way they expect.

3.5   Difference: Failing ATs Are OK

Integrated unit tests must always be in a passing state. This is a key requirement for XP teams and a fundamental part of the continuous integration process. If there are failing unit tests, it is of primary importance for the team to fix them as quickly as possible.

Acceptance tests, like unit tests, should be written and executed before starting any implementation. However, while unit tests will typically go from red to green in a few minutes, acceptance tests might not reach a passing state a few days. Failing acceptance tests must not be a barrier to integration if the team is to be able to integrate continuously. Hence, over the course of the iteration, there will be some integrated partially-implemented acceptance tests. The key goal for the team is to ensure that all acceptance tests are passing by the end of the iteration. If all acceptance tests are not passing by iteration end, it means that there are some stories that are still incomplete.

As some acceptance tests failures are legitimate, it is important to be able to distinguish which of the tests are failing because their story hasn't been fully implemented and which failing tests signal genuine problems. A typical strategy for dealing with this is to create a facility that enables you to mark which tests are complete and ready to be released. It is insufficient to just skip the incomplete acceptance tests, as showing the results of these tests is still important for the customer so that she can track the progress of development. However, these failures need to be clearly distinguished from real failures.

3.6   Difference: ATs Have Serious Side Effects

Unit tests are designed to be simple. Each unit test typically tests a single simple interaction with the class under test. This simplicity is necessary when practicing Test-Driven Development (TDD) both to drive the design of the code and to ensure that it is fully tested. Unit tests also are designed to be orthogonal by testing each unit in isolation. This means that problems in a particular unit will cause only the tests associated with that unit to fail. This helps in quickly identifying the cause of the failure and in maintaining the tests.

Acceptance tests, on the other hand, are written at the level of a story. Each test describes a particular scenario in which a user interacts with the system and defines how the system should respond. As they are written at such a high-level, acceptance tests tend to be end-to-end. They test the interaction of the different layers in the system and that the system correctly interoperates with its external dependencies. This means that acceptance tests require the external systems to be accessible and operating correctly.

Because of these external dependencies, acceptance tests can require considerable work to set up the environment properly before test execution and then clean it up when the test is done. For unit tests, the set up and tear down methods in a test fixture are primarily a vehicle for code reuse between the tests, and are generally quite simple. However, for acceptance tests, the set up and tear down code can be very complex and may need to be shared across multiple acceptance test fixtures.

This dependency on external systems can also create concurrency issues when running the tests simultaneously on different machines. For some dependencies, such as databases, concurrency issues can be avoided by ensuring that every developer workstation (and the integration server) has separate, local copies of the external systems. However, for any external system outside of the control of the development team, such as legacy systems or third party web services, this can be a serious bottleneck. If concurrency becomes a problem, some sort of token system may be required to allow synchronised access to external systems.

Because of their coarse granularity, there tends to be a lot of overlap between different acceptance tests. This overlap means that failures in one part of the system can cause a slew of tests to break. Going through and diagnosing the problem can be difficult, especially as acceptance tests are usually slow to run and the problems may have percolated up through many layers in the system. One common problem that we have faced is failures due to unreliable external systems. Instead of trying to look through a host of failed acceptance test to determine the cause of the failure, try writing some very fine grained integration tests that test the interface to the external system directly. These will immediately tell you if the external system is up and working properly, and if not, where exactly the problem is.

This overlap between acceptance tests can cause maintenance problems as well. Changes to the functionality in one part of the system could require updating a large number of tests. Identifying which tests to update and verifying their correctness can be quite an arduous task. The easiest way around this problem is to apply the same principles that we use as programmers and extract that duplication into a single, common place. This typically involves discussing the duplication with the customer and agreeing to add some new keyword to the language that represents the encapsulated test code (a common initial target is 'Login'). The customer may request some facility to see what test steps are encapsulated by the new keyword.

The overlap between acceptance tests is necessitated by the fact that areas of functionality within the system cannot be accessed directly. It is often necessary to pass through numerous intermediary screens setting up data along the way. Redundantly testing this functionality through the user interface of the application can be extremely slow. Providing hooks into the application that can invoke this functionality directly can greatly increase the speed and simplify the maintenance of complex acceptance tests.

4   Conclusion

By exploring the differences between unit testing and acceptance testing, I have identified some of the key features of acceptance tests and provided some practical advice for getting started with acceptance testing on your project:

– Communicate the importance of acceptance testing to your team, focussing on convincing your customer;
– Work with the customer to investigate potential sources of acceptance tests in your environment and begin to work towards defining a common domain language for defining requirements;
– Help the customer to write a couple of simple acceptance tests for new stories and try implementing them as you write the story;
– Investigate available acceptance testing frameworks like FIT or FAT or spike building your own framework;
– Discuss with the customer the best environment for them to use to write and execute the tests and develop a tool;
– Integrate the acceptance tests into your build process, but keep them in a separate test package so that if they fail, they won't break your build.

The greatest hurdle to acceptance testing is getting started, but by following the steps above you too can become acceptance test-infected.

Acknowledgements

Thanks go out to Rob Styles, who helped me assemble this material for the original presentation at XPDay in London (Dec. 2003), and to all the people who reviewed this paper and gave me feedback.

References

1. Various authors. *http://c2.com/cgi/wiki?AcceptanceTest.*
2. Auer, K, Miller, R. Extreme Programming Applied: Playing To Win. Addison-Wesley. (2002)
3. FAT Acceptance Testing Framework. *http://sourceforge.net/projects/fat/.*
4. FIT Acceptance Testing Framework. *http://fit.c2.com/.*
5. FitNesse Acceptance Testing Framework. *http://www.fitnesse.org/.*
6. Fowler, M. TestingLanguage. *http://martinfowler.com/bliki/TestingLanguage.html.*
7. JAccept. *http://www.roywmiller.com/papers/acceptanceTesting.htm*
8. Jeffries, R. What is Extreme Programming. *http://www.xprogramming.com/xpmag/whatisXP.htm.*
9. Hanly, S. BuildYourOwnAcceptanceTestFramework. Presentation from XPDay (London) *http://www.xpday.net/scripts/view.pl/Xpday2003/Program.* (2003)
10. Hunt, A., Thomas, D. The Pragmatic Programmer: From Journeyman to Master. Addison-Wesley (2000)

The Role of Process Measurement
in Test-Driven Development

Yihong Wang and Hakan Erdogmus

Software Engineering Group, Institute for Information Technology,
National Research Council of Canada
Montreal Road, Building M50, Ottawa, Ontario, Canada K1A 0R6
{hakan.erdogmus,yihong.wang}@nrc-cnrc.gc.ca

Abstract. Test-Driven Development (TDD) is a coding technique in which programmers write unit tests before writing or revising production code. We present a process measurement approach for TDD that relies on the analysis of fine-grained data collected during coding activities. This data is mined to produce abstractions regarding programmers' work patterns. Programmers, instructors, and coaches receive concrete feedback by visualizing these abstractions. Process measurement has the potential to accelerate the learning of TDD, enhance its effectiveness, aid in its empirical evaluation, and support project tracking.

1 Introduction

Test-Driven Development (TDD) [1-3] is a coding technique that relies on writing tests before implementation. The tests are written by the programmer using a unit testing framework such as JUnit [4]. Unit tests are incrementally added and all tests are periodically executed. Consequently, the program is regression tested as it is being developed.

This paper presents an unobtrusive approach for improving the effectiveness of TDD based on an analysis of programmers' coding and testing activities. First, we formalize the TDD process as a sequence of *programming cycles*, called a *cycle trace*. Cycle traces are visualized in different ways to obtain high-level information about the work patterns of programmers. This information in turn supports personal process improvement, education, empirical evaluation, and project tracking.

A single programming cycle involves writing unit tests and production code, and ends with a successful execution of tests. The formalization of a programming cycle allows a high-level representation of the programmer's coding and testing activities to be extracted from a record of low-level actions. These actions are captured using a third-party tool [5] that is integrated into the development environment. The logged actions track tool usage (JUnit) and changes to project resources; they are time-stamped and augmented with basic code metrics. Once the cycle trace is extracted in tabular form, further abstractions are produced that zoom in on different aspects of the process followed by the programmer. These abstractions are presented as charts, which are visualized and interpreted.

C. Zannier et al. (Eds.): XP/Agile Universe 2004, LNCS 3134, pp. 32–42, 2004.
© Springer-Verlag Berlin Heidelberg 2004

Section 2 elaborates on the motivation of the work. Section 3 presents the approach. Section 4 presents the tabular representation of a cycle trace and discusses the interpretation of various charts derived from this representation. Finally, Section 5 presents conclusions and discusses future work.

2   Motivation

Inevitably, programmers with different experience levels, preferences, reasoning processes, and established work patterns will apply TDD in different ways. With meaningful feedback, programmers can correlate any changes in productivity and code quality with the way the technique is being applied. In turn, the awareness of the process followed helps programmers discover rhythms and patterns that work best in a given context. In addition, process data can provide useful insight regarding the status of the project, both in terms of progress and in terms of product quality. Johnson et al. [6] stress the importance of process measurement in personal process improvement and project tracking, but not specifically in the context of TDD.

Concrete, measurement-based feedback is also important from a pedagogical point of view. Although students who are exposed to TDD find it useful [7, 8] and obtain better productivity scores [8] and course grades [9], many students find TDD counterintuitive [10] and a majority find it more difficult to apply compared to conventional programming. In addition, students with higher skill ratings are able to leverage TDD better, and achieve more dramatic productivity improvements compared to students with lower skill ratings [8]. These findings imply that TDD may initially appear counterintuitive to novices and the effective application of this technique demands both discipline and mastery. Therefore, coaches and instructors can take advantage of process measurement to teach TDD to newcomers and to advance the skill level of veterans.

Discrepancies in empirical findings [8, 9, 11-14] [12] constitute a significant impediment to drawing generalized conclusions, and consequently, the findings remain valid only in the contexts in which they were produced. While several factors may account for the discrepancies (such as differences in populations, experiment tasks, teaching methods and materials, the technique with which TDD is compared), all of the studies mentioned suffer from a common pitfall of empirical software engineering: *process conformance* [8]. Process conformance is a threat to construct validity [15] related to the ability and willingness of subjects to follow a prescribed process. How do we know that the subjects apply TDD in the same way, or in the manner expected, both within and across studies? Although it is impossible to address process conformance in a fully objective manner, measurement should reduce the construct threat that it poses. Researchers often rely on self-assessment through questionnaires to gauge process conformance. Measurement can complement self-assessment by allowing the comparison of the subjects' process measures with idealized patterns. In addition, measurement is useful in assessing maturation (achievement of sufficient experience in the investigated technique), which is a concern in TDD studies: productivity and quality measures taken will be more meaningful and valid if the subjects gain reasonable mastery beforehand. Therefore reasonable mastery beforehand. Therefore process measurement can play an important role in empirical evaluation, in terms of both enhancing the validity of the results and facilitating the comparison and aggregation of findings from multiple studies.

3   Approach

This section explains the process measurement approach taken. Section 3.1 formalizes the TDD process in terms of a cycle trace. Section 3.2 defines the high-level architecture for data collection and analysis of our prototype implementation. This architecture relies on a third-party tool for data collection. Section 3.3 explains how to mine the process data collected to recognize cycle traces.

3.1   Formalization of TDD Process

We represent the TDD process as a sequence of *programming cycles*, called a *cycle trace*. Each programming cycle in turn is composed of more elementary *blocks* representing three distinct types of activities. A TestCode block is defined as a contiguous sequence of coding activities that involves only writing or revising tests. A TestCode block is typically followed by a ProductionCode block, which is a contiguous sequence of activities that involves only writing or revising production code. The Test-Code-ProductionCode sub-cycle can be repeated several times, but usually a ProductionCode block is immediately followed by the execution of a series of tests. A contiguous sequence of test executions is a TestExecution block. A TestExecution block that is (100%) successful (represented by a green bar in JUnit) indicates the end of a programming cycle. An unsuccessful, or failing, TestExecution block (represented by a red bar in JUnit) marks the end of a sub-cycle, which we call a CycleElement. Thus, a single programming cycle is composed of several CycleElements, the last of which ends with a successful TestExecution block.

Formally, a cycle trace is defined by the following regular expressions:

$$\text{CycleElement}(x) = (\text{TestCode} \mid \text{ProductionCode})^+ \text{ TestExecution}(x)$$

$$\text{ProgrammingCycle} = \text{CycleElement}(\text{fail})^* \text{ CycleElement}(\text{pass})$$

$$\text{CycleTrace} = \text{ProgrammingCycle}^+$$

Here $x \in \{\text{fail, pass}\}$ differentiates between failing and successful TestExecution blocks and CycleElements. Note that the regular expressions describe a generic process that is not strictly TDD-compliant. For example, they recognize variant cycles where the programmer writes the tests after the production code. Such non-compliant cycles should be occasionally expected in TDD, but they are normally not persistent if TDD is faithfully applied. The regular expression pattern also recognizes more legitimate variants such as pure refactoring [16] cycles during which the programmer does not add new functionality, but improves the design by typically revising the test code or the production code. Whereas the cycle trace of a faithful TDD programmer will contain a large number of short cycles, the traditional programmer who follows a waterfall-like process will have a cycle trace that contains a fewer number of long cycles.

The formalization assumes that unproductive or dead-end cycles always conclude with the restoration of a former stable state of the code. In a stable state, all tests must run 100% successfully. Once a stable state is achieved, the programmer verifies this condition, thereby delimiting an unproductive or dead-end cycle with a successful TestExecution block.

3.2 Architecture for Data Collection and Analysis

To recognize cycle traces, we need to collect fine-grained data regarding the programmer's coding and testing activities. For this purpose we chose Hackystat [5, 17], a lightweight tool available from the University of Hawaii's Collaborative Software Development Laboratory. Hackystat client sensors are available for several development environments including Eclipse [18]. Once the sensors are installed and configured on the programmer's computer, they work transparently in the background to collect the data. The Hackystat sensor periodically sends the locally cached data to a Hackystat server, where it is stored permanently and can be retrieved on demand in XML form.

To generate a representation of the cycle trace for a given time period, the client runs the analysis tool locally. The analysis tool downloads the associated logged data from the Hackystat server and generates an Excel spreadsheet containing a tabular representation of the client's cycle trace as well as the associated charts.

3.3 Mining Hackystat Data

Hackystat sensors collect multiple types of data from the client. We take advantage of the data types *Activity*, *UnitTest* and *FileMetric*. Hackystat logs changes to project artifacts in *Activity* data. Unit test executions are logged in *UnitTest* data along with the test results. *FileMetric* data contain static structural metrics on project artifacts.

Figure 1 shows how Hackystat data is aggregated to recognize programming cycles. The blocks that make up the cycles (TestCode, ProductionCode and TestExecution Block) are composed of a set of related cycle entries, where each cycle entry has a duration (Active Time) and an associated project artifact (Active File). For TestCode and ProductionCode blocks, the project artifact is obtained by cross-referencing the test case names recorded in the Hackystat *UnitTest* data with the file names recorded in the Hackystat *Activity* data. The project artifacts (i.e., test classes) of a TestExecution block are obtained from *UnitTest* data alone. The duration of the cycle entry is estimated using Hackystat timestamps. When no Hackystat entries are logged for a project artifact for a certain period of time (e.g., two minutes), the excess time is recorded as "Idle Time," which is excluded from "Active Time" to account for interruptions.

"T/P Ratio" tracks the amount of test code produced relative to the amount of production code. This metric is calculated using the *UnitTest* and *FileMetric* data. Since a cycle entry may affect the size of a project artifact, T/P Ratio is recomputed at the end of each cycle based on the timestamp of the last modification from the

of each cycle based on the timestamp of the last modification from the *FileMetric* data.

The number of tests attempted and the number of tests passed from *UnitTest* data together identify successful and failing test executions.

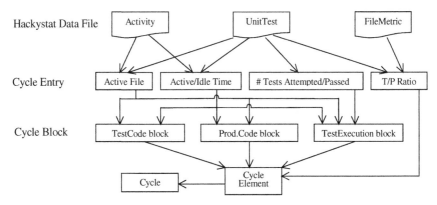

Fig. 1. Recognizing programming cycles using Hackystat data types.

Aggregation of cycle entries into blocks proceeds in a bottom-up fashion. Since test executions delimit CycleElements, TestExecution blocks are formed first using *Activity* and *UnitTest* data types. If there is no *Activity* entry whose timestamp is between the timestamps of two *UnitTest* entries, then the two *UnitTest* entries are grouped into one TestExecution block; otherwise, they belong to different TestExecution blocks. Once the TestExecution blocks are identified, remaining activities can be grouped into ProductionCode and TestCode blocks by comparing their timestamps with the delimiting timestamps of the TestExecution blocks. Finally CycleElements and Cycles are constructed based on the sequencing of the blocks. The output of this procedure is illustrated in the next section.

4   Analysis of Cycle Traces

In this section, we present the output of our prototype analysis tool for Eclipse [18], called TestFirstGauge. We also show with several examples how the output can be interpreted to support personal process improvement, learning, process conformance, and project tracking. The data used in the examples are collected during various programming tasks from an experienced programmer who was learning TDD. Section 4.1 explains the tabular representation of a cycle trace generated by the tool. Section 4.2 illustrates the analysis of cycle time and T/P Ratio using two different charts. Finally, section 4.3 discusses testing effort analysis.

4.1   TDD Report

Figure 2 illustrates the cycle trace report generated by the TDD analysis tool.

Cycle	Activity	Active File	Tests		Active Time	Idle Time	T/P
			Attempted	Passed	(sec)	(sec)	Ratio
19	Test Code	TestActionSet.java			17.77	0	0.37
	Prod Code	ActionSet.java			13.65	120	
	JUnit Run	TestActionSet	2	1	0.14		
		TestTransition	4	4	0.02		
	Test Code	TestActionSet.java			1.57	0	
	JUnit Run	TestActionSet	2	2	0.08		
		TestTransition	4	4	0.04		
	Cycle Total				33.27	120	
20	Test Code	TestActionSet.java			16.38	0	0.07
	JUnit Run	TestActionSet	2	2	0.06		

...

100	Prod Code	Controller.java			163.78	2640	0.32
		ActionSet.java			0.00	0	
		TransBridge.java			94.75	61440	
	Test Code	TestController.java			34.46	960	
	JUnit Run	TestController	3	3	0.39		
	Cycle Total				293.38	65040	

Fig. 2. Sample TDD report.

The first column shows the cycle number. The second column gives the type of the cycle entry, which depends on the block to which the cycle entry belongs. (The entries labeled "JUnit Run" belong to TestExecution blocks.) The third column lists the project artifacts associated with each cycle entry. For JUnit runs (TestExecution blocks), the numbers of tests attempted and passed are given in the next column. The column labeled "Active Time" gives the duration of the cycle entry (excluding idle time). Last column provides the (cumulative) ratio of test code to production code. The total duration of each cycle is indicated in the row "Cycle Total". Whereas Cycle 19 is a TDD cycle, Cycle 100 is a non-TDD cycle because it begins with a ProductionCode rather than a TestCode block.

4.2   Cycle Time and T/P Ratio Analysis

Figure 3 shows an example of the *cycle active time* chart. We can use this chart to support learning, assess process conformance and support project tracking.

Ideally, with faithful application of TDD, the chart should have short cycles of comparable length, representing a steady progress. Cycles from 40 to 100 are typical and conform to the ideal pattern. The spikes towards the beginning (long cycles) are possibly due to the initial TDD learning curve. The spikes towards the end correspond to integration-related tasks during which TDD was not applicable.

With regard to project tracking, persistent long cycles could be indicative of design complexities, which make adding new functionality difficult. Such patterns can be used to identify opportunities for refactoring to improve the design.

Figure 4 depicts the *cycle pattern* associated with another programming task. The x-axis denotes cumulative cycle time measured in minutes. Long cycles now appear as large gaps between consecutive vertical bars, each of which marks the beginning of a new cycle. In the middle section, the programmer performs a series of large refactorings. Towards the end, a steadier pattern is gradually reached as evidenced by increasingly tightly spaced vertical bars. The height of each bar indicates the ratio of test code to production code (T/P Ratio) at the end of the associated cycle. We see that during the refactoring activity, the T/P Ratio increased: the programmer added more tests most likely to better support the design changes. Towards the end, the T/P Ratio gradually reverted back to its previous level.

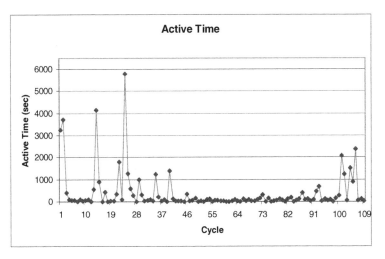

Fig. 3. Cycle Active Time.

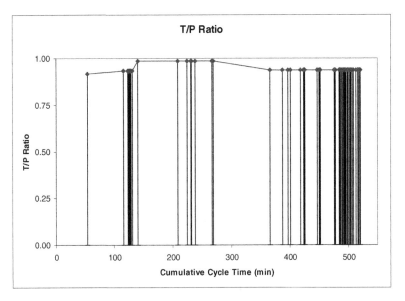

Fig. 4. Cycle Pattern with T/P Ratio.

4.3 Testing Effort Analysis

Analysis of testing effort is particularly useful for project tracking.

Figure 5 shows historical test code effort (bottom bars) relative to production code effort (top bars) as a function of cycle number. Test execution time is excluded from this analysis. Two explanations are possible for the absence of testing activity in the middle section of the chart. The first explanation is that the programmer could have neglected testing. In this case the chart can be used to look up the production code classes associated with the middle cycles in the TDD report to identify sections of the code as the focus of subsequent coverage analysis. The second explanation is that the middle section corresponds to refactoring activities during which no tests were added or modified. Again the TDD report can be analyzed further to verify this hypothesis.

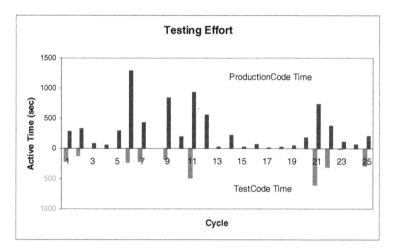

Fig. 5. Testing effort.

4.4 Cycle Time Distribution

Beck states [2] (page 83) that his JUnit usage (minutes between successive JUnit runs) has a particular U-shaped distribution. However, how often JUnit is run provides little information about how quickly a TDD programmer completes a programming task within a single cycle and how fine-grained the tasks are themselves. To gauge their speed and the granularity of the incremental process followed, TDD programmers should be more interested in the distribution of the duration of the programming cycles than the distribution of time between successive JUnit runs.

Figure 6 illustrates the cycle time distribution for a typical TDD session. The chart has been produced after the programmer has acquired experience with TDD. As expected with proper application of TDD, smaller cycles exhibit a higher frequency than larger cycles. As the mastery of TDD increases, the programmer should get better at task decomposition and follow an increasingly finer incremental process. Consequently, the head of the distribution should get fatter while the tail thins out.

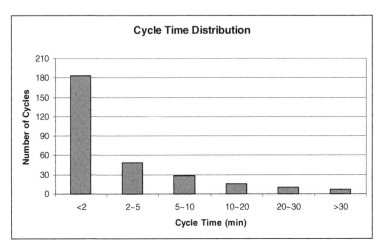

Fig. 6. Cycle time distribution.

5 Conclusions

Measurement supports process improvement not only at project and organizational levels, but also at a personal level. We presented an approach based on process measurement to support Test-Driven Development, an incremental coding technique that demands discipline. The goal of the approach is to:

- increase the mastery of TDD by providing concrete visual feedback to programmers regarding their past work patterns and rate of progress,
- facilitate teaching by allowing coaches to demonstrate target patterns and identify slippages,
- aid in project tracking by identifying sections of code that are candidates for closer scrutiny, and
- improve empirical evaluation by controlling process conformance.

At the centre of the approach is the concept of a programming cycle, which leads to the formalization of the process underlying TDD. A tool then extracts traces of such cycles from programmers' activity logs, and produces various time-series charts that are easy to interpret. We provided examples of how to interpret a subset of these charts. The tool generates additional charts that were not discussed in this paper.

Our prototype tool works with Eclipse, JUnit, Microsoft Excel and Hackystat. The tool is freely available under GPL upon contacting the authors.

Although the espoused benefits of our TDD process measurement approach in research settings are well founded, its impact on education and personal process improvement is speculative at this point. Future efforts will focus on further improvements to the tool and on the evaluation of the approach in different settings. Work is already under way. The tool will be tested in an industrial case study of TDD and in future replications of the TDD experiment mentioned in [8]. Regarding additional analysis capabilities, we have made progress in two fronts: incorporation of test coverage information into cycle traces using a commercial tool and automatic recognition of refactoring cycles.

Acknowledgments

Maurizio Morisio's relentless obsession with process conformance and Marco Torchiano's arguments were instrumental in convincing the authors of the usefulness of an automatic measurement approach for TDD. Discussions with Philip Johnson led to the development of a mockup for the TestFirstGauge tool. Alain Desilets, Joel Martin, and Janice Singer gave valuable feedback on an early version of the tool. The IIT Software Engineering Group members provided comments to improve the readability of the paper.

References

1. D. Astels, G. Miller, and M. Novak, *A Practical Guide to Extreme Programming*. Upper Saddle River, NJ: Prentice Hall, 2002.
2. K. Beck, *Test-Driven Development: by Example*: Addison Wesley, 2003.
3. K. Beck, "Aim, fire (test-first coding)," *IEEE Software*, vol. 18, pp. 87-89, 2001.
4. JUnit.org, *www.junit.org*.
5. P. M. Johnson, H. Kou, J. M. Agustin, Q. Zhang, A. Kagawa, and Takuya Yamashita, "Practical automated process and product metric collection and analysis in a classroom setting: Lessons learned from Hackystat-UH," University of Hawaii, Collaborative Software Development Laboratory, Technical Report (submitted to 2004 International Symposium on Empirical Software Engineering) csdl2-03-12, December 2003.
6. P. M. Johnson, H. Kou, J. Agustin, C. Chan, C. Moore, J. Miglani, S. Zhen, and W. E. J. Doane, "Beyond the personal software process: metrics collection and analysis for the differently disciplined," presented at 25th International Conference on Software Engineering (ICSE 2003), Portland (OR), USA, 2003.
7. M. M. Müller and W. F. Tichy, "Case study: Extreme Programming in a university environment," presented at International Conference on Software Engineering (ICSE), Toronto, Canada, 2001.
8. H. Erdogmus, M. Morisio, and M. Torchiano, "A Controlled Experiment on the Effectiveness of Test-Driven Development," *Submitted for publication*, 2004.
9. S. H. Edwards, "Using test-driven development in the classroom: Providing students with concrete feedback on performance," presented at Proceedings of the International Conference on Education and Information Systems: Technologies and Applications (EISTA'03), August 2003.
10. M. Morisio and M. Torchiano, "Perception of XP Practices in a University Environment," Dipartimento di Informatica e Automatica, Politecnico di Torino, Technical Report 2003.
11. B. George and L. Williams, "An Initial Investigation of Test Driven Development in Industry," presented at ACM Symposium on Applied Computing, Melbourne, Florida, 2003.
12. L. Williams, E. M. Maximilien, and M. Vouk, "Test-Driven Development as a Defect-Reduction Practice," presented at 14th Internation Symposium on Software Reliability Engineering (ISSRE '03), 2003.

13. M. M. Müller and O. Hagner, "Experiment about Test-First Programming," presented at Empirical Assessment in Software Engineering (EASE), Keele, UK, 2002.
14. M. Long, "A Meta Analysis of the Quality and Productivity Benefits of Pair Programming and Test Driven Design," Christopher Newport University, 2003
15. C. Wohlin, P. Runeson, M. Host, M. C. Ohlsson, B. Regnell, and A. Wesslen, *Experimentation in Software Engineering: An Introduction*: Kluwer Academic Publishers, 2000.
16. M. Fowler, *UML Distilled*: Addison Wesley, 2000.
17. "Hackystat," http://csdl.ics.hawaii.edu/Tools/Hackystat/
18. "Eclipse Platform Technical Overview," Object Technology International, 2003, http://www.eclipse.org/whitepapers/eclipse-overview.pdf

Acceptance Test Driven Planning

Richard J. Watt[1] and David Leigh-Fellows[2]

[1] ThoughtWorks, UK
rwatt@thoughtworks.com
[2] Egg, UK
David.Fellows@Egg.com

Abstract. The experience of XP planning for many is not a successful one. We have found that by making acceptance tests not only central to the definition of a story but central to our process itself, they can be used to drive the entire development. This paper describes an adaptation, or evolution to XP style planning based around acceptance testing which takes the existing planning practices (with some additions) and organises them in a way that we believe can lead to better planning and more predictable results.

1 Introduction: How Do We Know When We Are Done?

One of the defining questions for a development team is "do we know when they are done?". The question sounds simple but too often the answer is not as obvious as it should be. Acceptance tests are an effective way of expressing requirements in a way that provides an unambiguous answer to this question. As others have found, writing acceptance test definitions before coding begins on an iteration has both obvious and more subtle benefits. Given these benefits, why is it not more common for acceptance tests to be written before iteration planning begins? What are the obstacles and how can they be overcome? We have sought to find answers to these questions in the last year and in doing so have developed an adaptation of XP style iteration planning that has some key benefits over the traditional approach.

2 Iteration Planning: A Typical Experience

Our experience of iteration planning was perhaps typical. As a team fully signed up to the agile cause, we all agreed that this approach to planning was better than anything else we had tried. We also agreed that in our shared experience the process had never been wholly successful. Maybe we were doing something wrong but the more people we spoke to the more we realised our experience of planning was at least not uncommon.

As an illustration of our plight, below is a description of a typical iteration planning session:

We gathered all interested parties into a room which for us meant 10 developers, our customer, our QA engineers, an interaction designer, our project manager, iteration manager and coach – all empowered to contribute to the planning process.

C. Zannier et al. (Eds.): XP/Agile Universe 2004, LNCS 3134, pp. 43–49, 2004.
© Springer-Verlag Berlin Heidelberg 2004

Our customer would describe each of the stories in turn. The developers would ask questions and discuss solutions before producing a list of tasks for each story and an updated estimate of the effort it would take to implement the story. Unfortunately, this process of discussion often took a long time and was once described by our customer as feeling more like a "techno babble" session than a planning one. From the developers' perspective, it was very difficult to produce confident estimates when the customer could not provide the information they needed in the meeting - this resulted in best-guess estimates on the incomplete information available. Even though our customer tried to consider all of the likely angles they couldn't anticipate all of the questions that were going to be asked during the session. What seemed like a sensible approach to start with did not feel so good after a few painful, marathon planning meetings. The team was starting to lose confidence in the process.

The real pain came when we measured our velocity at the end of the iteration and discovered the discrepancy between what we had signed up for and what we had achieved. There are, of course, many reasons why a team could have a poorer than expected velocity but once we had investigated further we discovered that the main issue was that we hadn't identified a complete set of tasks for each story. We could all see that the developers were working really hard and the results produced were good but in hindsight it was if they had started a 400m race but didn't know where the finishing line was and just kept going round the track. Our understanding of the work was incomplete, which meant it was unclear when we were done. This also meant everyone was very tired and nobody was very happy - we knew we had to do something.

3   Getting Our Stories Straight

One of the biggest problems we had in our planning sessions was that our customer felt that no matter what they did to prepare there were still many questions they could not answer without time for further analysis and/or investigation. Our solution was simple: a day or two before the end of the iteration the customer would sit down with the QA engineer and a developer to begin the process of writing acceptance tests for the upcoming stories, or in our terms, "Getting our Stories Straight". In short, we still ended up asking the same questions but by doing this activity before the planning session we were able to find more answers earlier and thus be better prepared for when we did gather the full team into a room. This is not a return to "big up front analysis" but an acknowledgement that as we approach the end of an iteration we already have a good idea of what is going to be completed in this iteration and the customer has a good idea of what stories they want to include in the next.

Our principal aim at this stage was simply to better prepare the customer for our planning session so that developers could get more of the answers they needed at the time they needed them, but we soon discovered there were many more benefits:

- **Are our tests any good?** Writing acceptance tests is a skill, our QA engineer helps our customer make sure the acceptance criteria specify the expected behavior and external quality[1]. One of our developers is on hand to make sure that there is no technical reason why the functionality required to pass the acceptance tests cannot be implemented. If we liken this to UML use cases, a story becomes the title of the use case and the acceptance tests become the use case itself detailing the main success scenario, alternate and error scenarios. [2].

- **Are our stories too big?** One of the positive side-effects of this process is that it often highlights if a story is likely to be too big for the development team to estimate before we even get to the planning session. The simple correlation between the size and number of acceptance tests and the size of the story has proven to be a reliable predictive indicator.

- **The chance to improve our estimates:** For a story that appears too large we may choose at this stage to break it into two or more smaller stories. In our experience, smaller stories are easier to estimate accurately. We strive to have stories that can be ideally completed in 1 to 3 days.

- **Customer requirements vs. QA requirements:** The testing interests of our QA engineer may go beyond what is needed to define the requirements for the story, but over time we have found that the difference is much smaller than we expected.

The last point is an important one. Using acceptance tests as our "single source of truth" means the needs of both the customer and the QA function are served by a single artefact. We would later see how the same acceptance tests could be used to improve our task breakdown and estimates. The key to these additional benefits was our decision to choose acceptance tests as our focal point for all planning and development activities – it is perhaps too easy to think of acceptance testing as merely as a form of black box testing and miss their greater significance as a multi-use form of requirements specification.

With our stories "straight" the next thing to improve was how we ran our planning sessions.

4   The Planning Workshop

In Acceptance Test Driven Planning the typical XP planning session is refactored into something we call the Planning Workshop. The objectives remain the same as the XP planning session (updates to our story estimates with a clearer picture of their dependencies), but we find the quality of the information provided is much improved.

The Planning Workshop is split into two phases, "Task Identification" and "Present and Challenge".

4.1   Task Identification

As a result of us "Getting Our Stories Straight" we now have a set of candidate stories for the next iteration, their acceptance tests, some existing high level estimates and a vague understanding of what dependencies exist between stories.

The Planning Workshop begins with the customer presenting the candidate stories to the rest of the team - each story is described along with its acceptance tests. The developers then group themselves into triples and each mini team signs up to a subset of the stories for further analysis. We organise ourselves into triples because we've found that 3 is the optimum number of people to have in a mini team; we find that 3 people are able to fit around a pair station and the fact that we have an odd number always results in a mediator in case of disagreement. Once each candidate story has a triple assigned we move into the phase designed to drive out the tasks required to pass the acceptance tests. Each triple heads back to a workstation and pulls up the acceptance tests for their candidate stories. The customer and QA float between the triples answering any questions that may arise to make sure that everyone is clear on what is required in the story. At this stage the existing acceptance tests may be altered or (more rarely) added to.

It is useful and illustrative to consider what we did before and the reasons which led us to this process of task identification. In previous iterations, it became obvious to us that there was a discrepancy between the tasks identified for a story and the actual work that was required to complete a story. It was common to find a developer saying that they had finished the tasks for a story and now only had the acceptance tests to implement. The problem was that that it took the same time to implement the acceptance tests as it had taken them to complete the tasks. Their original task breakdown, with all the best intentions, was incomplete. We quickly found that by using the acceptance tests as the focus of the task identification exercise we were able to produce a list of tasks which was much more representative of the work that we would need to do to complete a given story. With the increase in confidence we gained from a more structured approach to task identification, we also found our estimates improved too.

4.2 Present and Challenge

The next phase of our planning workshop is called "Present and Challenge". The idea is that each triple presents their solution for a given story back to the rest of the team, and the rest of the team are then given the opportunity to challenge the list of tasks to see if we can refine the task list and the estimates given. This works well on two levels as it is a useful tool for exploring (at a high level) the proposed solution with the whole team present, whilst also acting as a double-check to ensure we have considered all of the tasks.

In addition, this process gives the team members an opportunity to practice their presentation and debating skills. We have also found it can be useful in establishing team rapport – the sessions are designed to be challenging and we manage them carefully to avoid challenge turning into conflict.

5 Putting It All Together

We have spoken specifically about "Getting Our Stories Straight" and "The Planning Workshop", but where do these activities fit into the bigger picture?

In a two week iteration we are now able to limit the impact of planning activities down to a single day for nearly all of our developers.

The morning marks the end of the existing iteration and begins with a show-and-tell session to allow interested (and paying) parties to come along and see what the team has achieved in the iteration. There are usually few surprises here as the customer and QA will have seen each story as it was completed during the iteration, but it is a useful opportunity for the team to appreciate all that has been achieved. We then follow this with a short retrospective [3] where we discuss those things that went well, not so well, things that still puzzle us and any actions we need to take to improve.

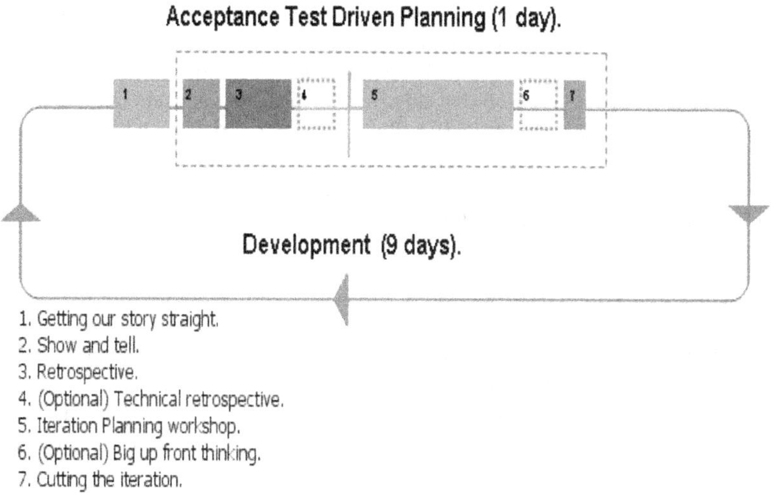

Acceptance Test Driven Planning (1 day).

Development (9 days).

1. Getting our story straight.
2. Show and tell.
3. Retrospective.
4. (Optional) Technical retrospective.
5. Iteration Planning workshop.
6. (Optional) Big up front thinking.
7. Cutting the iteration.

Fig. 1. ATDD Timeline

An optional addition to the morning programme is a technical retrospective that we have used on occasion when there have been significant changes to the code base which not all members of the team have been directly involved in. This of course is a "smell" of sorts but, regardless, is often a useful way to get everyone back on the same page before we begin the next iteration. After a break for lunch, a new iteration begins and we are in the "Planning Workshop" for most of the afternoon.

A "Big Up Front Thinking" session at the end of the day is also optional but is sometimes used by the team to draw broad brush impressions (class and simple interaction diagrams mostly) of how the code might evolve for the set of stories we are just about to begin working on. Big up front design? Not really. It is just a way to share ideas and get clear in people's minds current ideas on where we might go next.

The planning part of our process is time-boxed and now takes 2-3 hours as compared to our previous and much less effective 6-8 hour marathon session.

The day is over and it is time to go home and look forward to another iteration.

6   Conclusion

The 12 practices of XP can broadly be seen to fall into either one of two camps: planning or development type activities. The familiar mantra of test-code-refactor, combined with continuous integration and source control has given us a development environment with all the right ingredients and a fairly prescriptive recipe on how they should be practiced. The writings on planning are less prescriptive in how they should be practiced, especially for those used to more traditional heavyweight planning processes. In our experience development rather than planning practices are given more attention and yet successful planning is often more difficult to achieve.

This paper describes an adaptation, or evolution to XP style planning based around acceptance testing which takes the existing planning practices (with some additions) and organises them in a way which we believe can lead to better planning and more predictable results. In developing the process, we have aimed, at every juncture, to find the least amount of work we could do and still make informed, quality decisions. Experience has taught us that this balance point is not easily found.

Over time we have recognised that this form of planning appears to have a 'Goldilocks' like quality – any more process and we feel the overhead, and any less and the process begins to fail. We do, of course, continue to look for ways in which we can improve the process but after many months and many projects, the balance we have found by planning and driving the development in this simple way feels "just right".

Biographies of the Authors

Richard Watt: Richard is a coach and developer working with ThoughtWorks in the UK. In the last three years Richard has spent a large part of his time coaching and mentoring teams in XP and other Agile development methods. Richard has over 10 years experience of commercial software development and has been a practitioner (and passionate advocate) of XP since late '99.

David Leigh-Fellows: David Leigh-Fellows is an Agile coach and Iteration manager. He has run half a dozen XP software projects since he came across Kent Beck three years ago. Dave has 12 years experience of commercial software development and enjoys helping teams realize their true potential by helping them find their own way.

Acknowledgements

To Owen Rogers and Ivan Moore for their contribution to the early development of some of the ideas presented in the paper; for being smart; and being great fun to work with.

To Alan Francis, Areiel Wolanow, and Ally Stokes for their constructive feedback in the earlier drafts; to Rachel Davies, Alex Howson, and Stuart Blair for their time and support in helping get the paper into a fit and proper state as the deadline loomed.

To Mary Poppendieck for her valued feedback and the ongoing support of our ideas.

And finally, to my colleague Rebecca Parsons for her hard work and encouragement in helping us make sure our work was best represented.

Bibliography

1. Roy Miller, Acceptance Testing, http://www.xpuniverse.com/2001/pdfs/Testing05.pdf
2. Johan Andersson, Geoff Bache, Peter Sutton. XP with Acceptance-Test Driven Development: A rewrite project for a resource optimization system.
   http://www.carmen.se/research_development/articles/ctrt0302.pdf
3. Lisa Crispin, Tip House, Testing Extreme Programming. Addison Weseley; 2002; ISBN 0321113551
4. Kent Beck, Martin Fowler, Planning Extreme Programming, p88. Addison Wesley, 2001; ISBN 0201710919.
5. Kent Beck, Test-Driven Development. By Example. Addison Wesley, 2003; ISBN 0321146530.

References

1. Lisa Crispin Senior Consultant Boldtech Systems Denver, CO USA 1.303.722.7964, lisa.crispin@att.net, Is Quality Negotiable?,
   www.xpuniverse.com/2001/pdfs/Special02.pdf
2. Alistair Cockburn, Writing Effective Use Cases, Addison-Wesley, 2000;
   ISBN 0201702258
3. Norm Kerth, Project Retrospectives: A Handbook for Team Reviews, Dorset House Publishing Co, 2001; ISBN 0932633447

An Agile Customer-Centered Method:
Rapid Contextual Design

Hugh Beyer[1], Karen Holtzblatt[1], and Lisa Baker[2]

[1] InContext Enterprises, Inc., 2352 Main St., Suite 302, Concord, MA 01742 USA
{beyer,karen}@incent.com
[2] LANDesk Software, Inc., 698 West 10000 South, Suite 500, South Jordan, Utah 84095 USA
lisa.baker@landesk.com

Abstract. Agile methods have proven their worth in keeping a development team focused on producing high-quality code quickly. But these methods generally have little to say about how to incorporate user-centered design techniques. Also the question has been raised whether agile methods can scale up to larger systems design. In this paper we show how one user-centered design method, Contextual Design (CD), forms a natural fit with agile methods and recount our experience with such combined projects.

1 Introduction

Agile software development methods [1, 2, 3] propose a new approach to the old problem of quickly developing reliable software that meets users' needs. But their strong focus on improving the engineering process neglects questions about how other disciplines fit in, and how agile methods fit in with the larger organization. The role of interaction design, user interface design, and usability in an agile team is unclear. It is also unclear how well the approaches work with larger teams and projects [4, 5].

At one level there should be no problem – the developers of agile processes are very clear that developers should work closely with their customers [1]. Customer orientation is built into the basic method. Rather than provide complex techniques for requirements elicitation or user research, agile approaches make customers part of the release planning and iterative development process. But customer-centered design provides a range of techniques for focusing on the needs of users and customers as the central concern. How do these techniques of fit with the agile approach? Do they apply before agile methods start – or are these techniques are superceded by continual customer contact throughout the project? How exactly is this relationship reconciled?

Furthermore, customer-centered design assumes that initial research, design, and planning happens at the start of the project. This may well look to agile practitioners like "big design up front" – a bad thing in the agile programming rule book. To reconcile these different world-views we, along with people such as Constantine [6] and Kane [7], are incorporating customer-centered design and usability techniques into our agile development efforts. This requires some adjustment to these techniques.

In this paper we analyze the underlying assumptions of agile methods from the point of view of classic user-centered design. Each of these assumptions presents a process challenge, and agile methods incorporate ways to solve them. But the challenges themselves are not new. In developing Contextual Design (CD), our customer-

C. Zannier et al. (Eds.): XP/Agile Universe 2004, LNCS 3134, pp. 50–59, 2004.
© Springer-Verlag Berlin Heidelberg 2004

centered systems definition method [8], we encountered many of the same issues – as, indeed, any practitioner must. While working with teams committed to XP as a development methodology, we have adapted our approach to a quick-turnaround, short-development-lifecycle project. This has given us some insight into strengths and weaknesses of both approaches. In this paper, we will show how integrating the approaches fill the gaps in agile methods for both fast-turnaround iterative projects as well as the large-scale, high-impact, enterprise projects. We will describe our experience with such an integrated approach, which we call *Rapid CD*.

1.1 Contextual Design as a Customer-Centered Design Approach

Customer-centered or user-centered methods encompass a broad class of techniques that define systems by building an in-depth understanding of the people who will be supported by them. We make a distinction between the *user* and the *customer*; the user is the individual who interacts with the system being designed directly. They use it to accomplish their job. But "customer" is a larger term – a customer may be a user or may depend on the output of the system, prepare input for a system, decide on the need for a system, or approve the purchase of a system. A customer, as the Total Quality people say, is anyone standing between you and a sale – or between you and acceptance of your system in practice. Understanding the users is key to getting the design right – but understanding the other customers of the system may be key to getting it accepted.

CD is a well-respected customer-centered design method that has been around for over 10 years. It provides techniques covering the entire front end of systems design, from figuring out who your users are and how they work through designing the detailed user interface and functionality of the system. CD has been used on very large scale projects – defining complex business processes, corporate web sites, and portals – on software tools, and on small, self-contained parts of many products and systems.

CD in its classic (non-agile) form is as follows:

Contextual inquiry. Field interviews with customers in their work places while they work, observing and inquiring into the structure of their own work practice. This ensures that the team captures the real business practice and daily activities of the people the system is to support, not just the self-reported practice or official policies..

Interpretation sessions and work modeling. Team discussions in which the events of the interview are retold, key points (affinity notes) are captured, and models representing the customer's work practice are drawn (including as-is sequences of tasks). This disciplined, detailed debriefing allows the team to share the findings, build a common understanding of the customer, and capture all the data relevant to the project in a form that will drive the design.

Consolidation and affinity building. The data from individual customers is consolidated to show a larger picture of the work of the targeted population. The affinity notes from all customers are brought together into an *affinity diagram*, a hierarchical representation of the issues labeled to reflect customer needs. Work models are consolidated, showing the common work patterns and strategies across all customers – the "as-is" work process.

Visioning. Together, the team reviews the models and invents how the system will streamline and transform the work people do. This is captured as a hand-drawn sketch on flip chart paper. This *vision* represents the big picture of what the system could do to address the full work practice. It can subsequently be broken down into coherent subsets so that the vision can be implemented over a series of releases. Alternatively, in a smaller project the team may simply brainstorm solutions.

Storyboarding. The new design for work tasks are sketched out using pictures and text in a series of hand-drawn cells. A storyboard includes manual practices, initial UI concepts, business rules, and automation assumptions. This becomes the "to-be" work model.

User Environment Design (UED). A single representation of the system showing all functions and how they are organized into coherent places in the system to support user intent. The UED is built from the storyboards. This ensures a large system is coherent and fits the work. It provides a basis for prioritization and rational segmentation of the system.

Paper prototypes and mock-up interviews. User interfaces are designed on paper and tested with the system's actual users, first in rough form and then with more detail. This ensures the basic system function and structure work for the users, and that the basic UI concept is sound.

A Contextual Design project exploits just those CD techniques needed for the project at hand. (Rapid CD uses just a few of them.) But each technique exists to solve a particular problem in managing a development project, just as the techniques of agile methods do.

1.2   Experience with Contextual Design and Agile Methods

Two of the authors are from InContext, a company specializing in customer-centered design. The third is from LANDesk, which provides integrated solutions for managing systems. When we came together to collaborate on a development project, our challenge was to make agile methods work with a strong customer focus. LANDesk is committed to XP as a development method, so all our customer inquiry and design work had to be reconciled with this way of doing development. Our success in creating an effective methodology has resulted in the following perspective on agile methods.

Agile methods seem to be based on what we will call axioms – principles or assumptions that are almost self-evident. Some of these axioms have been listed explicitly in the literature [1]; others have not, perhaps because they seem so obvious. Each axiom presents a challenge to the traditional development process, and agile methods propose a solution to each that makes sense from the engineering perspective. (As Alan Cooper said, these methods seem to have been created by engineering to defend itself from the failings of the parent organization [9].)

But the community of customer-centered researchers and practitioners have been dealing with variations of these issues for years [10, 11, 12, 13]. What is the customer-centered design perspective on these problems? Here is a discussion of these axioms and our experience with customer-centered design alters our approach to the issues:

Axiom 1: Separate Design from Engineering. Much of the distinctiveness (and much of the value) of agile methods comes from the clear separation of responsibilities they bring to the development process. Developers write code and design the implementation of systems – that is what they are good at. They are not good at understanding how people work, creating effective and intuitive user interfaces, or making an interface usable.

The great strength of agile methods is that they focus the engineers on doing what engineers do best. The weakness of agile methods is that they give little guidance in figuring out what to tell the engineers to do. This is the job of the customer role, whether played by the actual customer or a surrogate, but how is the customer to accomplish it?

In particular, how is the customer to answer questions such as:

What is the scope of the system? What problem will it solve, and what tasks will it affect? Will these tasks be streamlined through the introduction of technology or replaced entirely by automated system? What will the overall effect on the business be? For an XP team to begin developing User Stories, these questions must already have been answered.

These design questions fall into the domain traditionally known as "systems analysis" or "requirements analysis" and are not covered by agile methods at all. In practice, some organizations have product marketing scope out the product release according to business and marketing needs; then they hand off a high-level overview of the user stories to engineering.

CD provides Contextual Inquiry, work modeling, consolidation and affinity building, and visioning to bring customers and developers together and make the customer needs explicit.

What should the basic function and structure of the system be? Someone must decide how a system will be structured to support user tasks, how functions will be grouped into coherent user interfaces to support coherent parts of a task, and what those functions do. There is no good support for these design activities in traditional programming methodologies – even the word "design" is reserved for the design of the internal structure of the system. But to the user, the user interface *is* the system.

The new concepts of "user experience architecture" and "user interaction" have been coined to cover these activities. Agile methods do not provide specific techniques to address them. Instead, agile methods send each completed iteration off to designated customers so engineering can receive feedback earlier in the process. Engineering then cleans up and fixes the UI afterward based on user feedback. (The XP saying is: the earlier you get it to the customer, the earlier you can fix it.)

In CD, we define overall structure and basic function using Storyboards and User Environment Design. These define exactly the level of structure needed to provide coherent and effective User Stories.

What is the user interface? Screen layout, button labels, tree views, drag and drop, hyperlinks, pulldown menus, etc. must be assembled into coherent, pleasing, and transparent screens that support the user's work in the new system.

This is classic user interface (UI) design, and it is the orphan child of software development methodologies. Is it design? Is it analysis? Does a requirements specification include the UI or does it not? There is no consistent practice.

Regardless of where UI design is situated organizationally, a successful agile development project depends on the skill being available, even if a team does not explicitly assign such a role. Because the UI is the interface between the user and the system's function, the only way to test the system is through the UI. Effective UI design is a prerequisite for agile methods to work, but the methodology provides no separate focus or testing. In our own past XP agile projects, we have included user interface mockups as part of the story definition and acceptance testing criteria for the iteration. But this practice is incomplete because it focuses on individual stories and does not create an explicit, cohesive view of the product and work practice.

CD recognizes and staffs UI design as a separate discipline – which fits the agile approach of focusing developers on code. The UED (when needed) or vision provides requirements for UI design and the paper mockups permit the UI to be considered and tested on its own, independent of the developer's underlying implementation.

Taken together, these elements of CD dovetail with agile processes to ensure that what the customer representatives communicate is what the customers actually need. These processes support the thinking and design needed for the release planning and User Stories to be effective.

Axiom 2: Make the User the Expert. Agile and customer-centered approaches agree in recognizing the user as the final authority and only arbiter of what makes a good system. But how to make this voice heard? The agile approach is to put the customer on the team, and if there are multiple customers, assign one as the representative who makes all choices. [3, p. 68] But there are some drawbacks to this approach:

People cannot articulate their own work practice. When asked what they do, people give their impression of what they do – which may or may not be accurate [10, 14]. In one example from our own experience, system managers told our project team that most of their job was troubleshooting. Later field interviews revealed that in fact, they spent most of their time doing simple tasks such as installs and user management.

So it is not sufficient to put a customer on the team and asking them to explain how they do things and what they need – or worse, how *others* do things and what *others* need. This is likely to lead to an incomplete understanding of the work practice and consequently, a system that does not work for its users.

A "representative" user never is. No one person can embody all the customers of a real enterprise system. All the stakeholders in the system – direct users, secondary users, management, upstream and downstream roles in the process – must also be considered. The divide between the users, who are focused on doing the work, and the other customers of the system may be quite wide.

Furthermore, the more the "representative" customer becomes part of the engineering organization, the less useful they are as a user surrogate. They learn too much about the technology and they become invested in the team's thinking. They become more empathetic to the engineer's challenges and less connected to the challenges they faced in their previous job. We have made our users members of our XP teams, and have found that they are just too nice to us. They become so understanding of the difficulties the development team faces that their feedback simply is not tough enough.

Customers are not designers, any more than engineers are. They know where their shoes pinch but not what the technical possibilities are, and they cannot easily envision what a future work practice might be. Consider the "make it fit" feature that first appeared in WordPerfect – the users were asking for a faster print preview. Only through on-site interviews did the design team discover they were using print preview to squeeze their documents onto a page. An experienced person's work is habitual and automatic, which makes it hard to envision a new and different world supported by an unknown technology.

If the customer representative cannot accurately communicate customer needs, the project will fail no matter how well development does their end of the work. Customer-centered design makes the customer a powerful and accurate voice on the team. CD gives the team a way to understand all their customers and users. CD says: if you want to learn about the customer's work, apprentice yourself to your customers. Don't ask them to talk about their work out of context. Go to their workplace and watch what they do, discussing it with them. Represent their voice in the data and design to the data.

Axiom 3: Keep Up-Front Planning to a Minimum. Agile methods distrust up-front planning intensely. Business needs change, the business climate changes, or the customer discovers they did not really understand what they needed after all. So agile methods view time invested in up-front planning as probable time wasted. Up-front planning is kept short, relatively informal, and focused on just the next release – which is also short.

CD takes a different tack towards the relationship between requirements and plans, because of its different starting point:

Work practice changes very little over time. The initial focus in CD is on understanding customer work practice, as opposed to defining a particular system. The work patterns, strategies, and intents discovered during this phase are fundamental to how people work and change little over time or across a wide range of users. It is feature implementations or underlying technology that changes rapidly. After developing a full set of CD models to represent a user population, we find those models are still useful years later. We return to them when starting new projects serving the same population. These models are *more* accurate and robust than the voice of a single customer representative who has not made a formal study of the work. Compared to hiring an on-site user, the CD models are useful longer and over time cost significantly less.

A solid understanding of the user leads to speed. Once the work practice of the user is understood, you can rapidly iterate the design and implementation. The data drives the current release, suggests the focus for the next, and provides a base understanding for each iteration. On our XP teams, velocity slows each time the engineers come upon a new storyline. They churn, questioning the basis of the user requirements and the details (or lack thereof) included in the story definitions.

'Minimum planning' depends on project scope. A small, quick-iteration project only needs a small amount of planning. We have completed field studies of 5-8 users, quickly consolidated and brainstormed solutions, all within a week or two. This small CD investment is enough for a fast-turnaround release and makes the user presence on the project unnecessary. But a large project introducing disruptive technology will require much more up-front data gathering and planning and will need more time to budget resources and market priorities. Bankston's concept of an "architectural spike" [15] is a useful way to think about this more detailed planning – just as you might devote an iteration to solving an implementation problem, devote an iteration to requirements definition.

So the CD philosophy is: Do only the planning you need to do; use team-based, high-communication processes to drive quickly to a common understanding of the problem and the solution; and create only the artifacts you need for the next step of design.

Axiom 4: Work in Quick Iterations. The classic design methodologies are frequently criticized for lacking prompt feedback – a two-year project would typically get its first real customer feedback a year and a half into it, when it first went to field test. At this point, it was far too late to discover that the project should have been addressing a different problem, or that it was addressing the right problem the wrong way. Any user feedback was thrown onto the feature pile for the next release. To compensate for this, agile methods prescribe rapid iterations in development (we plan 3-week iterations in our XP projects) and short release cycles. Each iteration is developed through test-first development – write the test, then write the code to satisfy it.

But creating code – no matter how fast it is created – only to rework it later is wasteful. Instead, CD pushes both these ideas earlier in the process: begin the iterations and start testing even before coding begins.

Test and iterate the spec before code. XP's "Developer's Bill of Rights" states: "You have the right to know what is needed, with clear declarations of priority in the form of detailed requirements and specifications." But the specification will never be correct unless it is tested with users to ensure it fits their real – as opposed to espoused – needs.

But how can a user test a specification? Few people can foresee the impact of a proposed system change merely by hearing such a change described. Instead, CD uses paper mockups to present a proposed new system to its users as though it were real. Users can work through their own actual work problems in the paper system, with the designer manipulating it to show the system's responses. When problems arise, user and designer change the system together, immediately, to better fit the user's work practice. Rough paper mockups are sufficient to show that the right system, the right structure, and the right functions are being defined.

Test and iterate the UI before code. Once the basic system has been proved, paper mockups can be refined to represent the proposed user interface. This ensures the basic UI concept is suitable before the team starts iterating it in code.

Test and iterate in code when needed. Once the spec and basic UI are in place, agile development's short iterations become the central driver for testing. Each iteration is a working version of the system, albeit with limited functionality. These iterations can be used to test the final UI and actual behavior of the system with customers to ensure low-level usability concerns are identified and dealt with early.

Testing iterations with customers as they are completed and using the results to refine the team's direction is good. But there's no reason to wait until after code is cut. CD makes the fast iteration and course-correction part of the specification process itself.

2   Building a New Process: *Rapid CD*

The above discussion suggests how a customer-centered design approach such as CD can coexist with agile methods – indeed, how the two complement each other so well that they form a very strong combination. *Rapid CD* [16] is a fast, effective, customer-centered way to design a product when quick turnaround is desired.

Here is an overview of the process, step by step, with typical time estimates for each step. This is essentially the process we have used for several versions of our own shipping commercial systems. (Different projects have been able to do more or less of the idealized process outlined below.) We assume that the customer role will be played by customer representatives working with a team of at least two UI designers. This brings design ability, knowledge of what the technology can do, and knowledge of what makes a good user interface to the "customer" side of the project.

1. **Set project focus.** Determine the complexity of the project and the level of innovation required. Identify the 1 or 2 key customer roles this product release will support and plan customer visits. (½ day for discussions, but expect 2-3 weeks to set up visits from a standing start. Once you have relationships and organizational expertise, it is easier.)

2. **Contextual inquiry with potential customers.** Gather data from at least 3 people in each role. In a week, a team can do 8 interviews with people from 4 organizations and interpret that data, producing affinity notes and sequence models (as-is tasks). Ideally, this is done in a cross-functional team of UI people, marketing, and developers. In practice, we find that developers are usually finishing up their previous project and we bring them up to speed later. (1 week)

3. **Build an affinity** showing the scope of issues from all customers, and sequence models (task models) showing how specific tasks to be supported by the project are now done. This is a representation of the "as-is" customer work practice. (3 to 4 days)

4. **Introduce the larger team** (including the full development team) to the customer roles and customer data. Summarize key findings, then walk the team through the affinity to allow the team members to comprehend the customer environment. Ask each team member to note questions and design ideas.

5. **Identify issues.** Key team members determine what issues will be addressed by the project (typically product marketing, development leads, and human factors participate in this). Collect issues from the affinity, choosing the most critical issues that can be addressed within the project scope. Brainstorm ideas of how to better support the work. Record and save big ideas for future high-impact projects. (2 days)

6. **Build User Stories** in response to these issues. User Stories are guided by the sequence models and show how the system will resolve the issues.

7. **Run the Planning Game** with the User Stories. Use conceptual diagrams and high level UI mockups to facilitate team communication. Without a completed UI the team can't know exactly how difficult implementation will be, but within the context of an organization the team can know the typical complexity of the UI's they define, so they can supply a rough estimate. Organize the User Stories into Iterations, groups of stories that deliver coherent subsets of function. Prioritize and eliminate stories as necessary to meet resource budget for the release. (We always save some budget for additional user stories that will reveal themselves once we begin getting user feedback.)

8. **Design detailed user interfaces** to support the User Stories in the first Iteration. UI design is its own discipline – don't mix it with the implementation work of coding the User Story. (1-2 days)

9. **Test UIs with users** in paper with mock-up interviews. User Stories are a fairly fine-grained definition of system functionality; many User Stories can be covered in a single paper prototype test. Test these UIs with 3 to 4 users and use the results to refine the design. Do a second round of tests with a more detailed UI if you have the time and resources. A third round of testing will happen with live code. (2 weeks for both rounds)

10. **Deliver to development.** Provide the User Stories and completed UIs to the development team for implementation. With detailed UIs, developers can very accurately cost their work for the iteration. In addition, testing can incorporate UI mockups into their acceptance tests, providing development with a clear end point to their task.

11. **Continue iterations in parallel.** During implementation of the first Iteration, the UI team develops the UIs for the second Iteration's User Stories and tests them with users in 2 rounds of paper before the code for the first Iteration is complete. When the code for the first Iteration is completed, the UI team gives developers the next set of stories and UIs and the developers start on the second Iteration. Meanwhile, the UI team designs the UIs for the third iteration and tests them with users in paper. Simultaneously, if desired, they test the running code of the first iteration with users to get quick feedback on the actual product. (Our projects have done this with customers every second or third iteration.)

At the end of the second iteration, the UI team gives the User Stories and UI designs for the third iteration to the development team and the testing feedback is incorporated into the plan. This process repeats until the release is done.

If user testing suggests changes to future User Stories, the changes are made and the work estimate for those stories changed if necessary. When user feedback indicates you must change work the team has already done, plan additional User Stories and schedule them in as needed. (Be aware this *will* happen as the system comes alive and low-level issues reveal themselves. Be careful not to schedule yourself too tight in your initial resourcing. The team will need to save some of its resource budget to accommodate these additional stories.)

This plan assumes a separate UI design team exists that will work out the details of the interface within the context of the User Stories. In practice, UI design is usually a separate skill held by different people on the team. Our experience is that this sort of handoff – once the developers have come to recognize the value of the skill – is very easy. (In fact, once developers figure out how much time and effort the UI designers save them, the developers are prone to complain that the UI designers haven't told them *enough* about what to do and have left them with too many choices.) We also find it promotes better understanding to have developers accompany the UI designer on some user tests.

For highly complex or highly innovative projects, a more traditional CD process can be used to determine customer needs and system requirements. In such a process, the full set of CD customer work models represents the complete "as-is" work practice to ensure the existing process is really understood. The CD vision is used to synthesize a coherent design response to the work problem.

The UED model becomes the key representation of the behavior of the new system. It shows all the parts of the system and all the function, to maintain the coherence of the system as a whole. It also shows how the system can be broken into coherent chunks for implementation. Each of these chunks becomes input to an agile team – the release planning and user stories are oriented towards delivering that chunk and the UED keeps the work of the multiple teams in sync.

3   Conclusion

Agile methods address the difficulties of development in real organization by putting practices in place to make engineering effective. But these practices depend on a correct and complete understanding of customer needs – of what the system is to do and how it is to be structured to support the customer organization. Agile techniques in general do not try to address the question of how this understanding is generated and communicated to the team.

Customer-centered design techniques *do* address exactly this question. In our projects, we have found that we can draw on both disciplines to support agile teams that work from an in-depth understanding of their customers. We have used that experience to define the process outlined above. This process incorporates the customer voice and provides room for UI and user interaction design as part of the agile process. It also suggests how significantly large projects could be addressed in an agile manner.

References

1. K. Beck, *Extreme Programming Explained: Embrace Change*. San Francisco: Addison-Wesley, 2000.
2. A. Cockburn, , *Agile Software Development*, Addison Wesley, Reading, MA, 2002.
3. J. Highsmith, *Adaptive Software Development: A Collaborative Approach to Managing Complex Systems*. New York: Dorset House, 2000.
4. B. Boehm and R. Turner, "Observations on Balancing Discipline and Agility" presented at *Agile Development Conference 2003*, Salt Lake City, Utah, and archived at http://agiledevelopmentconference.com/2003/files/P4Paper.pdf
5. J. Grenning, Using XP in a Big Process Company, article at http://www.agilealliance.com/articles/articles/XPInABigProcessCompany.pdf
6. L. Constantine, "Process Agility and Software Usability: Toward Lightweight Usage-Centered Design," in ForUse Conference Proceedings, 2003.
7. D. Kane, "Finding a Place for Discount Usability Engineering in Agile Development: Throwing Down the Gauntlet," at the *Agile Development Conference 2003*, as archived at http://agiledevelopmentconference.com/2003/files/P5Paper.pdf
8. H. Beyer and K. Holtzblatt, Contextual Design: *Defining Customer-Centered Systems*, Morgan Kaufmann Publishers Inc., San Francisco (1997).
9. A. Cooper, as reported by E. Nelson in *Extreme Programming vs. Interaction Design* at FTPOnline: article at http://www.fawcette.com/interviews/beck_cooper/default.asp
10. J. Whiteside, J. Bennett, and K. Holtzblatt, "Usability Engineering: Our Experience and Evolution," *Handbook of Human Computer Interaction*, M. Helander (Ed.). New York: North Holland, 1988.
11. L. Suchman, *Plans and Situated Actions*, Cambridge University Press, Cambridge, 1989.
12. T. Winograd, *Bringing Design to Software*, ACM Press, NY, NY, 1996.
13. P. Seaton and T. Stewart, "Evolving Task Oriented Systems," *Human Factors in Computing Systems CHI '92 Conference Proceedings*, May 1992, Monterey, California.
14. M. Polanyi, *The Tacit Dimension*, Routledge and Kegan Paul, 1967.
15. A. Bankston, *Usability and User Interface Design in XP*, article at http://www.ccpace.com/resources/documents/UsabilityinXP.pdf
16. K. Holtzblatt, *Rapid CD*, Morgan Kaufmann Publishers Inc., San Francisco (forthcoming).

Suitability of FIT User Acceptance Tests for Specifying Functional Requirements: Developer Perspective

Grigori Melnik, Kris Read, and Frank Maurer

Department of Computer Science, University of Calgary
Calgary, Canada
{melnik,readk,maurer}@cpsc.ucalgary.ca

Abstract. The paper outlines an experiment conducted in two different academic environments, in which FIT tests were used as a functional requirements specification. Common challenges for functional requirements specifications are identified, and a comparison is made between how well prose and FIT user acceptance tests are suited to overcoming these challenges from the developer's perspective. Experimental data and participant feedback are examined to evaluate whether developers can use requirements in the form of FIT tests to create a design and implementation.

1 Introduction

It is common knowledge that two thirds of all software projects today fail (either by being terminated, going overtime, going over-budget, or because they deliver only partial functionality). Ambiguous or incomplete software requirements along with poor quality control are two of the biggest contributors to these failures [7].

Despite the fact that quality control is a major cause of project failure, it is still often overlooked by project teams. Eighty-three percent of organizations' software developers don't like to test code [2]. One of the reasons is simply a lack of time to perform diligent and proper testing, which is frequently the result of inadequate planning and time overruns in other activities. When testing is performed, often it is done at the level of unit tests by the development and/or testing team. However, the goals and mentality of testers may not entirely correspond with those of the customer. Acceptance tests are needed to ensure customer satisfaction with the final product. Acceptance tests also serve as regression tests, to ensure that previously working functionality continues to behave as expected. These tests are often created based on a requirements specification, and serve to verify that contractual obligations are met. This creates a dependency between the requirements specification and acceptance test suite, a dependency that may involve a great deal of overhead. Changes to one side necessitate changes to the other, and effort is needed to ensure that the written requirements correspond precisely to the expected test results (and vice versa). Moreover, this dependency means that problems in the requirements specification will directly impact quality control.

It is estimated that 85 percent of the defects in developed software originate in the requirements [9, 1]. "Irrespective of the format chosen for representing requirements, the success of a product strongly depends upon the degree to which the desired system is properly described" [8]. Most software requirements are not specified using formal languages, but instead are written as some form of business requirement document. Normally such documents are written using natural languages and pictures. There are several "sins" to avoid when specifying requirements, some of which are listed by Meyer[1] [6]. The first such sin is *noise*, which manifests as information not relevant to the problem, or a repetition of existing information phrased in different ways. Noise may also be the reversal or shading of previously specified statements. Such inconsistencies between requirements make up 13 percent of requirements problems [4]. A second hazard is *silence*, in which important aspects of the problem are simply not mentioned. Omitted requirements account for 29 percent of all requirements errors [4]. *Over-specification* can happen when aspects of the solution are mentioned as part of the problem description. Requirements describe what is to be done but not how they are implemented [3]. *Wishful thinking* is when prose describes a problem to which a realistic solution would be difficult or impossible to find. *Ambiguity* is common when natural languages allow for more than one meaning for a given word or phrase. Often this is problematic when jargon includes terms otherwise familiar to the other party [6]. Prose is also prone to *reader subjectivity* since each person has a unique perspective (based on their cultural background, language, personal experience, etc). *Forward references* mention aspects of a problem not yet mentioned, and cause confusion in larger documents. *Oversized documents* are difficult to understand, use and maintain. *Customer uncertainty* appears when an inability to express specific needs results in an inclusion of vague descriptions. This, in turn, leads to developers making assumptions about "fuzzy" requirements: it has been estimated that incorrect assumptions account for 49 percent of requirements problems [4]. Making requirements understandable to the customer and verifiable by the developer might lead to the creation of *multiple representations* of the same requirements. Preserving more than one document can then lead to maintenance, translation and synchronization problems. Requirements are sometimes lost, especially non-functional requirements, when the use of *tools for requirements capture* only supports a strictly defined format or template. Lastly, requirements documents are often poor when written with *little to no user involvement*, instead being compiled by requirements solicitors, business analysts, domain experts or even developers [7].

This paper examines the suitability of FIT as a format for communicating functional requirements to the developer, and explores whether this format helps mitigate the "sins" listed above. In this context, we define "suitability" as the degree to which the functional requirements are found to be unambiguous, verifiable, consistent, and usable by developers for designing and implementing the system.

There are possibly other desirable properties of requirements. For example, from the customer's perspective, the ease of specifying and understanding the requirements by all stakeholders is important. However our paper focuses only on those properties listed above.

---

[1] Meyer's classification is well known; we have added some additional difficulties to the traditional "seven sins". Meyer's classification has been frequently referenced (see pp.232-233 in [8] for example)

2   Acceptance Testing with FIT

By definition, acceptance tests assess whether a feature is working from the customer's perspective. Acceptance tests are different from unit tests in that the later are modeled and written by the developer, while the former is at least modeled and possibly even written by the customer. Acceptance tests can be specified in many ways, from prose-based user stories to formal languages. Because the execution of acceptance tests is time consuming and costly, it is highly desirable to automate this process. Automating acceptance tests gives an objective answer when functional requirements are fulfilled. At the same time, making the requirements too formal alienates the user, as in the case of definition using formal languages.

FIT was named from the thesaurus entry for "acceptable". The goal of FIT is an acceptance test that an ordinary person can read and write[2]. To this end, FIT tests come in two parts: tests are defined using ordinary *tables* (usually, written by customer representatives, see Fig. 1 and Fig. 2, left side), and later fit *fixtures* are written to execute code using the data from table cells (implemented by the developers, see Fig. 1 and Fig. 2, right side). By abstracting the definition of the test from the logic that runs it, FIT opens up authorship of new tests to anyone who has knowledge of the business domain.

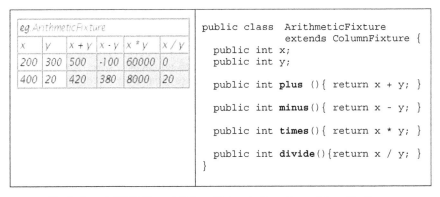

Fig. 1. Sample FIT table and ColumnFixture in Java. Excerpt from fit.c2.com

FIT tables can be created using common business tools, and can be included in any type of document (HTML, MS Word, MS Excel, etc). This idea is taken one step further by FitNesse[3], a Web-based collaborative testing and documentation tool designed around FIT. FitNesse provides a very simple way for teams to collaboratively create documents, specify tests, and even run those tests through a Wiki Web site. The FitNesse wiki[4] allows anyone to contribute content to the website without knowledge of HTML or programming technologies.

---

[2]   We leave it to a future experiment to show whether or not FIT tests can be easily read or written by customers. The present experiment focuses on whether developers can use functional requirements for their purposes when specified as FIT acceptance tests

[3]   http://www.fitnesse.org and http://fit.c2.com

[4]   http://wiki.org/wiki.cgi?WhatIsWiki

```
public class    Browser
                extends ActionFixture {
  ...
  public void select(int i) {
    MusicLibrary.
    select(MusicLibrary.library[i-1]);
  }

  public String title() {
    return MusciLibrary.looking.title;
  }

  public String artist() {
    return MusciLibrary.looking.artist;
  }
  ...
}
```

Fig. 2. Simple FIT table and ActionFixture in Java. Excerpt from fit.c2.com

Although acceptance tests are often written based on user requirements, we see that with FIT it is not necessary to create a written requirements document before creating an acceptance test. FIT tests are a tabular representation of customer expectations that can be understood by human beings. All that is needed to write a FIT table is a customer expectation and the ability to precisely and unambiguously write it down. In this way they are very similar to written functional requirements[5]. If the expectations themselves adequately explain the requirements for a feature, can be defined by the customer, and can be read by the developer, there may be some redundancy between the expression of those expectations and the written system requirements. Consequently, it may be possible to eliminate or reduce the size of prose requirements definitions. An added advantage to increased reliance on acceptance tests may be an increase in test coverage, since acceptance testing would both be mandatory and defined early in the project life cycle. To this end an experiment has been designed to evaluate the understandability of FIT acceptance tests for functional requirements specification.

3 Instrument

The goal of our experiment was to determine the suitability of using FIT tests as the functional part of a requirements specification. A project was conceived to develop an online document review system (DRS). This system allows users to submit, edit, review and manage professional documents (articles, reports, code, graphics artifacts etc.) called submission objects (so). These features are selectively available to three types of users: Authors, Reviewers and Administrators. More specifically, administrators can create repositories with properties such as: title of the repository, location of the repository, allowed file formats, time intervals, submission categories, review

---

[5] http://c2.com/doc/xpu02/workshop.html

criteria and designated reviewers for each item. Administrators can also create new repositories based on existing ones. Authors have the ability to submit and update multiple documents with data including title, authors, affiliations, category, keywords, abstract, contact information and bios, file format, and access permissions. Reviewers can list submissions assigned to them, and refine these results based on document properties. Individual documents can be reviewed and ranked, with recommendations (accept, accept with changes, reject, etc) and comments. Forms can be submitted incomplete (as drafts) and finished at a later time.

For the present, subjects were required to work on only a partial implementation concentrating on the submission and review tasks (Fig. 3). The only information provided in terms of project requirements was:

1. An outline of the system no more detailed than that given in this section.
2. A subset of functional requirements to be implemented (Fig. 3).
3. A suite of FIT tests (Fig. 4)

Specification

1. Design a data model (as a DTD or an XML Schema, or, likely, a set of DTDs/XML Schemas) for the artifacts to be used by the DocumentReviewSystem. Concentrate on "Document submission/update" and "Document review" tasks for now.

2. Build XSLT sheet(s) that when applied to an instance of so's repository will produce a subset of so's. As a minimum, queries and three query modes specified in DrsAssignmentOneAcceptanceTests must be supported by your model and XSLT sheets.

3. Create additional FIT tests to completely cover functionality of the queries.

Setup files

- drs_master.xml⬈ - a sample repository against which the FIT tests were written

- DrsAssignmentOneAcceptanceTests.zip⬈ - FIT tests, unzip them into FITNESSE_HOME\FitNesseRoot\ directory.

Fig. 3. Assignment specification snapshot[6]

Requirements in the FIT Test Suite of our experiment can be described generally as sorting and filtering tasks for a sample XML repository. Our provided suite initially consisted of 39 test cases and 657 assertions. In addition to developing the code necessary to pass these acceptance tests, participants were required to extend the existing suite to cover any additional sorting or filtering features associated with their model. An example FIT Test finding a document by exact match of author name, with results sorted by title in descending order is shown in Fig. 5.

Participants were given two weeks (unsupervised) to implement these features using XML, XSLT, Java and the Java API for XML Processing (JAXP). A common online experience base[7] was set up and all students could utilize and contribute to this

---

[6] http://mase.cpsc.ucalgary.ca/EB/Wiki.jsp?page=SENG513w04AssignmentOne
[7] http://mase.cpsc.ucalgary.ca/EB/

knowledge repository. An iteration planning tool and source code management system were available to all teams if desired.

DRS Assignment One Acceptance Test Suite

Startswith Author Search

DrsAssignmentOneAcceptanceTests.FindByAuthorUnsorted
DrsAssignmentOneAcceptanceTests.FindByAuthorSortByTitle
DrsAssignmentOneAcceptanceTests.FindByAuthorSortByTitleDescending
DrsAssignmentOneAcceptanceTests.FindByAuthorSortByType
DrsAssignmentOneAcceptanceTests.FindByAuthorSortByDate
DrsAssignmentOneAcceptanceTests.FindByAuthorSortByDateDescending

Contains Author Search

DrsAssignmentOneAcceptanceTests.FindByAuthorContainsUnsorted
DrsAssignmentOneAcceptanceTests.FindByAuthorContainsSortByTitle
DrsAssignmentOneAcceptanceTests.FindByAuthorContainsSortByTitleDescending
DrsAssignmentOneAcceptanceTests.FindByAuthorContainsSortByType
DrsAssignmentOneAcceptanceTests.FindByAuthorContainsSortByDate

---

Fig. 4. Partial FIT Test Suite. The suite contains test cases and can be executed. For example, the test FindByAuthorUnsorted results in an unsorted list of items matching an author name

We hypothesized that:

A) FIT acceptance tests describe a customer requirement such that a developer can implement the feature(s) for that requirement.
B) Developers with no previous FIT experience will quickly be able to learn how to use FIT given the time provided.
C) 100% of developers will create code that passes 100% of customer provided tests.
D) More than 50% of the requirements for which no tests were given will be implemented and tested.
E) 100% of implemented requirements will have corresponding FIT tests.

4   Sampling

Students of computer science programs from the University of Calgary and the Southern Alberta Institute of Technology (SAIT) participated in the experiment. All individuals were knowledgeable about programming and testing, however, no individuals had any advance knowledge of FIT or FitNesse (based on a verbal poll).

Twenty five (25) senior undergraduate University of Calgary students were enrolled in the course *Web-Based Systems*[8], which introduces the concepts and techniques of building Web-based enterprise solutions and includes comprehensive hands-on software development assignments. Seventeen (17) students from the Bachelor of Applied Information Systems program were enrolled in a similar course, *Internet Software Techniques*[9], at SAIT. The material from both courses was presented consis-

---

[8] http://mase.cpsc.ucalgary.ca/seng513/W2004/
[9] http://mase.cpsc.ucalgary.ca/apse504/W2004/

tently by the same instructor in approximately the same time frame. This experiment spans only the first of six assignments involving the construction of a document review system.

fit.ActionFixture		
start	seng513.w04.drs.fixtures.FindActionFixture	
enter	repository	drs_master.xml
enter	querytype	findbyauthor
enter	querymode	isexact
enter	sortorder	title
enter	sortdirection	descending
enter	query	Maurer, Frank
press	find	
enter	select	3
check	author	Read, Kristopher
check	author	Maurer, Frank
check	author	Melnik, Grigori
check	author	Liu, Lawrence
check	title	Advantages of Tablet Usage by Software Development Teams
check	type	tex
check	dateSubmitted	2003-12-25
enter	select	2
check	author	Melnik, Grigori
check	author	Read, Kristopher
check	author	Maurer, Frank
check	title	Distributed Extreme Programming
check	type	rtf
check	dateSubmitted	2003-11-21
enter	select	1
check	author	Maurer, Frank
check	author	Chau, Thomas
check	title	Knowledge Management in Scrum
check	type	pdf
check	dateSubmitted	1999-03-15

Fig. 5. A sample FIT test (after execution)

Students were encouraged to work on programming assignments following the principles and the practices of extreme programming, including test-first design, collective code ownership, short iterations, continuous integration, and pair programming.

The University of Calgary teams consisted of 4 to 5 members, and additional help was available twice a week from two teaching assistants. SAIT teams had 3 members[10] each; however they did not have access to additional help outside of classroom lectures. In total, there were 12 teams and a total of 42 students.

---

[10] SAIT teams had fewer members so that we would have an equal number of teams at each location.

5 Observations

Our first hypothesis was that FIT acceptance tests describe a customer requirement such that a developer can implement the feature(s) for that requirement. Our experiment provided strong evidence that customer requirements provided using good acceptance tests can in fact be fulfilled successfully. On average (mean) 82% of customer-provided tests passed in the submitted assignments (SD=35%), and that number increases to 90% if we only consider the 10 teams who actually made attempts to implement the required FIT tests (SD=24%)[11] (Fig. 6). Informal student feedback about the practicality of FIT acceptance tests to define functional requirements also supports our first and second hypotheses. Students generally commented that the FIT tests were an acceptable form of assignment specification[12]. Teams had between 1 and 1.5 weeks to master FIT in addition to implementing the necessary functionality (depending on if they were from SAIT or the University of Calgary).

	University of Calgary						SAIT				
Team	1	2	3	4	5	6	1	2	4	5	6
Customer Tests Pass Ratio	100%	100%	0%	100%	100%	100%	79%	26%	100%	100%	100%

Fig. 6. Customer test statistics by teams

Seventy-three percent (73%) of all groups managed to satisfy 100% of customer requirements. Although this refutes our second hypothesis, our overall statistics are nonetheless encouraging. Those teams who did not manage to satisfy all acceptance tests also fell well below the average (46%) for the number of requirements attempted in their delivered product (Fig. 7).

	University of Calgary						SAIT				
Team	1	2	3	4	5	6	1	2	4	5	6
% of Requirements Attempted	87%	55%	42%	77%	42%	68%	32%	10%	59%	32%	35%

Fig. 7. Percentage of attempted requirements. An attempt is any code delivered that we evaluate as contributing to the implementation of desired functionality

Unfortunately, no teams were able to implement and test at least 50% of the additional requirements we had expected. Those requirements defined loosely in prose but given no initial FIT tests were largely neglected both in terms of implementation and test coverage (Fig. 8). This disproves our hypothesis that 100% of implemented requirements would have corresponding FIT tests. Although many teams implemented

---

[11] One team's data was removed from analysis because of a lack of participation from team members. One other team (included) delivered code but did not provide FIT fixtures.

[12] It should be noted that an academic assignment is not the same as a real-world requirements specification.

requirements for which we had provided no customer acceptance tests, on average only 13% of those new features were tested (SD=13%). Those teams who did deliver larger test suites (for example, team 2 returned 403% more tests than we provided) mostly opted to expand existing tests rather than creatively testing their new features.

Team	Number New Tests	New Test Pass Ratio	Number New Assertions	New Assertions Pass Ratio	% Additional Tests	% Additional Assertions	% New Features Tested	% Attempted Features Tested	
1	19	100%	208	100%	49%	32%	32%	67%	
2	157	100%	5225	100%	403%	795%	26%	100%	University
3	0	0%	0	0%	0%	0%	0%	0%	
4	116	100%	2218	100%	297%	338%	32%	75%	
5	9	100%	99	100%	23%	15%	16%	100%	
6	41	93%	616	95%	105%	94%	37%	100%	
1	0	0%	0	0%	0%	0%	0%	80%	
2	0	0%	0	0%	0%	0%	0%	100%	
4	56	100%	1085	100%	144%	165%	11%	66%	SAIT
5	0	0%	0	0%	0%	0%	0%	100%	
6	5	100%	64	100%	13%	10%	5%	100%	

Fig. 8. Additional features and tests statistics

Customers do not always consider exceptional cases when designing acceptance tests, and therefore acceptance tests must be evaluated for completeness. Even in our own scenario, all tests specified were positive tests; tests confirmed what the system should do with valid input, but did not explore what the system should do with invalid entries. For example, one test specified in our suite verified the results of a search by file type (.doc, .pdf, etc.). This test was written using lowercase file types, and no-where was it explicitly indicated that uppercase or capitalized types be permitted (.DOC, .Pdf, etc). As a result, 100% of teams wrote code that was case sensitive, and 100% of tests failed when given uppercase input.

6   Conclusions

Our hypotheses (A and B) that FIT tests describing customer requirements can be easily understood and implemented by a developer with little background on this framework were substantiated by the evidence gathered in this experiment. Considering the short period of time allotted, we can conclude from the high rate of teams who delivered FIT tests (90%) that the learning curve for reading and implementing FIT tests is not prohibitively steep, even for relatively inexperienced developers.

Conversely, our hypotheses that 100% of participants would create code that passed 100% of customer provided tests (C), that more than 50% of the requirements for which no tests were given would be tested (D), and that 100% of implemented requirements would have corresponding FIT tests (E) were not supported. In our opinion, the fact that more SAIT teams failed to deliver 100% of customer tests can be attributed to the slightly shorter time frame and the lack of practical guidance from TA's. Given more time and advice we believe that a higher rate of customer satisfaction can be achieved. The lack of tests for new features added by teams may, in our opinion, be accredited to the time limitations placed on students, the lack of motivation to deliver additional tests, and the lower emphasis given to testing in the past academic experiences of these students[13]. At the very least, our observation that feature areas with fewer provided FIT tests were more likely to be incomplete supports the idea that FIT format functional requirements are of some benefit.

The fact that a well defined test suite was provided by the customer up front may have instilled a false sense of security in terms of test coverage. The moment the provided test suite passed, it is possible that students assumed the assignment was complete. This may be extrapolated to industry projects: development teams could be prone to assuming their code is well tested if it passes all customer tests. It should be noted that writing FIT tests is simplified but not simple; to write a comprehensive suite of tests, some knowledge and experience in both testing and software engineering is desirable (for example, a QA engineer could work closely with the customer). It is vital that supplementary testing be performed, both through unit testing and additional acceptance testing. The role of quality assurance specialists will be significant even on teams with strong customer and developer testing participation. Often diabolical thinking and knowledge of specific testing techniques such as equivalence partitioning and boundary value analysis are required to design a comprehensive test suite.

From the outcome of our five hypotheses, along with our own observations and feedback from the subjects, we can suggest how FIT acceptance tests perform as a specification of functional requirements in relation to the criteria stated in our introduction. We believe that *noise* is greatly reduced when using FIT tests to represent requirements. Irrelevant information is more difficult to include in well structured tables than in prose documents. Also, tests which shade or contradict previous tests are easily uncovered at the time of execution (although there is no automatic process to do so). Acceptance tests can be used as regression tests after they have passed in order to prevent problems associated with possible noise. We discovered that *silence* is not well addressed by the FIT framework, and may even become a more serious problem. This was well demonstrated by the failure of our teams to test at least 50% of the requirements for which no tests were given. Our example of case-sensitive document types also clearly demonstrates how a lack of explicit tests can lead to assumptions and a lack of clarifications. Prose documents may be obviously vague, and by this obviousness incite additional communication. *Over-specification* is not a problem since FIT tests do not allow any room for embedded solutions in the tests themselves. FIT tables are only representations of customer expectations, and the fixtures become the agents of the solutions. Although it can be argued that specifying an ActionFixture describes a sequence of actions (and therefore a solution), when writing FIT tables these actions should be based on business operations and not code-level events. *Wishful thinking* is largely eliminated by FIT, since defining tests requires that

---

[13] Despite the fact that the importance of testing was repeatedly emphasized, students are not accustomed to writing test code. Students were aware that the majority of marks were not being assigned based on new tests.

the customer think about the problem and make very specific decisions about expectations.

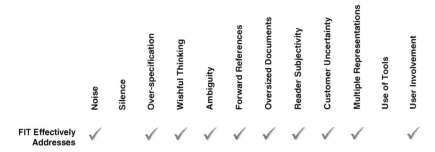

Fig. 9. Evaluation of FIT for requirements specification. Check marks indicate that FIT effectively addresses the issue (although it could be only partial)

Ambiguity may still be a problem when defining requirements using FIT tests if keywords or fields are defined in multiple places or if these identifiers are open to multiple interpretations. However, FIT diminishes ambiguity simply because it uses fewer words to define each requirement. *Forward references* and *oversized documents* may still be an issue if large numbers of tests are present and not organized into meaningful test suites. In our experiment, the majority of groups categorized their own tests without any instruction to do so. *Reader subjectivity* is greatly reduced by FIT tests. Tables are specified using a format defined by the framework (*ActionFixture*, *ColumFixture*, etc). As long as tests return their expected results when executed, the developer or customer knows that the corresponding requirement was correctly interpreted regardless of the terminology used. *Customer uncertainty* may manifest as the previously mentioned problem of silence, but it is impossible for a defined FIT test not to have a certain outcome. FIT tests are executable, verifiable and easily readable by the customer and developer, and therefore there is no need for *multiple representations* of requirements. All necessary representations have effectively merged into a suite of tables. Requirements gathering *tools* can be problematic when they limit the types of requirements that can be captured. FIT is no exception; it can be difficult to write some requirements as FIT tests, and it is often necessary to extend the existing set of fixtures, or to utilize prose for defining non-functional requirements and making clarifications. However, FIT tests can be embedded in prose documents or defined through a collaborative wiki such as FitNesse, and this may help overcome the limitations of FIT tables.

In addressing the characteristics of suitability (as defined in Introduction), our findings demonstrate that FIT tests as functional requirements specifications are in fact unambiguous, verifiable, and usable (from the developer's perspective). However, insufficient evidence was gathered to infer consistency between FIT tests.

Although our results did not match all of our expectations, valuable lessons were learned from the data gathered. When requirements are specified as tests, there is still no guarantee that the requirements will be completed on-time and on-budget. Time constraints, unexpected problems, lack of motivation and poor planning can still result in only some requirements being delivered. As with any type of requirements elicitation, it is vital that the customer is closely involved in the process. FIT tests can be executed by the customer or in front of the customer, and customers can quickly evaluate project progress based on a green (pass) or red (fail) condition. In conclusion, our study provides only initial evidence of the suitability of FIT tests for specifying functional requirements. This evidence directly supports the understandability of this type of functional requirements specification by developers. There are both advantages and disadvantages to adopting FIT for this purpose, and the best solution is probably some combination of both prose-based and FIT-based specifications.

7 Validity

This paper provides only initial evidence supporting the use of FIT tests to communicate functional requirements to developers. There are several possible threats to the validity of this experiment that should be reduced through future experiments. One such threat is the limitation of our experiment to a purely academic environment. Although we spanned two different academic institutions, industry participants would be more relevant. Another threat is our small sample size, which can be increased through repeated experiments in future semesters. Moreover, all of the FIT tests provided in this experiment were written by expert researchers, which would not be the case in an industrial setting. Although this was an academic assignment, it was not conducted in a controlled environment. Students worked in teams on their own time without proper invigilation.

8 Future Work

This experiment is the first in a series of six FIT-related experiments planned for the next eight months. Given more time and advice, we believe, that a higher rate of customer satisfaction can be achieved. This will be investigated using the same teams as the experiment continues this semester. All insights gained from the analysis of our observations will be verified and validated with additional trials on the current teams as well as new trials with a new sampling of subjects.

An upcoming experiment will have the subjects refactor current tests to adapt to new and changing requirements. In addition, there will be increased emphasis on more complete, negative testing. In a third experiment, subjects will be asked to specify a suite of FIT requirements for a remote team at a different institution.

An experiment with industry practitioners is part of our ongoing research. It will test the understandability of functional requirements specified as FIT tables. We invite any interested party to contact the authors for further discussion. FIT training, onsite or off-site, will be provided free of charge.

Acknowledgements

We would like to thank all participants from the University of Calgary and SAIT who participated in this study and provided us with their valuable feedback. This ongoing research is partially sponsored by NSERC and iCore.

References

1. Ben-Menachem, M., Marliss, G. *Software Quality: Producing Practical, Consistent Software*, International Thomson Publishing, London, UK, 1997.
2. CenterLine Software, Inc. A Survey of 240 Fortune 1,000 companies in North America and Europe, Cambridge, MA, 1996. Online http://www.computerworld.com/news/1997/story/0,11280,17522,00.html. Last accessed February 29, 2004.
3. Davis, A. *Software Requirements Revision Objects, Functions, & States*, Prentice Hall PTR, Englewood Cliffs, NJ, 1994.
4. Hooks, I., Farry, K. *Customer-Centered Products: Creating Successful Products Through Smart Requirements Management*. American Management Association, New York, NY, 2001.
5. Jones, C. Patterns of *Software Systems Failure and Success*. International Thompson Computer Press, Boston, MA, 1996.
6. Meyer, B. On Formalism in Specifications. *IEEE Software*, 2(1):6–26, 1985.
7. *The CHAOS Chronicles*. The Standish Group International, West Yarmouth, MA. Online http://www1.standishgroup.com//chaos/intro2.php. Last accessed January 20, 2004.
8. Van Vliet, H. *Software Engineering: Principles and Practice*, 2/e, John Wiley & Sons, Chichester, UK, 2000.
9. Young, R. *Effective Requirements Practices,* Addison-Wesley, Boston, MA, 2001.

Using Storyotypes to Split Bloated XP Stories

Gerard Meszaros

ClearStream Consulting Inc.,
3710– 205 – 5th Avenue S.W.
Calgary, Alberta Canada T2P 2V7
gerard@clrstream.com

Abstract. An ideal XP project is composed of stories defined by the customer that are of the right size and focus to plan and manage according to XP principles and practices. A story that is too large creates a variety of problems: it might not fit into a single iteration; there are a large number of tasks that must be coordinated; it can be too large to test adequately at the story/functional level; too much non-essential functionality is bundled early in development causing essential functionality to be deferred. Teams new to XP find managing the size of stories especially challenging because they lack the experience required to simplify and breakdown large stories. This experience report describes four heuristics (storyotypes) we have used on our XP projects to successfully manage the size of stories.

1 Introduction

At ClearStream Consulting, we have helped many clients learn how to apply eXtreme Programming (XP) on their projects. A common problem they face is getting the right granularity for their stories; most projects start off with "bloated stories" that later need to be split into smaller stories.

Teams that have experience using "use cases" find it particularly difficult because use cases can have many scenarios. These scenarios can vary greatly in business value and should not be included in a single "use case story".

To help these clients learn how to structure their stories, we have come up with a set of four "storyotypes". We ask them to identify which storyotypes a particular story-candidate exhibits and if it exhibits more than one, we have them discuss the value of splitting the story into smaller stories, ideally one for each storyotype.

The focus of this paper is to share our experiences with managing the size of stories within XP projects. We start by describing the problems in managing the story size. We then describe the four storyotypes we have encountered on information system projects and how they are used to mitigate these problems.

1.1 The Problem with Stories

To understand the problems that are generally experienced with story granularity, a quick review of the XP concept of a story is helpful. Stories were first described in [1] & [2]. The customer is responsible for defining the functionality of the system in short "stories" of one or two sentences. Each story should describe functionality that has

C. Zannier et al. (Eds.): XP/Agile Universe 2004, LNCS 3134, pp. 73–80, 2004.

real business value to the customer. From a planning perspective, the story is the unit of prioritization, scheduling, and progress tracking that is visible to the customer.

An XP project has frequent small releases, each of which contains a number of time-boxed iterations. Release planning involves scheduling one or more stories in a particular release, based on the priority and size of the story. The entire story must be finished within the release for which it is scheduled otherwise no value is delivered to the customer. A large story creates problems in three areas: Release Planning, Task Coordination, and Story Testing.

1.2 Release Planning

The first problem that large stories create for an XP team is in release planning. The larger the stories, the fewer will fit into a release. (Larger stories are also harder to estimate.) This gives the customer less flexibility to pick and choose what gets done. Too much functionality bundled into a single story will often squeeze out other equally important core functionality from early releases thus delaying a meaningful demo unnecessarily. If the stories remain too large throughout the project essential core functionality may be squeezed out (differed indefinitely), because the earlier bloated stories contained non-essential functionality that consumed development resources.

1.3 Task Coordination

Task coordination is the second area in which problems can arise. A large story either generates a larger number of tasks or larger tasks. We have found the integration of these tasks can be problematic.

Our XP projects typically do not require micro-management of tasks to the extent that detailed grouping and dependencies of the tasks do not have to be worked out as long as the stories are kept reasonably small. With larger stories, extra overhead must be incurred to orchestrate the sequencing of cohesive tasks to ensure that the team makes progress towards a common sub-goal at any one point in time within the iteration.

1.4 Story Testing

The third problem experienced is that the granularity of the story testing is too large. The customer is responsible for specifying and signing off on customer tests. As a story becomes larger, there must be more extensive testing to deal with all the interactions of the functionality. These interactions are difficult for customers to test all at once. We have found the completeness of customer tests drops as the number of tests needed by a story exceeds 10 tests. Smaller stories tend to have more complete testing than larger stories.

2 Using Storyotypes to Split Stories

Splitting of stories is described [1] & [2] as one of the basic techniques of managing scope on XP projects. A story should meet the following criteria:

- *Each story should describe functionality that has real business value to the customer.*
- *The stories should not have any value if they are further subdivided.*
- *The functionality described in a single story should have the same importance to the customer.* That is, the relative priority should be the same.
- *The functionality should have the same level of certainty.* That is, if some functionality is completely understood and some needs to be discussed in more detail with the business, there should be at least two different stories because one is ready to be built now and the other is not.

Further guidelines are provided for the "bootstrap story" (the first story built; a special case on every project) in [3].

These guidelines help newcomers to XP, but they don't help them figure out how to make a story the right size. Those coming from a use case world have a tendency to want to use the functionality described by a use case as the basis for their stories. But use cases are the wrong granularity for stories. They are both too big and too small at the same time.

Use Cases Are Too Small. Many use cases cannot be tested independently of other functionality. That is, while they might be executed independently, the results cannot be verified without using some other use case to inspect the state of the system. Or, the use case may depend on some other use case to set up the state of the system before it can be exercised.

Use Cases Are Too Big. While there are many definitions of what constitutes a use case, most definitions agree that it includes all the possible ways a user can achieve some goal or desired outcome. Typically, a use case has several or many scenarios. Some of these scenarios are used very often (the "happy path" scenario and a few others) while others may be pathological cases that occur so rarely that it is not worth automating them. That is, they provide insufficient "business value" to justify the investment to automate them through software.

Usage Scenarios Are Better but Not Enough. Use cases typically consist of several or many scenarios (the "alternate paths" through the use case) that describe how the use cases works with various prior states of the system. Each scenario can be considered a candidate for a separate story so that it can be prioritized independently of the other scenarios. To address the "Use cases are Too Small" problem, they often need to be combined with scenarios of other use cases to make a truly testable story. And even scenarios can be too big to build in a single release.

2.1 Four Storyotypes

To make it easier for new XP teams to come up with the right story granularity, we have devised the following four "storyotypes" (short for "story stereotypes".) These storyotypes are used to characterize each story and provide a means to split a "bloated story" into smaller but still valuable pieces. While the following storyotypes descriptions frequently refer to use cases, these storyotypes can be applied to any story whether they are more like a use case like or a larger XP story. Use cases just happen to be the best understood and most broadly used form of prose-based requirements capture so they form a good point of reference for these storyotypes descriptions.

Storyotype: New Functionality. This storyotype describes new functionality that is fairly independent of functionality previously described in other stories. In the use case world, these stories could be characterized as the happy path of one use case or several interrelated use cases. If several use cases, the use cases must be co-dependent (like chickens and eggs): it would be difficult to test one without the other. A common example is the CRUDing (Create, Read, Update and Delete) of a business entity; it would be very difficult to update an entity that has not yet been created and it would be difficult to verify the update was successful without being able to read it. So, the create, update and read of a basic business entity might be grouped into a single "basic functionality" story.

The use case functionality included in this story should be restricted to a single scenario, with no conditional processing. The other storyotypes describe additional functionality related to (extensions of) this basic new functionality.

If a user interface is required as part of this story, the user interface should be "the simplest UI that could possibly work". That is, the most basic windows, fields, buttons, or menu items required to provide the functionality. Anything else related to the UI belongs in the *UI Enhancement* storyotype.

Storyotype: Variation of Existing Functionality. Stories with this storyotype describe a variation of functionality introduced in another story (most commonly, in a *New Functionality* story.) This can involve one or more extensions or exceptions (as described in [4]). This is the kind of story that introduces conditional logic into the software as each of these variations typically involves checking some condition and executing a different path when the condition is true.

When a *Variation* story involves several use cases, they will typically be the same use cases as described in the *New Functionality* story that the *Variation* story extends.

User interface work related to this storyotype should be restricted to the addition of any data field to the screens required to enter or view data used to make the decisions.

Storyotype: New Business Rule. *New Business Rule* stories (often called "input validation" or "edit checks") extend *New Functionality* and *Variation* stories with additional constraints that need to be enforced by the software. This kind of story introduces conditional logic into the software in the form of guard clauses or assertions as each of these variations typically involves checking some condition and raising some sort of error condition when the condition is true. Any user interface work included in this storyotype should be restricted to whatever is needed to communicate the error condition to the user and the means for them to rectify the problem.

Storyotype: User Interface Enhancement. User interface design and development is a complex discipline that can quickly become a major "time sink" if not managed well. It is one of the areas ripest for scope creep and the most fruitful for adjusting scope to match available resources. As such, it is very worthwhile explicitly separating the stories that relate to developing complex user interfaces from those that develop the underlying business functionality.

Stories with this storyotype should focus on a specific form of enhancement of the user interface and should not include any business functionality. If there are several "dimensions" of interface improvement required (e.g. drag&drop, multi-selection list boxes and voice recognition,) each should have a separate story or stories to enable the customer to chose the functionality they need most without dragging in other bits of less important (to them) functionality.

2.2 Refactoring Stories Based on Storyotypes

Having identified the storyotypes occurring in each story, we can make conscious decisions to split the stories into single storyotype stories or leave multiple storyotypes in some stories. There is a cost to having too many (and therefore too small) stories; combining them into larger stories results in fewer stories to estimate and keep track of.

We rarely find it useful to combine stories with different storyotypes. The main exception to this is when the single-storyotype stories are so small as to only require a single task to build them. This occurs most frequently during the bug-fixing or minor enhancements phase of a project.

We do find it useful to combine two stories with the same storyotype (e.g. two Business Rule stories) as it can be pretty arbitrary whether we call them a single story or several. Again, the size of the stories is a key determinant; we don't want the resulting story to be too large to be completed in a single iteration and we don't want to force the customer to "pay for" work they might not want just because it is lumped in with other functionality in the same story.

2.3 Managing User Interface Enhancement Stories

The style of the user interface is a "cross-cutting concern" that spans the different kinds of functionality provided by the system. Changes to the style of the user interface can involve visiting a lot of software. The key challenge when building *User Interface Enhancement* stories is to avoid excessive revisitation of each part of the user interface in successive attempts to build a highly usable user interface. It may take several (e.g. 3 or 4) tries to find a user interface metaphor that the users are happy with. Without careful management of the process, we may have to apply each *User Interface Enhancement* story to every part of the application's user interface as we learn what the customer really wants.

We have found the most effective strategy is to build the system with a simple UI initially and to do some UI enhancement stories targeted on a particular part of the system. This provides a way to get feedback on the UI technology and style without making a massive investment in the UI for the entire system. Once the users are happy with the UI in the pilot area of the system, the same UI paradigm can be applied to the rest of the system (typically in later iterations or releases). This can greatly reduce the churning of the UI code those results if the UI evolution involves the entire system. (This is one area where it really is worthwhile avoiding rework by using Options Thinking [4] to delay the bulk of the work until the high impact decisions have been made.)

3 A Caveat on Combining Stories

Regardless of the storyotypes involved, we would only choose to merge two or more stories when they have identical business value and the level of specification certainty is the same. We also want to be sure that the value/certainty won't change before we build them. This is an excellent argument for "early splitting; late merging"!

4 Example

Consider an application that prepares invoices for various customers of a service. To show the applicability of storyotypes regardless of the approach used to come up with the stories, we will provide both a "use case" and a "bloated story" description of the functionality requested for the application. The intention is not that one would first generate the "bloated story" description from the use cases but rather that either could act as the starting point for the refactoring exercise.

4.1 Use Cases Example

The system includes a number of use cases including: Maintain Customer, Maintain Billing Cycle, Generate Invoices and Send Invoices. The Maintain XXX use cases include the ability to create, modify and either delete or obsolete the corresponding business concept as appropriate.

Use case "Generate Invoices" is used to produce the actual invoices that can then be viewed, regenerated, finalized and sent. Invoices may contain charges based on simple subscription (e.g. monthly charges), usage (e.g. so much per unit) and manual charges (special cases). It can be used to generate the invoices for all customers or only selected customers.

The user would like to be able to select the customer using a multi-selection list, by pressing a button to add the customer to the list of invoices to be generated or by dragging and dropping the customers onto the list of invoices to be generated. They would also like the system to remember the last group of customers used. And the system should not allow generating an invoice for a customer who has not yet been approved by the sales manager.

Use case "View Invoice" allows the user to see the list of available invoices and to select one for viewing in more detail.

Use case "Finalize Invoice" is used to "lock down" the invoice so that it cannot be regenerated. An invoice cannot be sent to the customer until it is finalized.

4.2 Bloated Stories Example

A team that is not familiar with use cases may have come up with the following stories for the same functionality.

Story 1: Invoice Generation. Generate an invoice consisting of a single subscription charge for one or all customer. View the resulting invoice. The user can select the customers whose invoices are to be generated using a multi-selection list box or using Add/Remove buttons to move the customers from the All Customers pane to the Selected Customers pane. The system should remember the last set of customers for whom an invoice was generated. An invoice cannot be generated for a customer until the sales manager has approved them. An invoice cannot be generated for a customer until all mandatory data elements have been provided. These include name, contact information (mailing address, phone #), title, and company name. Customers can be created with as little as just a name but they cannot be invoiced.

Story 2: Send Invoice to Customer. When the user is satisfied with the invoice for a customer, they may finalize it and then send it to the customer. Once finalized, the invoice cannot be regenerated or modified in any way.

Story 3: Usage-Based Charges. Generate an invoice that includes usage-based charges. The usage data is read in from a flat file and the usage rate can be set via a user interface. Generate the invoice and view it to verify the rate is being applied correctly. View the resulting invoice.

4.3   Characterizing the Bloated Stories Using Storyotypes

Consider a story that describes the process of generating an invoice. This "use case story" includes many storyotypes:

Generating the invoice for all customers is an example of the *New Functionality* storyotype. Generating them for a subset of customers is an example of the *Variation of Functionality* storyotype.

Because there are three different UI metaphors being described, we can infer that there are at least two candidates for *UI Enhancement* stories.

4.4   Splitting the Story Based on Storyotypes

Now that we've identified the various storyotypes, we can refactor the story into the following single-storyotype stories:

New Functionality: Generate a very simple invoice consisting of a single subscription charge for the customer. View the resulting invoice. Note: This is an example of a "bootstrap story" as described in [3].

New Functionality: Finalize and Send an invoice to a customer.

Variation: Generate an invoice that includes usage-based charges. The usage data is read in from a flat file and the usage is charged at a rate of $1 per unit of usage. View the resulting invoice.

Variation: The usage rate can be set via a user interface. Generate the invoice and view it to verify the rate is being applied correctly.

Variation: Use a multi-selection list box of customers to select the customers whose invoices are to be generated.

Variation: Remember the last set of customers for whom an invoice was generated.

UI Enhancement: Select the customers for whom to generate the invoices (or finalize the invoice) using a simple dual list box with add/remove buttons UI metaphor.

Business Rule: An invoice cannot be sent to a customer until it has been finalized.

Business Rule: An invoice that has been finalized cannot be regenerated or modified in any way.

Business Rule: An invoice cannot be generated for a customer until the sales manager has approved them. This also requires a simple UI to approve the customer (probably described in the Maintain Customer use case.)

Business Rule: An invoice cannot be generated for a customer until all mandatory data elements have been provided. These include name, contact information (mailing address, phone #), title, and company name. Customers can be created with as little as just a name but they cannot be invoiced.

Business Rule: Only the sales manager can approve the customer. This implies some kind of login capability so that the system can be aware of who is using the system. Authentication (that is, security) could be another story.

4.5 Combining Stories Based on Storyotypes

Now, we can make conscious decisions to keep each instance of a storyotype in a separate story or to merge two (or more, but not recommended) storyotypes into a single story. In our example, we will choose to treat the two business rules related to when an invoice can be generated as a single story (that still has a single storyotype). We might call this story "Invoice Generation Business Rules".

We would only choose to merge them when we know their business value and certainty is the same and we are sure that they won't change. For example, we could choose to include both subscription charges and usage charges in the same invoice generation story. We would do this knowing the consequences of having done so rather than out of ignorance.

5 Conclusions

The story is the foundation for describing, planning, and managing an XP project. Getting the granularity of the stories right is crucial for making the release planning game function efficiently. The four storyotypes we present here are a useful tool for understanding the size and complexity of the stories planning regardless of whether the stories are based on use cases or are bloated for other reasons. They give the neophyte XP team a set of heuristics they can use when making decisions about the how to refactor stories while doing release planning. These storyotypes came from our experiences using XP while building enterprise information systems; teams working in other problem domains may find it useful to identify storyotypes specific to their domain.

Acknowledgements

The author would like to thank all the ClearStream colleagues who shared their experiences and insights in managing stories on a variety of XP projects and especially Ted O'Grady who encouraged me and gave me valuable feedback on early drafts.

References

1. Beck, Kent. Extreme Programming Explained: Embrace Change, Addison-Wesley, 2000; ISBN 201-61641-6.
2. Beck, Kent. Martin Fowler, Planning Extreme Programming, Addison-Wesley, 2001; ISBN 0-201-71091-9.
3. Andrea, Jennitta. Managing the Bootstrap Story in an XP Project, in Proceedings of XP2001, 2001.
4. Cockburn, Alistair. Writing Effective Use Cases, Addison-Wesley, 2001; ISBN 0-201-70225-8.
5. Poppendieck, Mary and Tom. Lean Software Development, An Agile Toolkit, Addison-Wesley, 2003; ISBN 0-321-15078-3.

Distributed Pair Programming: An Empirical Study

Brian F. Hanks

School of Engineering
University of California, Santa Cruz
brianh@soe.ucsc.edu

Abstract. Pair programming provides many benefits, both to the programmers and to the product that they develop. However, pair programming is limited to those situations in which the developers can collocate, preventing its benefits from being enjoyed by the widest possible audience. A software tool that allowed the pair to work from separate locations would address this limitation. This paper presents some initial results from a distributed pair programming experiment in which students in an introductory programming class used such a tool. Student perceptions of distributed pair programming are also discussed.

1 Introduction

Pair programming [1] transforms what has traditionally been a solitary activity into a cooperative effort. In pair programming, two software developers share a single computer monitor and keyboard. One of the developers, called the *driver*, controls the computer keyboard and mouse. The driver is responsible for entering software design, source code, and test cases. The second developer, called the *navigator*, examines the driver's work, offering advice, suggesting corrections, and assisting with design decisions. The developers switch roles at regular intervals. Although role switching is an informal process, a typical interval is 20 minutes.

Initial studies suggest that two programmers working together in the pair programming style produce code with fewer errors, with only a slight increase in total programmer time [2]. In addition, programmers who pair report improved mentoring [2], increased confidence in their solutions [3, 4], and increased job satisfaction [2, 5].

At the university level, pair programming has been used in computer science courses as a teaching tool [3, 4]. McDowell et al. [4] found that allowing students to pair in an introductory programming course resulted in a greater percentage of students completing the course. These students also were more likely than non-pairing students to select computer science related majors within one year of completing the course. Compared with students who work alone, students who pair are more likely to turn in solutions to their programming assignments, and these solutions are of higher quality [6, 7].

One major drawback of pair programming is that both members of the pair must be collocated. Although research has shown that collocated work has significant advantages over work by distributed teams [8], there are many factors motivating distributed work. More workers are telecommuting, and many organizations have offices in multiple locations, resulting in geographically dispersed project teams.

This trend towards distributed teams conflicts with the collocation requirement of pair programming. By removing the collocation requirement, the benefits of pair

C. Zannier et al. (Eds.): XP/Agile Universe 2004, LNCS 3134, pp. 81–91, 2004.

programming could by enjoyed by a wider audience. A tool that supports *distributed pair programming*, in which the driver and navigator pair from separate locations, would remove this impediment to the adoption of pair programming. I have developed such a tool, and have conducted a controlled experiment to evaluate its effectiveness.

2 Related Work

Schumer and Schumer [9] and Maurer [10] have conducted research in this area that suggests that distributed pair programming (DPP) can work. However, their research was more focused on distributed XP, and provides only anecdotal evidence that DPP is effective. No quantitative results are provided and no comparison is made between distributed and collocated pair programming.

More recent work by Baheti et al. [11] suggests that distributed pairing can be as effective as collocated pairing. Students who virtually paired using Microsoft's Net-Meeting performed similarly to collocated pairs in terms of the grades they received on their project. Because student pairs worked on separate, self-selected projects direct comparison of their performance is difficult.

Canfora et al. [12] studied virtual pairing by having students use a screen sharing application along with a text-based chat application. No audio channel was provided to the students. They found that distributed pairs tended to stop cooperating and began to work as two solo programmers. Based on these results, they made some suggestions for features that should be supported in a distributed pair programming tool. However, these suggestions may not be valid because the distributed pairs in this study did not have a method of speaking with each other.

Stotts et al. [13] provides further evidence of the potential success of distributed pairing. They describe an on-going series of experiments and case studies in which students virtually paired. Although distributed pairs successfully completed their programming assignments, they complained of their inability to point or gesture. As Stotts observed, "pairs need better capabilities for indicating areas of interest".

While this research provides compelling evidence that DPP can be effective, it seems clear that a tool that supported the needs of the distributed pair would enhance DPP. The next sections describe such a tool, an experiment that I conducted to evaluate its effectiveness, and some initial experimental results and user experiences.

3 VNC for Pair Programming

The tool described here is based on the open source screen sharing application Virtual Network Computing (VNC) [14]. VNC allows a user's desktop to be replicated onto multiple computers (in particular, two in the case of pair programming). Application output is displayed on both computers, while keyboard and mouse input from either computer is sent to the applications.

I decided to use a screen sharing approach in the development of this tool, instead of developing collaboration-aware distributed pair programming development tools. This choice was motivated by the fact that screen sharing applications allow single user applications to be shared by multiple users without modification [15]. I believe that this is especially important for complex tasks such as software development.

Software developers use a large set of tools in their work, such as compilers, editors, debuggers, and testing tools. It is critical for a distributed pair of developers to be able to use their preferred development tools, and the screen sharing approach supports this requirement.

While VNC can be used as-is for DPP, it is not ideal for this. Both users have active keyboards and mice. If both partners use the keyboard simultaneously, their keystrokes are interlaced into an unintelligible stream. There is also only one cursor, which makes it difficult for the navigator to point at areas of the screen. [13]

I have modified VNC to provide a second cursor that can be controlled by the navigator. This cursor is displayed when the navigator presses the F8 key to enter 'gesture mode'. In gesture mode, a second cursor (in the form of a red hand with a pointing index finger) is added to the user interface. The navigator's mouse controls the movements of this cursor, while the driver retains control of the standard cursor. While the navigator is in gesture mode, keyboard and mouse button events are ignored, and mouse movement events are used to control the position of the gesturing cursor.

Fig. 1. Gesturing Mode

This second cursor allows the navigator to point at areas of the screen without affecting the driver's state. Figure 1 shows a portion of the driver's desktop while the navigator is gesturing. In this figure, the driver is typing in an editor window while the navigator is pointing at the previous line where there is a missing semicolon.

While many synchronous groupware applications provide a separate cursor for each user [16], my approach differs from the typical one in that the cursor is transient and only present when the navigator requests it. A benefit of this approach is that the navigator's intent is clear to the driver, because the second cursor only appears when the navigator wants to gesture. A continuously present second cursor would not be as noticeable to the driver, and gesturing might not be as readily observed.

The shape of the cursor also plays a role in its usability [17]. In an earlier version of this tool the gesturing cursor was arrow-shaped. It was changed to its current hand shape based on early user feedback.

In addition to frequent gesturing, collocated pair programmers converse regularly during a pairing session [1]. It is essential for partners in a distributed pair to be able to speak with each other. One obvious solution is for the partners to use telephones. However, in the experiment described in this paper, the students who participated did not have always have access to telephones. Instead, they used a voice-over-IP application (such as AOL Instant Messenger) and computer headsets to converse. This also allowed them to use the chat window of AIM to transmit items that are difficult to convey verbally, such as URLs, long path names, and complex method names.

4 The Experiment

In the fall 2003 quarter, 76 students in two sections of an introductory programming course at the Santa Cruz campus of the University of California volunteered to participate in an experiment to evaluate distributed pair programming. All students in these sections pair programmed, even if they were not experimental volunteers. Students were not paid to participate in the experiment.

Potential volunteers were told that I was studying a new tool to support pair programming, but they were not given any details regarding the tool. In particular, they were not told that the tool would allow them to work from separate locations.

Separate instructors taught these two classes. Although the courses covered the same material, the programming assignments and exams were different. The number of programming assignments also differed between the two sections – one section had five graded assignments while the other had seven. The author was the instructor of the section with seven assignments, which is identified as section 2 in the discussion that follows.

Volunteer pairs were randomly assigned to one of two groups. One group was allowed to pair program using the tool described here, while the second group paired while collocated. The pairs in the tool group were allowed to use the tool as much or as little as they wanted. They could still pair while collocated if it was convenient for them, such as immediately before or after class.

Although allowing students in the tool group to pair while collocated was not ideal from an experimental viewpoint, it is important to remember that the experiment was being conducted in a classroom setting. Because of this, it would not have been ethical to force the students in one group to act in a way that might have negatively impacted their classroom performance.

Students in both groups initially worked on their programming assignments while collocated, so that they could establish good working relationships with their partners before attempting distributed pairing. One reason for this is the pair jelling factor noted by Williams [3], which indicates that students have to learn to pair. Student pairs became more effective in comparison to individuals after they had completed their first assignment. A second reason for having students work together before attempting distributed pairing is that I believe that they are more likely to have established a cooperative relationship. This is substantiated by Rocco's [18] findings that individuals who had prior face-to-face interaction were more likely to cooperate in a distributed game than those who had never met. Stotts et al. [13] also noted that face-to-face meetings helped distributed pairs work effectively.

After this initial period of collocated work, the pairs in the tool group were instructed in its use. Computer headsets were loaned to these students. These students were allowed to pair while using the tool on the remainder of their programming assignments. The students in the control group continued to pair while collocated.

Student volunteers filled out surveys at the beginning and end of the experiment. These surveys contained questions about the students' demographic data, experience, and opinions about pair programming. The students in the tool group were asked additional questions about their experience using the tool.

The volunteers also answered a few questions (using a form on a web site) when they turned in their programming assignments. Each student was asked how much time they spent driving, navigating, and working alone, how confident they were in their solution to the assignment, and how satisfied they were with their working relationship with their partner on the assignment.

5 Experimental Results

To be successful in an academic setting, a tool must not have a negative impact on student performance. One measure of student performance is the final exam. Another measure is the students' confidence, as this directly influences their success in computer science courses.

It is also important to measure user satisfaction with the distributed pairing process. Subjects were asked to rate the utility of the gesturing feature, and comment on what they liked and disliked about distributed pairing.

5.1 Final Exam Performance

Of the 76 students who volunteered for the experiment, 72 took the final exam. This was an individual, in-class, written exam with a variety of question types. Students were expected to understand and create short programs, methods, or classes. Table 1 shows the final exam scores for these students. Because the students in the two sections did not take the same final exam, the results for the two sections cannot be compared directly. The categories in the table are (1) All: all student volunteers as a group, (2) Non Tool Group: the collocated students, (3) Tool Group: the students who were allowed to use the tool, and (4) Tool Users: those students in the tool group who actually used the tool. As shown in the table, students in the collocated and distributed groups performed equally on the final exam. Distributed pairing did not negatively affect student performance on the final exam.

Table 1. Final Exam Score

	Group	Final Exam Score	Number of Subjects
Section 1	All	79.0	31
	Tool Group	78.6	15
	Non Tool Group	79.3	16
	Tool Users	83.0	4
Section 2	All	69.7	41
	Tool Group	69.8	21
	Non Tool Group	69.7	20
	Tool Users	73.6	14

Curiously, those students in the Tool Group who actually used the tool on their homework assignments performed better on the final exam, although this difference is not statistically significant. A possible explanation for this difference is that higher performing students are more likely to make the effort to try a new software tool.

5.2 Confidence

When they turned in their programming assignments, each student was asked to respond to the following question: "On a scale from 0 (not at all confident) to 100 (very confident), how confident are you in your solution to this assignment?". Table 2 shows the mean values of the responses and associated statistical significance for the students in the two sections of the class.

In section 1, students in the tool group began using the tool on their third programming assignment. In section 2, they began using the tool on the fourth assignment. There were no statistically significant differences in student confidence in either section on any of the programming assignments, either before or after the students began using the tool.

Table 2. Student Confidence

	Assignment	Non Tool Group	Tool Group	ANOVA	p
Section 1	1	94.57	95.73	$F(1,27) = 0.28$	0.60
	2	97.31	85.13	$F(1,26) = 2.75$	0.11
	3	96.92	92.81	$F(1,27) = 2.10$	0.16
	4	70.11	84.40	$F(1,22) = 1.19$	0.29
	5	45.45	67.28	$F(1,23) = 1.73$	0.20
Section 2	1	97.79	95.56	$F(1,31) = 2.27$	0.14
	2	83.58	84.63	$F(1,31) = .015$	0.91
	3	89.61	94.11	$F(1,34) = 0.74$	0.41
	4	92.88	91.12	$F(1,32) = 0.34$	0.56
	5	91.78	89.37	$F(1,32) = 0.31$	0.58
	6	73.80	58.36	$F(1,27) = 1.44$	0.24
	7	90.88	82.44	$F(1,31) = 2.34$	0.14

5.3 Gesturing

To evaluate the effectiveness of the gesturing feature in enabling DPP, the students who used the tool were asked to indicate their level of agreement with the statement,

"The gesturing feature was very useful to me." The response was given on a 7 point Likert scale, where 1 meant "strongly disagree", 4 meant "neutral", and 7 meant "strongly agree".

Figure 2 shows the students' responses. The mean response was 5.47. Although one student disagreed with the statement and two were neutral, the other 14 were in agreement. These results are encouraging, and indicate that the gesturing feature aids the distributed pairing process.

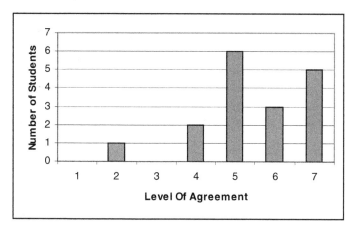

Fig. 2. Gesturing Feature was Useful to Me

6 Student Experiences with the Tool

To gain more understanding of the benefits and drawbacks of DPP, students were asked what they liked and disliked about using the tool. I was also interested in learning why some students in the tool group chose not to use it.

6.1 Student Likes

Students gave a variety of answers to the question, "What did you like about the distributed pair programming tool?". Many of the responses addressed convenience and effective use of time. A representative sample of these responses includes:

- "Well, besides it allowing us to work in the comforts of our own homes without ever getting out of our chairs, it also helped to overcome some schedule conflicts, and the time that would have been wasted just walking to the other person's computer was instead turned into productive programming time!"
- "You don't have to go all the way to a computer lab to pair program."
- "It made pair programming very easy and convenient. We didn't have to meet on campus or at each other's houses so we could always pair program w/out the effort of getting together. I think the class would have required a lot more time w/out the tool."

Another set of responses addressed student satisfaction with the tool itself. These responses indicated that the students felt that the tool was an effective way for them to pair program without having to physically meet. Responses of this type include:

- "If we didn't meet in person, this combined with AIM almost perfectly emulated working side by side. We could work on it any time and take long breaks."
- "The pair programming tool allowed us to work together from two different places. The pointing function of the program also made it easier to point out errors and not accidentally type while my partner was typing."

An interesting group of responses came from students who used the tool *while collocated*. These students found that using the tool improved the pairing process even when they weren't separated. In fact, some of these students never used the tool from separate locations, but still found it valuable. Comments from this group of students includes:

- "I like the flexibility it offers in case two partners can't meet and work together. I liked being able to work on separate terminals while working side by side in the lab."
- "Easier than sharing computer"
- "Being able to switch driver/navigator easily"

These students felt that the typical physical setup in the campus computing labs made role switching difficult. These labs are set up for solo work, and it is sometimes difficult to get two chairs in front of one workstation. The limited desk space also makes moving the keyboard and mouse difficult, and hinders the role switching process. The tool eliminated these problems, and allowed the students to use any campus computing lab as if it were a pair programming lab.

One particularly interesting comment was made by a female student, who said, "The tool was useful at night when we couldn't work in the lab together because we live on opposite sides of campus." This comment suggests that some students may feel uncomfortable on campus at night, and that tools such as this would allow them to work in a safe environment.

6.2 Student Dislikes

Students were also asked what they disliked about the distributed pairing tool. Many of the comments had to do with problems with the computing environment, such as poor quality audio, or the lack of a Macintosh version of the tool.

Some students seemed to feel disconnected from their partner while distributed. Typical comments from these students include:

- "Communication with the partner is still awkward"
- "The tool was difficult to use when we were programming something we had never programmed before – for instance, when we first used arrays."
- "We sometimes wrote over each other's work and sometimes presenting things in person kept each others' interest."
- "AIM is not a good way to communicate, even with the headsets. Sometimes it is difficult to explain something through the air."

One particularly interesting comment came from a student who felt that distributed pairing was antisocial:

- "Discourages human contact. One of the things I like best about pair programming is that the two people are physically in the same place together, talking and interacting face-to-face. This helps foster community and social interaction. The tool makes face-to-face contact unnecessary, and this can encourage a retreat into the "lone-wolf" mode, an aspect that troubles me"

6.3 Reasons for Not Using the Tool

The students in the tool group did not have to use it, and some of them chose not to. I asked these students the question, "Why didn't you use the distributed pairing tool?".

One common reason for not using the tool was that they didn't find it necessary. Many of the pairs found it easy to physically meet with their partner, and therefore did not see any reason to use the tool. Comments from these students included:

- "We never had any need to. It was easier to meet in person."
- "Because we were able to find time together working on it at one person's place"
- "It was not necessary for us. It was very easy for us to meet in lab and talk face to face"

Some students found it challenging to get the program running. They had to start up a server application, connect with the partner using AIM, and then run the VNC client. Comments from these students include:

- "Too many programs to do a simple thing."
- "It was a hassle trying to get the program up and running than just simply meeting up with your partner at the lab. "

It is clear that some students don't see any need for distributed pairing. It was easy for them to meet with their partner, and they were happy to do so.

The tool may have helped some of the other students in the tool group who did not use it. These students gave up in their attempts to use the tool because it was not easy enough for them to set up. It is important to remember that these students are not necessarily experienced computer users, and the steps required to establish a distributed pair programming session may have been too complex. This suggests that more work needs to be done to make the tool simpler to setup.

7 Concluding Remarks

Although previous research has shown that DPP is possible, none of this research investigated tools specifically designed to support distributed pairing. This paper describes a tool that was developed specifically to support distributed pairing, and reports results showing that students who used the tool performed as well as collocated students, had similar levels of confidence, and found the tool beneficial.

Students in the control and experimental groups performed equally well on the final exam. Although it is not statistically significant, students who used the tool performed better on the exam than the students in the control group. Students in both experimental groups were also equally confident in their programming solutions.

Students agreed that the gesturing feature was useful to them. Further research is needed to verify the usefulness of the gesturing feature by comparing the performance of pairs using this tool with that of pairs using VNC without the gesturing feature.

This paper discusses student performance in terms of final exam scores. This is not the best measure of pair programming performance, for a couple of reasons. First, the final exam is an individual effort. Second, it measures student understanding of the course material, but does not directly measure programming ability. The students' grades on their programming assignments would provide a better indication of the impact of distributed pair programming on student performance. This analysis remains to be done.

The results reported here may not generalize to other populations. The experimental subjects were students who were learning to program; therefore, these results may not be applicable to DPP with experienced software developers. Similarly, the experimental subjects were allowed to establish working relationships with their partners before using the tool, and those in the tool group were also allowed to pair while collocated. The results reported here may not apply to those situations where partners are not able to physically meet before or while pairing.

As noted earlier, there are many situations where collocated pair programming cannot be done. The availability of an effective DPP tool would allow the benefits of pair programming to be enjoyed by a larger audience. Although much work remains to be done to develop a commercial grade tool, the results presented here show that such a tool can facilitate distributed pairing.

Acknowledgements

This research is supported by National Science Foundation grant DUE-0341276. Plantronics, Inc. also supported this research by generously donating computer headsets. Any opinions, findings, and conclusions or recommendations expressed in this paper are those of the author and do not necessarily reflect the views of the National Science Foundation or those of Plantronics.

References

1. Laurie Williams and Robert Kessler. *Pair Programming Illuminated*. Addison-Wesley, 2002.
2. Alistair Cockburn and Laurie Williams. The costs and benefits of pair programming. In Giancarlo Succi and Michele Marchesi, editors, *Extreme Programming Examined*, pages 223 - 247. Addison-Wesley, 2001.
3. Laurie A. Williams. Strengthening the case for pair programming. *IEEE Software*, 17(4):19 - 25, July/August 2000.
4. Charlie McDowell, Linda Werner, Heather Bullock, and Julian Fernald. The impact of pair programming on student performance, perception and persistence. In *Proceedings of the International Conference on Software Engineering (ICSE 2003)*, pages 602 - 607, May 3 - 10, 2003.
5. John T. Nosek. The case for collaborative programming. *Communications of the ACM*, 41(3):105-108, March 1998.

6. Charlie McDowell, Brian Hanks, and LindaWerner. Experimenting with pair programming in the classroom. In *Proceedings of the 8th Annual Conference on Innovation and Technology in Computer Science Education*, 2003.

7. Brian Hanks and Charlie McDowell. Program quality with pair programming in CS1. To appear in *Proceedings of the ninth annual conference on innovation and technology in computer science education (ITiCSE)*, June 28 - 30, 2004.

8. Judith Olson, Stephanie Teasley, Lisa Covi, and Gary Olson. The (currently) unique advantages of collocated work. In Pamela Hinds and Sara Kiesler, editors, *Distributed Work*, pages 113-135. The MIT Press, 2002.

9. Till Schummer and Jan Schummer. Support for distributed teams in extreme programming. In Giancarlo Succi and Michele Marchesi, editors, *Extreme Programming Examined*, pages 355-378. Addison-Wesley, 2001.

10. Frank Maurer. Supporting distributed extreme programming. In *Extreme Programming and Agile Methods - XP/Agile Universe 2002*, number 2418 in LNCS, pages 13-22. Springer, 2002.

11. Prashant Baheti, Edward Gehringer, and David Stotts. Exploring the efficacy of distributed pair programming. In *Extreme Programming and Agile Methods - XP/Agile Universe 2002*, number 2418 in LNCS, pages 208-220. Springer, 2002.

12. Gerardo Canfora, Aniello Cimitile, and Corrado Aaron Visaggio. Lessons learned about distributed pair programming: What are the knowledge needs to address? In *Proceedings of the Twelfth IEEE International Workshops on Enabling Technologies: Infrastructure for Collaborative Enterprises (WETICE03)*, pages 314-319, 2003.

13. David Stotts, Laurie Williams, Nachiappan Nagappan, Prashant Baheti, Dennis Jen, and Anne Jackson. Virtual teaming: Experiments and experiences with distributed pair programming. In *Extreme Programming and Agile Methods - XP/Agile Universe 2003*, number 2753 in LNCS, pages 129-141. Springer, 2003.

14. Tristan Richardson, Quentin Stafford-Fraser, Kenneth R. Wood, and Andy Hopper. Virtual network computing. *IEEE Internet Computing*, 2(1):33-38, January-February 1998.

15. Saul Greenberg. Sharing views and interactions with single-user applications. *ACM SIGOIS Bulletin*, 11(2-3):227-237, April 1990.

16. Stephen Hayne, Mark Pendergast, and Saul Greenberg. Gesturing through cursors: Implementing multiple pointers in group support systems. In *Proceedings of the 26th Hawaii International Conference on System Science*, volume 4, pages 4-12, 1993

17. Saul Greenberg, Carl Gutwin, and Mark Roseman. Semantic telepointers for groupware. In *Proceedings of the 6th Australian Conference on Computer-Human Interaction*, pages 54-61, 1996.

18. Elena Rocco. Trust breaks down in electronic contexts but can be repaired by some initial face-to-face contact. In *Proceedings of CHI 98*, pages 496-502, 1998.

Support for Distributed Pair Programming in the Transparent Video Facetop

David Stotts, Jason McC. Smith, and Karl Gyllstrom

Dept. of Computer Science, Univ. of North Carolina at Chapel Hill
Chapel Hill, NC 27599-3175 USA
{stotts,smithja,gyllstro}@cs.unc.edu

Abstract. The Transparent Video Facetop is a novel user interface concept that supports not only single-user interactions with a PC, but also close pair collaborations, such as that found in collaborative Web browsing, remote medicine, and in distributed pair programming. In this paper we discuss the use of a novel video-based UI called the Facetop [16] for solving several problems reported to us by teams doing distributed pair programming. Specifically, the Facetop allows a distributed pair to recapture some the facial expressions and face-to-face communications contact lost in earlier distributed sessions. It also allows members of a distributed pair to point conveniently, quickly, and naturally to their shared work, in the same manner (manually) that they do when seated side-by-side. Our results enhance the ability of organizations to do effective XP-style agile development with distributed teams.

1 Distributed Pair Programming

Previous research [17,19] has indicated that pair programming is better than individual programming in a co-located environment. Do these results also apply to distributed pairs? It has been established that distance matters [18]; face-to-face pair programmers will most likely outperform distributed pair programmers in terms of sheer productivity. However, the inevitability of distributed work in industry and education calls for research in determining how to make this type of work most effective. Additionally, Extreme Programming (XP) [1,2] usually has co-located pairs working in front of the same workstation, a limitation that ostensibly hinders use of XP for distributed development of software.

We have been investigating a video-enhanced programming environment for the past year for use in distributed Pair Programming and distributed Extreme Programming (dPP/dXP) [1,2]. Pair programming is a software engineering technique where two programmers sit at one PC to develop code. One types ("drives") while the other reviews and assists ("navigates"); roles swap frequently. The benefits of pair programming are well known in co-located situations [3]; we have been exploring if they remain in distributed contexts [6,7,15].

Video was one issue discussed at a workshop on distributed pair programming at XP/AU 2002. This workshop was attended by over 30 people, many of whom had tried some form of distributed pair programming and were working on tools to improve the effectiveness of such activities. The consensus on video was that "web cam" style video – small image and low frame rate – was of little value in enhancing communications or sense of presence in a distributed pairing. However, it was felt

C. Zannier et al. (Eds.): XP/Agile Universe 2004, LNCS 3134, pp. 92–104, 2004.

that video, if large enough and real enough was of potential value and worth further research. We have been doing that research since that time.

2 The Facetop Basics

The transparent video Facetop [16] is a novel enhancement of the traditional WIMP user interface, so nearly ubiquitous on today's computers. In the Facetop, the user sees him/her self as a "ghostly" image apparently behind the desktop, looking back at the icons and windows from the back. Instead of a traditional desktop, we see a *"face" top*. This self-image is used for visual feedback and communications both to the user as well as to collaborators; it is also used for desktop/application control and manipulation via a fingertip-driven "virtual mouse".

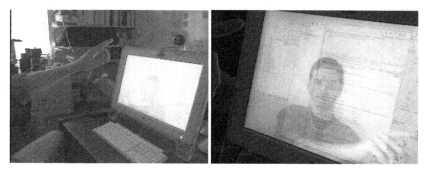

Fig. 1. Facetop physical setup, with iBot video camera

Figure 1 shows the physical setup for a computer with a Facetop being displayed on a monitor. Note the video camera sitting on top the LCD panel pointing back at the user; in our current work we use a $100 Sony iBot, giving us an image that is 640 x 480 pixels of 24-bit color, captured 30 frames per second. The Facetop video window shows the PC user sitting at his/her workspace; we reverse the image horizontally so that when the user moves a hand, say, to the left, the image of the hand mirrors this movement on the screen. In software, and using a high-performance 3D-graphics video card, we make the video window semi-transparent and composite it with the desktop image itself.

Once we have the full screen video with transparent image compositing we get the illusion of the user watching the desktop from behind. Mirroring means if the user physically points to an icon on the desktop, the Facetop image points to the icon as well (with proper spatial calibration of the camera and user locations). Using image analysis techniques we then track the user's fingertip in the backing window, and optionally drive the mouse from this tracker. Figure 2 shows this finger tracking (the desktop image is more transparent and the user face more opaque to emphasize the tracking). The user can then manipulate the desktop of a *projected* computer, for example, from his seat while successfully communicating the areas of interest on the screen to others watching the projection.

2.1 Transparency Combined with User Self-view

The Facetop combines and extends work from several different domains of computing research. Gesture-based computer controls have existed for a while, for example. The Facetop, however, is unique among these for two reasons. The first is transparency: the Facetop blends the traditional desktop with a video stream of the user, mirrored and made semi-transparent. The second is the video cues the user image gives: the user is *in* the desktop, as live background wallpaper, rather than making detached gestures apart from the image of the desktop. These video cues have proven very effective at giving fine and intuitive control of the cursor to the user in various tasks and applications we have experimented with.

Fig. 2. Facetop finger tracking (low user transparency)

We allow the user to dynamically control the transparency level of the Facetop window, altering it from fully opaque (all user face, a communications tool) to fully transparent (all desktop) during execution for varying useful effects. Figure 3 shows the near extremes.

3 Dual-Head Collaborative Facetop

Though the previous presentation has been in the context of a single-user PC interface, an equally interesting domain of application for the Facetop is in collaborative systems – specifically in systems for supporting synchronous paired tasks. We have been investigating a two-head Facetop for the past year for use in distributed Pair Programming (dPP). This investigation is an extension of earlier studies we conducted to see if distributed pairs could pair program effectively communicating over the Internet [6,7,15].

In our previous dPP experiments, programmers worked as a pair using COTS software, including *pcAnywhere* (Symantec) and *Yahoo messenger* (for voice communications). The *pcAnywhere* shared desktop allows the two programmers effectively to work on a single host computer; each seeing exactly what the other sees, as they would sitting side-by-side at the host PC. Our experiments found that programmers working in this dPP environment were as effective as co-located pairs. In posttrial interviews, teams consistently told us 3 things:

- They missed facial expressions and the sense of presence
- They wanted a way to point at the shared work they were discussing via audio
- They wanted a whiteboard for drawing and design work

Fig. 3. Varying user transparency, from mostly user showing to mostly desktop showing

The Facetop provides potential solutions to each of these problems, via its video capabilities. Video was provided to the pairs in our previous dPP experiments; we gave each team "web cams" that generate small images at low frame rates. Each team turned off the video almost immediately, finding that the small, nearly still, images gave no useful information, but did consume considerable bandwidth. Maximal bandwidth was needed for fast update of the *pcAnywhere* shared desktop.

The video capabilities in Facetop are very different, however. The image is large, and frame rates run from 15 to 30 fps, showing facial details and fine motor movements of the fingers and lips. The video image is also tightly and seamlessly integrated with the shared workspace via transparency, thereby eliminating the "dual" nature of video teleconferencing solutions. Users do not have to switch their attention from desktop, to video, back to desktop.

For the dual-user Facetop, we have built a setup that has both video streams (each collaborator) superimposed on a shared desktop, illustrated for a projected environment in Figures 4 and 5. Each user sits slightly to the right so that the two heads are on different sides of the frame when the two streams are composited. In this "knitted together" joint image, we sit each user against a neutral background to control the possible added visual confusion of the dual Facetop image.

Collaborating users continue, as before, to communicate audibly while using the Facetop via an Internet chat tool like *Yahoo messenger*. The primary advantage the Facetop gives over other approaches is the close coupling of communications capabilities with examination of the content. Each user can see where the other points in the shared workspace; they can also use the Facetop as a direct video conferencing tool (by varying the transparency level to fade the desktop image) without changing applications or interrupting the work activities.

Fig. 4. Dual-head Facetop for collaborative browsing

Fig. 5. Varying levels of transparency in dual-head Facetop

3.1 System Features and Functions

The following sections briefly discuss a collection of features and functions of our current Facetop implementation.

Multiple varying transparency levels. In the dual-head Facetop, each user has transparency level controls that are independent of the settings chosen by the partner. A user can set the level (from opaque to transparent) of each video image separately (self and partner image), as well as level of the desktop (see Figure 5). In this way, each user can get different communications effects. If both user images are set to *highly visible*, and the desktop set *low*, the Facetop is a form of video conferencing system. Bring the desktop up to *visible* and the unique integration of user image with shared work happens, allowing pointing and discussion. Some users may wish not to see themselves and have only the partner image visible on the desktop; they can still effectively point by finger tracking and watching the mouse pointer.

Chalk passing. Passing locus of control among collaborators in a shared application is an important issue, called *floor control*, or *chalk passing*. The user who has "the chalk" is the one who drives the mouse and click on links when Web browsing.

Our tracker algorithm has a loss recovery mode that produces an interesting chalk passing behavior in the dual-user Facetop. When tracking, if the user moves the finger faster than the tracker can track, we detect that it is "lost" by noticing no data for processing in several consecutive frames. When this happens, the algorithm stops tracking in a local neighborhood and does an entire image scan; this is too computationally expensive to do each frame, but works well for the occasional frame. In this full-frame search, the tracker acquires and moves to the largest fingertip object it finds.

With two users, this means that chalk passing happens simply by the user with the mouse hiding (dropping, moving off screen) the finger. This "loses" the tracker and starts the full screen search algorithm. The mouse pointer immediately jumps to the other user's fingertip and "parks" in a corner until there is one.

Monitor or projector. The Facetop as a concept works fine on a PC with any display technology -- a monitor, a projector, an immersive device -- but its unique aspects are most pronounced and most effective in a projected environment. When projected, it is natural to point with hand and finger at the projected image on a wall, especially when several people in a room are viewing the projection.

Finger tracking on/off. One interesting feature in the Facetop is finger tracking. This function can be turned on or off and used as needed. Even if the user chooses not to use finger tracking, the Facetop has great value as a pure communication tool via finger pointing and facial expressions, especially in collaborative applications like dPP. However, tracking and mouse control does add some interesting and useful capabilities for users that wish to use them.

Figure 2 illustrates the tracking in a view of the Facetop when the user is fully opaque, showing the user and none of the underlying desktop or whiteboard. The highlighted box around the finger is the region the tracker operates in, and in this view we show the actual data bits being examined (a debugging mode that can be toggled on and off). As the user moved the hand around in view of the camera, the tracker constantly finds the center of mass off the fingertip and reports an $<x,y>$ coordinate location for each frame.

In the Facetop, the user's fingertip functions as a mouse driver, so applications like browsers can be controlled with finger motions rather than the mouse. The tracker provides the $<x,y>$ location information for moving the mouse; the more difficult problem is designing and implementing gestures that can serve as mouse clicks, drags, etc.

Fingertip mouse click activation. The Facetop tracker gives us mouse-pointer location and causes mouse motion, but the harder issue is how to click the mouse. The method we currently use is occlusion of the fingertip. When the mouse pointer has been positioned, the user makes a pinching fist of sorts, hiding the fingertip in the hand or between the other fingertips. The tracker notes the loss of the tip, and begins a timer. If the tip reappears (user raises the finger) in a ½ second, a single-click mouse event is generated at the mouse pointer location. If the tip remains hidden for between ½ and 1 second, a double-click event is generated. User studies (discussed in a later section) have so far shown that this motion is not hard to learn and even master. It is sufficient to open/close windows, drag them, resize them, select links in Web browsers, and even position the mouse between characters in documents.

Another interaction method we have implemented is voice commands. This is especially useful in rapidly altering the transparency level of the various Facetop camera images, as well as for hands-free mouse clicking where useful.

Video auto on/off. Another technique we use for managing visual clutter is to have the Facetop tracker recognize when the fingertip enters the video frame. When the fingertip enters, the user camera image is composited in. When the tip leaves, the user fades and the desktop remains. This is modal and can be turned on and off. It is especially useful for doing presentations in Web browsers and PowerPoint.

4   Initial User Evaluations

Controlled user evaluations are still ongoing, but we have some usability results to report from our first experiments. To date we have had 15 users try the basic Facetop to determine if live background video is a viable, usable concept as an interface for manipulating the PC environment. We set up the Facetop up in a room with white walls so that there would not be a busy background to add visual clutter to the screen image.

As might be expected, arm fatigue is a problem for continuous use of the fingertip-based mouse feature. For browsing a hypertext, this is not a major issue, as much time is spent reading vs. actually manipulating the screen. Users drop their arm during these quiescent periods, and then raise it to point when ready to navigate more. The video image on-screen gives the visual cues needed for nearly instant positioning of the mouse pointer directly where needed.

Another problem reported by several users is visual clutter. Most users adapted quickly and comfortably to the moving image as background "wallpaper"; transparency was set at different levels by different users, and there did not seem to be a preferred level of mixing of desktop with user-image other than to say that both were visible. The human eye/brain is able to pay attention (or ignore) the face or the desktop respectively, depending on the cognitive task – depending on whether the user wants to read the screen contents or to communicate (in the two-head version).

Users were queried specifically as to visual clutter or confusion. A few objected, but most found the adjustability of transparency fine-grained enough to get to a level where they were not distracted or hindered in using the desktop.

We also created a networked tic-tac-toe game for usability trials of the dual head version and had 11 pairs of users try it. The users were a class of 8-grade students who came to the department for research demonstrations. Five of the users took less that 5 minutes to become facile with the interface, learning to move and click the mouse well enough to Web browse. All users were able to successfully play the game (which involves clicking on GUI buttons) in the 30 minute time-frame of the trials.

4.1 Distributed Pair Programming Trials

We had five of the pairs involved in past dPP experiments (with audio and shared desktop only) try the Facetop environment for small pair programming "shakedown" tasks. Since all had tried the earlier environments, the trials were designed to see if the "video made large" features in Facetop overcame the lack of pointing ability and lack of facial expressions reported by these teams before (the lack of whiteboard they reported is still being investigated, and is discussed in the next section).

All teams were quite comfortable using the Facetop, and did not consider visual complexity or clutter an issue. We suspect this is due to concentration on program-ming focusing the attention on the various text windows of the desktop. All dPP teams were able to complete small programs with no problems.

They also reported setting varying levels of user image transparency to suit per-sonal taste. Given that the video images can be completely faded out, leaving nothing but desktop, the current Facetop is "no worse" than our previous audio-only environ-ments. However, no teams chose to completely fade out the video and use audio only. All teams left the user images visible to some extent and did use the video to point to code being discussed.

In post-trial interviews, the overall impression was that Facetop was an interesting improvement over the audio-only dPP environment used before. Each team was asked "if you were to do a longer dPP development, would you prefer to use Facetop or the original audio-only environment?" All teams expressed a preference for Facetop.

These simple usability trials do not reveal if the preference for Facetop was emo-tional or qualitative only, or if the added video and sense of presence increases pro-grammer effectiveness. We find these early usability trials compelling enough, though, to start larger, controlled experiments to see if Facetop can have an impact on quantitative aspects of software, such as design quality or error counts.

5 Further Distributed Pair Programming Investigations

Our studies have found that adding large, fast video via the Facetop to a dPP envi-ronment enhances the qualitative experience of the programmers. Our investigations are continuing; we are gathering quantitative data on productivity and product quality in follow-on trials. Current work is in two areas: whiteboard support, and universal access for impaired programmers.

5.1 Dual Camera Facetop for Whiteboard

One of the items noted earlier as wanted by dPP teams in past experiments was access to a good whiteboard. To solve this problem, we have a version of Facetop that works with two Firewire video cameras per workstation. In addition to the normal Facetop user camera, a second camera is situated to the side of the user and faces a white-board. The user sits near enough to the board to be able to comfortably reach out from the seat and draw on the whiteboard. This layout is shown in figure 6. Facetop takes both camera streams (user face and whiteboard) and composites them into the video stream that is laid semi-transparent on the desktop. As in the normal Facetop, the user face stream is mirrored (reversed horizontally) so that pointing is meaningful to the user. The whiteboard video image is not mirrored, so that words written on the board remain readable when composited into the Facetop video.

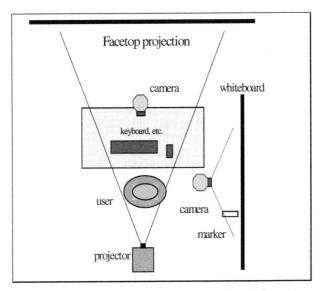

Fig. 6. Schematic of two-camera Facetop for whiteboard

   Since the whiteboard is neutral in appearance, compositing it into the Facetop im-age doesn't really alter the appearance over the traditional Facetop. When words or drawings are written on the whiteboard, they appear to "float" within the room/background of the user. Figure 7 shows this compositing of both video streams. By varying transparency levels of each camera, users can see whiteboard only, or whiteboard composited with their images. Key-press commands in Facetop allow instant swapping between whiteboard image and user image. User's hands show up as drawing is done, so each sees what the other is drawing.

5.2   Universal Access for Impaired Programmers

We are also investigating the use of the collaborative Facetop in providing access to pair programming, and other synchronous paired collaborations, for people with audio and visual impairments. For programmers with audio impairments, we are experi-menting with the Facetop video being used for support of signing and lip reading during pair programming. Programmers with audio impairments can do side-by-side pair programming with current technology, but they cannot participate in dPP using the audio-only environments we first experimented with.

For programmers with visual impairments, we are developing audio cues that will provide information about the state of a collaboration. Currently individual programmers with visual impairments use a screen reader like JAWS [20] for navigating a PC screen. Our extensions will function similarly, but will have to not only communicate screen information, but partner activity information as well.

Fig. 7. Whiteboard image composited into the Facetop user image

6   System Structure and Performance

Our single-user Facetop is implemented on a Macintosh platform. Our collaborative Facetop is also Mac-based but runs on a peer-to-peer gigabit network between two machines, to get the very high bandwidth we need for 30 fps video stream exchange. Current experimental versions are built for best-effort use of the switched Internet give about 18 frames a second. This is usable for dPP, but we need better for universal access and hearing-impaired signing.

A Macintosh implementation has several advantages. The desktop is rendered in OpenGL, making its image and contents not private data structures of the OS, but rather available to all applications for manipulation or enhancement. We also use dual-processor platforms, so that one processor can handle tracking issues and other Facetop-specific loads, while leaving a processor free to support the collaborative work, such as pair programming. Video processing is handled mostly on the graphics card.

Our implementation is beautifully simple, and potentially ubiquitous due to its modest equipment needs. Facetop uses a $100 Sony iBot camera, and runs with excellent efficiency on an Apple Powerbook, even when processing 30 video frames a second. No supplemental electronics are needed for wearing on the hand or head for tracking or gesture detection. Facetop is minimally invasive on the user's normal mode computer use.

The current prototype was generated with a Macintosh G4 with a high-end graphics card to perform the image transparency. It is implemented on MacOS X 10.2 by taking advantage of the standard Quartz Extreme rendering and composition engine. QE renders every window as a traditional 2D bitmap, but then converts these to OpenGL textures. By handing these textures to a standard 3D graphics card, it allows the highly optimized hardware in the 3D pipeline to handle the compositing of the images with varying transparency, resulting in extremely high frame rates for any type of image data, including video blended with the user interface.

The video application, with tracking capabilities, is run in a standard MacOS window, set to full screen size. Using OpenGL, setting the alpha channel level of the window to something under 0.5 (near-transparency) gives the faint user image we need.

Some of our experiments have been run with the two Power Mac's connected via peer-to-peer gigabit network. In this configuration, we get a full 30 frames per second video data exchange in each direction. This is possible due to the high network speeds, and due to our passing only the 640 x 480 camera image. Image scaling to screen size is handled locally on each machine after the 2 video signals and the desktop are composited into one image.

7   Related Prior Research

7.1   Pointing in Collaborative Applications

Several systems have dealt with the issue of two users needing to provide focus (point) at different, or independent locations on a shared screen. The common solution is to provide two mouse pointers and let each user control his/her own independently. Use of two mouse pointers is central to a dPP tool being developed by Hanks [21]. This is fundamentally different from using a human device (fingers) to point as in Facetop.

7.2   Collaborative Systems, Distributed Workgroups

One major use for the Facetop is in collaborative systems. There have been far too many systems built for graphical support of collaboration to list in this short paper. Most have concentrated on synthetic, generated graphics. *ClearBoard* [4] is one system that is especially applicable to our research. ClearBoard was a non-co-located collaboration support system that allowed two users to appear to sit face to face, and see the shared work between them. The ClearBoard experiments showed that face-to-face visibility enhanced the effectiveness of collaboration. However, the workstations required were expensive and used custom-built hardware. One of the advantages of the Facetop is its use of cheap and ubiquitous equipment.

One last project we use results from is BellCore's *VideoWindow* project [5]. In this experiment, two rooms in different buildings at BellCore (coffee lounges) were outfitted with video cameras and wall-sized projections. In essence, an image of one lounge was sent to the other and projected on the back wall, giving the illusion in each room of a double-size coffee lounge. The researchers discovered that many users found the setup to be very natural for human communication, due to its size. Two people, one in each room, would approach the wall to converse, standing a distance from the wall that approximated the distance they would stand from each other in face-to-face conversations. The conclusion: *Video, when made large, was an effective and convincing communication tool.* We have leveraged this finding in creating the dual-head Facetop that we use for synchronous, collaborative Web browsing.

7.3 Transparency, UI, Video, and Gestures

Many prior research projects have experimented with aspects of what we have unified in the Facetop. Several researchers have made systems that have transparent tools, windows, pop-ups, sliders, widgets that allow see-thru access to information below; these are primarily used for program interface components [8,11]. Many systems have some user embodiment and representation in them (avatars), especially in distributed virtual environments like [10], but these tend to be generated graphics and not live video. Giving your PC "eyes" is a growing concept, as is illustrated by this 2001 seminar at MIT [12]. A system being developed in Japan [9] uses hand activities as signals to programs; the system uses silhouettes to make recognition easier and faster. Our ideas for fingertip gesture control in the Facetop are related to the many efforts under way to recognize pen gestures and other ink-based applications; the Tablet PC based on Windows with ink is now commercially available from several manufacturers. They are also related to efforts in the past to recognize human facial features and motions.

The work most closely related to our Facetop video analysis is from the image-processing lab of Tony Lindberg in Sweden. Researchers there have developed tracking algorithms for capturing hand motions rapidly via camera input, and have developed demonstrations of using tracked hand motions to interact with a PC [13,14]. One application shows a user turning on lights, changing TV channels, and opening a PC application using various hand gestures while seated in front of a PC. Another experiment shows careful tracking of a hand as it display one, two, and three fingers, and scales larger and smaller. A third experiment uses hand gestures in front of a camera to drive the mouse cursor in a paint program. The missing concept in Lindberg's work (and in other hand-gesture work), one that we are exploiting for Facetop, is the immersion of the user *into* the PC environment to give video cues and feedback for control.

Acknowledgements

This work was partially supported by a grant from the U.S. Environmental Protection Agency, # R82-795901-3. It does not represent the official views or opinions of the granting agency.

References

1. Beck, K., *Extreme Programming Explained*, Addison-Wesley, 2000.
2. Wells, J. D., "Extreme Programming: A Gentle Introduction," 2001, available on-line at http://www.extremeprogramming.org/

3. A. Cockburn and L. Williams, "The Costs and Benefits of Pair Programming," *eXtreme Programming and Flexible Processes in Software Engineering -- XP2000*, Cagliari, Sardinia, Italy, 2000.
4. H. Ishii, M. Kobayashi, and J. Grudin, "Integration of inter-personal space and shared workspace: ClearBoard design and experiments," *Proc. of ACM Conf. on Computer Supported Cooperative Work*, Toronto, 1992, pp. 33-42.
5. R. S. Fish, R. E. Kraut, and B. L. Chalfonte, "The VideoWindow System in Informal Communications," *Proc. of ACM Conf. on Computer Supported Cooperative Work*, Los Angeles, 1990, pp. 1-11.
6. P.Baheti, L.Williams, E.Gehringer, and D.Stotts, "Exploring the Efficacy of Distributed Pair Programming," XP Universe 2002, Chicago, August 4-7, 2002; Lecture Notes in Computer Science 2418 (Springer), pp. 208-220.
7. P.Baheti, L.Williams, E.Gehringer, D.Stotts, "Exploring Pair Programming in Distributed Object-Oriented Team Projects," Educator's Workshop, OOPSLA 2002, Seattle, Nov. 4-8, 2002, accepted to appear.
8. Eric A. Bier, Ken Fishkin, Ken Pier, Maureen C. Stone, "A Taxonomy of See-Through Tools: The Video, Xerox PARC, Proc. of CHI '95,
   http://www.acm.org/sigchi/chi95/Electronic/documnts/videos/eab1bdy.htm
9. T. Nishi, Y. Sato, H. Koike, "SnapLink: Interactive Object Registration and Recognition for Augmented Desk Interface," Proc. of IFIP Conf. on HCI (Interact 2001), pp. 240-246, July 2001.
10. Steve Benford, John Bowers, Lennart E. Fahlén, Chris Greenhalgh and Dave Snowdon, "User Embodiment in Collaborative Virtual Environments,", Proc. of CHI '95,
    http://www.acm.org/sigchi/chi95/Electronic/documnts/papers/sdb_bdy.htm
11. Beverly L. Harrison, Hiroshi Ishii, Kim J. Vicente, and William A. S. Buxton, "Transparent Layered User Interfaces: An Evaluation of a Display Design to Enhance Focused and Divided Attention," Proc. of CHI '95,
    http://www.acm.org/sigchi/chi95/Electronic/documnts/papers/blh_bdy.htm
12. Vision Interface Seminar, Fall 2001, MIT, http://www.ai.mit.edu/~trevor/6.892/
13. Bretzner, L., and T. Lindberg, "Use Your Hand as a 3-D Mouse, or, Relative Orientation from Extended Sequences of Sparse Point and Line Correspondences Using the Affine Trifocal Tensor," Proc. of the 5th European Conf. on Computer Vision, *(H. Burkhardt and B. Neumann, eds.), vol. 1406 of Lecture Notes in Computer Science*, (Freiburg, Germany), pp. 141--157, Springer Verlag, Berlin, June 1998.
14. Laptev, I., and T. Lindberg, "Tracking of multi-state hand models using particle filtering and a hierarchy of multi-scale image features," Proc. of the IEEE Workshop on Scale-space and Morphology, Vancouver, Canada, in *Springer-Verlag LNCS 2106* (M. kerckhove, ed.), July 2001, pp. 63-74.
15. Stotts, D., L. Wiliams, et al., "Virtual Teaming: Experiments and Experiences with Distributed Pair Programming," TR03-003, Dept. of Computer Science, Univ. of North Carolina at Chapel Hill, March 1, 2003.
16. Stotts, D., J. McC. Smith, and D. Jen, "The Vis-a-Vid Transparent Video FaceTop," UIST '03, Vancouver, Nov. 3-6, 2004, pp. 57-58.
17. Nosek, J.T., "The Case for Collaborative Programming," *Communications of the ACM*, March 1998, pp. 105-108.
18. Olson, G.M., and J.S. Olson, "Distance Matters," *Human-Computer Interaction*, vol. 15, 2000, pp. 139-179.
19. Williams, L., "The Collaborative Software Process," *Ph.D. dissertation*, Dept. of Computer Science, Univ. of Utah, Salt Lake City, UT, 2000.
20. JAWS, Windows screen reader, Freedom Scientific, http://www.freedomscientific.com/
21. Hanks, B.," Distributed Pair Programming: An Empirical Study" XP/Agile Universe, Aug. 2004, Calgary, to appear.

Toward a Conceptual Framework of Agile Methods

Kieran Conboy[1] and Brian Fitzgerald[2]

[1] Dept. of Accountancy and Finance, National University of Ireland, Galway, Ireland
kieran.conboy@nuigalway.ie
[2] Dept. of Computer Science and Information Systems, University of Limerick,
Limerick, Ireland
brian.fitzgerald@ul.ie

Abstract. Since the software crisis of the 1960's, numerous methodologies have been developed to impose a disciplined process upon software development. It is now widely accepted that these methodologies are unsuccessful and unpopular due to their increasingly bureaucratic nature. Many researchers and practitioners are calling for these heavyweight methodologies to be replaced by agile methods. The Agile Manifesto was put forward in 2001, and several method instantiations, such as XP, SCRUM and Crystal exist. Each adheres to some principles of the Agile Manifesto and disregards others. This paper conducts a review of the literature on agility across many disciplines, in order to reach an all-encompassing notion of what agility is. This paper aims to develop a comprehensive framework of software development agility, through a thorough review of agility across many disciplines. We then elaborate and evaluate the framework in a software development context, through a review of software related research over the last 30 years.

1 Introduction

The formation of the Agile Alliance in 2001 and the publication of the Agile Manifesto [25] formally introduced agility to the field of software development (SD). Those involved sought to "restore credibility to the word *method*" [25]. The Agile Manifesto conveyed an industry-led vision for a profound shift in the SD paradigm, through 12 principles:

- Satisfy the customer through early and continuous delivery of valuable software
- Sustainable development is promoted, facilitating indefinite development
- Simplicity is essential
- Welcome changing requirements, even late in development
- Deliver working software frequently
- Working software is the primary measure of progress
- Continuous attention to technical excellence
- Business people and developers must work together daily
- Face-to-face communication is the best method of conveying information
- The team regularly reflects on how to become more productive and efficient
- The best work emerges from self-organising teams
- Build projects around motivated individuals

C. Zannier et al. (Eds.): XP/Agile Universe 2004, LNCS 3134, pp. 105–116, 2004.
© Springer-Verlag Berlin Heidelberg 2004

The Agile Manifesto and its principles represent quite pioneering work in coalescing and extending the critique of formalised software methods over the past decade or so (e.g [3, 22, 23] and have been well received by practitioners and academics.

2   Shortcomings of the Study of Agility in SD

There is no universally accepted definition of an agile method in the field of Information Systems Development (SD). Cockburn [13] even dismisses the existence of an agile method altogether, claiming that it is something that developers can only aspire to, and only hindsight can determine whether an agile method was actually adhered to.

Because there is no universal definition or framework of what agility is, there are many methods currently in use which are all categorised as agile by those that use these methods. Each of these focus on some of the principles of the agile manifesto, often at the expense of other principles. Given that such vague and diverse interpretations exist, it is impossible to reach any conclusions on agile methods and their use.

Agility is not a concept unique to software development. Indeed it first appeared in the mainstream business literature in 1991, when a group of researchers at the Iacocca Institute in Lehigh University introduced the term "agile manufacturing" [40]. The industry-based report aimed to provide the USA with a weapon to regain its pre-eminence in manufacturing, and described the emerging agile principles being adopted by US, European and Japanese firms as being the way forward. Since then manufacturing companies across many industries have gained a competitive advantage from such an agile philosophy [9].

However, a review of the agile manufacturing literature indicates that even now, 12 years later, those who study agile manufacturing are having the same problems as those studying agile methods in SD. There are many diverse and often contradicting definitions of agile manufacturing, and consideration is not given to the differences between industries and organisations [9].

Therefore, the search for a definitive, all-encompassing concept of agility is not to be found simply through an examination of agility in other fields. Rather it is to be found through an examination of the underlying concepts of agility, namely flexibility and leanness [60, 63] which have much older origins. For example, lean thinking can be traced back to the Toyota Production System in the 1950s with its focus on the reduction and elimination of waste [52], the production of the Spitfire airplane in World War 2 [10]and even as far back as the automotive industry in 1915 [18].

3   Research Method

The objective of this paper is to develop a comprehensive conceptual framework of SD agility that can be applied to any SD project, enabling the true level of its agility to be established. This objective is achieved through a four step research process:

- A literature review on the concepts of flexibility and leanness, and their relationship with agility, is carried out. This review includes research on agility across manufacturing, finance, management, labour and marketing among others, in order to appreciate the multi-disciplinary nature and evolution of these concepts.

- A clear definition of each term, based on the literature review, is proposed. Due to the broad nature of each of these terms, and to the diverse interpretations of these terms that exists, these definitions are constructed and adjusted in an incremental manner.
- The definitions of flexibility and leanness are then merged to form an initial working definition of agility. This initial definition is then subsequently refined in the light of further relevant research on the relationship between agility and the flexibility and leanness concepts. A conceptual framework of agility is then put forward, using this refined definition as a base. Given the diversity of the literature, the researchers sought to ensure that the framework represents agility in its most general sense.
- The final stage was to apply the framework to an SD context. This was done through a review of the 30 odd years of general SD literature, to extract any policies, actions or behaviours of SD teams which would be classified within this framework. The review had to be more inclusive than just agile methods *per se* as these did not appear until the late 1990s, although SD practitioners have been applying agile principles for much longer, even if they did not know it.

4   Towards a Framework of Agility for SD

4.1   Flexibility

Flexibility is often interpreted as per its simple dictionary definition as simply:

"the ability to adapt to change".

However, the body of research on the definition of flexibility indicates such an interpretation is too simple.

Firstly, the word "embrace" is a better reflection of flexibility than "adapt to". Hashimoto et al [34, 35] refer to *robustness* or *resilience* as a component of flexibility. Robustness or resilience is the ability to *endure* all transitions caused by change, or the degree of change tolerated before deterioration in performance occurs *without* any corrective action ([34, 35]. This concept indicates that in order to be truly flexible, an entity must not only be able to adapt to change by taking steps, but must also be able to embrace change by taking none. Also, the literature makes a distinction between defensive and offensive strategies [28]. This raises the issue that, when change occurs, not only can an entity attempt to return to its original state, but it can take advantage of the change to place itself in a better position. The term *"adapt to"* implies that an entity is homeostatic, and that its only objective in the face of change will be to return to its original state. *"Embrace"* implies that the entity may not only try to return to its original state but may capitalise on the change and improve on its position. As well as using flexibility to anticipate uncertainty, it can also be used proactively to permit a company to positively impact its environment [26]. This concept argues that proactive steps may "not just anticipate change, but may create it" [55]. The words "adapt to" implies that change is the driving force and the entity's actions are as a result of that force. "Embrace" signifies a *two-way process* where the entity not only reacts to change but can also influence it.

There is a difference between *proactive* and *reactive* flexibility [28] also known as *initiative* versus *response* [30]. This concept recognises the fact that an entity is not helpless while waiting for change to occur and that steps can be taken *in advance of change* as well as in response to it. The simple example of periodic inspection and preventative maintenance of equipment is a proactive approach to combating machine failure, as opposed to repair and replacement of equipment after failure, which is a reactive one [26].

It is important to note that *an entity itself is not flexible*. Rather, an entity obtains this flexibility through the various sub-systems, resources, and activities that comprise that entity. For example Correa's [14] opinion is that "an organisation is only as flexible as its people".

The literature also highlights a distinction between internal and external flexibility. This dimension of flexibility is defined as "the area in which the flexibility is created" [28]. It reflects the fact that an entity *may not be a closed system*. Rather it may interact with other systems in its environment and may be able to use these interactions to handle change. Goudswaard & de Nanteuil [31] illustrate this concept through labour flexibility referring to internal flexibility as the ability of an organisation to vary employee's duties, working hours or salaries, while external flexibility refers to the ability of an organisation to draw resources through subcontractors, short-term contracts or temp agencies.

Much of the literature indicates time as a primary measure of flexibility [20, 33, 64]. Golden & Powell [28] describe the temporal dimension of flexibility as the "length of time it takes for an organisation to respond to environmental change" or to "adapt within a given time frame". Furthermore, as change may arise due to environmental influences the temporal dimension must incorporate the length of time taken for an entity to recognise that change has occurred, to decide on what action to take, and to carry out that action. As time is such a central criterion to evaluating and measuring an entity's flexibility, it is imperative that it is referred to in the definition. However, careful wording is required, since speed alone should not be taken as a measure of success. Volberda [66] compares time taken to adapt to change against the variety of that change, acknowledging the fact that rapid response to familiar change is not necessarily better than a slow response to large, strategic change.

This research proposes the following refined definition of flexibility which reflects the robust, proactive, reactive and temporal dimensions of flexibility

> "the ability of an entity to proactively, reactively or inherently embrace change in a timely manner, through its internal components and its relationships with its environment."

4.2 Agility v. Flexibility

Lindbergh [45] and Sharafi & Zhang [60] indicate that agility is made up of two components. The first is flexibility, but it shares equal prominence with the second, which is *speed*. Essentially, an organisation must be able to "respond flexibly" and "respond speedily" [6]. Terms such as "speed" [62], "quick" ([17, 32, 44, 70], "rapid" [38] and "fast" [71] occur in most definitions of agility. This reference to speed was discussed within the context of flexibility. However, as research on the definition of agility has placed such emphasis on rapidity, it merits an adjustment to the definition before it can be applied to the term *agile*.

Another distinction between agility and flexibility is the assumption that change is *continuous* and embracing it is an ongoing activity. This assumption was laid down in the key contribution of Goldman, Nagel & Preiss [30], where they described agility in general terms as "a continual readiness to change". The flexibility literature, and therefore the definition as it stands, makes no reference to continual change as opposed to a once off change.

For some, agile means to apply the concepts of flexibility throughout different parts of the organisation, and not to a specific part such as manufacturing or production processes [42]. This has led to the coining of terms such as "agile supply chains" [11], "agile decision support systems" [39], and "agile workforce" [65]. However, some suggest that agility is flexibility with an "organisational orientation" [11], in that it is applied *collectively* throughout the enterprise [30, 57]. This notion would be in line with Golman & Nagel's [29] "agile enterprise", Nagel & Dove's [49] opinion that agility must be viewed in a "business-wide context", and that of Gunasekaran et al [32] which states that agility is "not a series of techniques but a fundamental management philosophy".

Our definition of flexibility can be amended to reflect these differences, and can therefore be said to subsume the flexible component of agility. The modified definition now reads as:

> "the continual readiness of an entity to rapidly or inherently, proactively or reactively, embrace change, through its collective components or its relationships with its environment".

4.3 Leanness

Unlike the concept of flexibility, the notion of leanness is relatively straight-forward. It is "the elimination of waste" [51, 52, 68] and "doing more with less" [63].

Different authors have conflicting opinions regarding the benefits and drawbacks of using a lean approach. However, there is a general consensus that such an approach broadly consists of the following principles [51, 52, 63, 68]

- Utilisation of all resources is maximised, and no unnecessary resources are maintained.
- Simplicity of tasks, information flow and information processes is maximised.
- A product or activity should pass through the necessary components of an entity and the components of its partners in a single flow.
- A high level of quality must be maintained through defect prevention not correction. A "root cause" approach is taken to problem solving to maximise added value.

The proposed definition of leanness is:

> "the maximisation of simplicity, quality and economy"

4.4 Agility v. Leanness

Some believe that although agility exhibits similar traits to *leanness* in terms of *simplicity* and *quality,* the literature has identified one major difference in terms of *economy* [69]. Ultimate leanness is to eliminate all waste. Agility requires waste to be eliminated, but *only to the extent where its ability to respond to change is not hindered.* As this does not remove the need to be economical, only lower its priority, it is important that the definition of agility is modified to incorporate all elements of leanness, which was defined above as "the maximisation of simplicity, quality and economy".

4.5 Proposed Definition of Agility

After consideration of the literature on flexibility and leanness and, after accounting for the differences between these concepts and the concepts of agility, the final definition of agility in this study is:

> "the continual readiness of an entity to rapidly or inherently, proactively or reactively, embrace change, through high quality, simplistic, economical components and relationships with its environment".

5 Conceptual Framework of Agility

This framework is a descriptive formulation of the agility process. It draws upon a framework of manufacturing agility proposed by Zhang & Sharifi [72] However, it is greatly modified to ensure it corresponds with the definition of agility proposed earlier. The main components of the framework are discussed next.

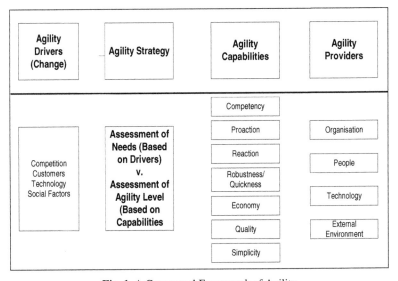

Fig. 1. A Conceptual Framework of Agility

5.1 Agility Drivers

Competition refers to the nature and behaviour of the collective organisations who strive for superiority in SD, and how such nature and behaviour drives an SD team to be agile. Examples include the increase in software customisation and Commercial-Off-The-Shelf (COTS) software applications which "carve days or weeks from a development schedule" [12]These developments are part of a larger trend known as the "industrialisation of IS development" [2]. Paulk recognises that the SD team in question also fits within this banner, stating that change can come from an internal "push" within the team, or an external "pull" from its competitors [54].

Customers refer to the nature and behaviour of the client, and how such nature and behaviour drives an SD team to be agile. The "faster metabolism of business today" [58] means that user needs are constantly evolving and form a "moving target" for developers [15]. Even if we could assume that the business remains unchanged, the client typically does not know the complete requirements in advance, causing back-tracking as these requirements are slowly discovered [3, 8, 53].

Changes in *technology* may require the SD team to be sufficiently agile to embrace that change. Technology can refer to any software, hardware, method or technique *used or developed* by the team. For example, many authors assert that developers have struggled to cope with the introduction of the internet, multimedia and hyperme-dia, and the technologies that accompany them [19, 46, 48, 56]. Such changes forces the team to decide if they are innovators (techies), early adopters (visionaries), early majority (pragmatists), late majority (conservatives), or laggards (skeptics) [47, 54].

Social factors is a catch-all term to refer to any agility driver in the general SD en-vironment that cannot be attributed to competitors, customers or technology. Exam-ples include:

- the growing importance of quality standards in the IS development field, such as the Capability Maturity Model (CMM) and ISO certification, and the emergence of these standards as "conditions of trade"[21].
- the growing number of system users, exemplified by the Internet where the users are the global population.
- The growing importance of legal issues, exemplified by the Internet, where information on a website must comply with the regulations of many countries.

5.2 Agility Strategy

This part of the framework indicates that it is pointless to argue whether agile meth-ods are superior to traditional methods. They are only better when the need to be agile and the capability of being agile coexist. The team must make an assessment of their agile needs and capabilities before assuming that an agile method is the way to go. The need for such an assessment has already been appreciated by the mainstream IS literature and two general schools of thought exist. Firstly, contingency factors re-search state that no single method is appropriate for every situation, and that an ap-propriate method should be selected from a portfolio of methods, depending on the specific characteristics of the development context. [16, 24, 50, 61]. Secondly, method engineering is an approach that requires methods to be developed or "engi-neered" to meet a particular IS development's needs, instead of selecting a method solely from an available library according to contingencies [7, 43].

5.3 Agility Capabilities

Competency refers to the SD team's ability to carry out the functions necessary the development of a successful system. If a team cannot carry out the fundamental ac-tivities related to SD, then it is irrelevant if they can carry them out quickly, proac-tively or economically for example.

Proaction refers to any action taken by an SD team in *advance of* change. Prototyping, for example, is used to elicit the "real" [67] requirements as soon as possible, mitigating the amount and impact of future requirement changes [5].

Reaction refers to any action taken by an SD team *after change has occured*, in order to reduce the impact or increase the benefit from that change. Changing design documentation, rewriting code and retesting in response to requirement changes are the simplest forms of reaction to change in the SD context.

Quickness refers to the speed of an SD team's proactions or reactions. *Robustness* is the team's inherent ability to endure change, or rather when the time needed to take action is zero.

Economy is the ability to eliminate waste through the minimisation of code and the avoidance of "documentation mountain ranges" [37]. It also refers to the maximum utilisation of developers and optimal development procedures. This is reflected in Level 5 of the CMM which requires that the documented, defined and institutionalised procedures required for ISO 9000 are in place, and that the software organisation is now ready to optimise its processes [41].

Quality refers to the ability to achieve high standards in terms of the software and supporting documentation produced, and also to the abilities of the SD team. Quite often, the focus is on the quality of the code, but documentation quality is ignored, resulting in high quality code being developed on the basis of low quality documentation that contains numerous anomalies [27]. Within the construct of quality, and more specifically Total Quality Management (TQM), lies the poka-yoke philosophy, which states that it is not enough to fix bugs when they occur, but to identify the root cause of the problem [59].

Simplicity refers to the straightforwardness of the software as well as the simplicity of the methods and techniques used to produce it.

5.4 Agility Providers

The *organisation* as a provider of agility refers to the structure of the development team and its decision-making process.

People refers to the persons who comprise the SD team and can provide agility by being highly skilled to allow role swapping, being able to see the big picture, and having a disposition to learning and change. However, the main constraint on software organisations is the availability of such people [1].

Technology such as automated code analysis and testing products can enhance an SD team's agility. Using automated products allow the new program to be retested quickly and thoroughly, whereas without such products a late change could result in a full phase of manual regression testing, delaying the project significantly [4, 36]. Also, CASE tools such as document control systems allow document changes to be made quickly and efficiently [37].

The *external environment* refers to any individual or organisation outside the SD team, including the client, the users and any vendors or third party suppliers.

6 Conclusions

Those who favour agile methods in SD have put forward many success stories to support their claims that agile methods are good, while any other method is not. This paper concludes that there is no consensus as to what constitutes an agile method, either in academia or in industry. Furthermore, the older, so called pre-agile methodologies exhibited many traits of agility.

A review of the literature indicates that an SD team that wishes to be truly agile must consider a lot more than they do at the moment. There are numerous capabilities that must be assessed and utilised, including competency, proaction, reaction, robustness, quickness, economy, quality and simplicity. Also they must ensure they examine all possible sources of these capabilities, namely the people on the team, the way they are organised, the hardware and software they use, and finally the clients, users and vendors that they interact with.

A further conclusion is that there is a fundamental problem with automatically declaring agile methods to be superior. There is a strong argument for assessing an SD team's need to be agile, and comparing that need to the capabilities that team has for being agile. In simple terms, if you don't need to be agile, or if you can't be agile, then don't be agile.

References

1. Baker, S.; McWilliams, G.; Kripalani, M., (1997) *The Global Search for Brainpower.* Business Week, 1997. **August 4**: p. 46-50.
2. Bansler, J.; Havn, E., (1994) *Information Systems Development With Generic Systems*, in *Proceedings of the Second European Conference on Information Systems*, W. Baets, Editor. 1994, Nijenrode University Press: Breukelen. p. 707-718.
3. Baskerville, R.; Travis, J.; Truex, D., (1992) *Systems without method: the impact of new technologies on information systems development projects.*, in *The Impact of Computer Supported Technologies on Information Systems Development*, K. Kendall, J. DeGross, and K. Lyytinen, Editors. 1992, Elsevier Science Publishers: North Holland. p. 241-269.
4. Bennett, P. A., (1994) *Software Development for the Channel Tunnel: A Summary.* High Integrity Systems, 1994. **1**(2): p. 213-220.
5. Berrisford, T.; Wetherbe, J., (1979) *Heuristic development: A redesign of systems design.* MIS Quarterly, 1979. **March**: p. 11-19.
6. Breu, K.; Hemingway, C.; Strathern, M., (2001) *Workforce agility: the new employee strategy for the knowledge economy.* Journal of Information Technology, 2001. **17**: p. 21-31.
7. Brinkkemper, S., (1996) *Method engineering: Engineering of information systems development methods and tools.* Information and Software Technology, 1996. **38**: p. 275-280.
8. Brown, P., (1985) *Managing Software Development.* Datamation, 1985(April): p. 133-136.
9. Burgess, T., (1994) *Making the Leap to Agility: Defining and Achieving Agile Manufacturing through Business Process Redesign and Business Network Redesign.* International Journal of Operations and Production Management., 1994. **14**(11): p. 23-34.
10. Childerhouse, P.; Disney, S.; Towill, D., (2000) *Speeding Up the Progress Curve Towards Effective Supply Chain Management.* International Journal of Supply Chain Management, 2000. **5**(3): p. 176-186.
11. Christopher, M., (2000) *The agile supply chin: competing in volatile markets.* Industrial Marketing Management, 2000. **29**(1): p. 37-44.
12. Clapp, J.; Taub, A., (1998) *A Management Guide to Software Maintenance in COTS-Based Systems.* 1998, Electronic Systems Center, MP 98B0000069.
13. Cockburn, A., (2002) *Agile Software Development Joins the "Would-Be" Crowd.* Cutter IT Journal, 2002. **Vol. 15**(1): p. 6-12.
14. Correa, H., (1994) *The Flexibility of Technological and Human Resources in Automotive Manufacturing.* Journal of Integrated Manufacturing Systems, 1994. **5**(1): p. 33-40.

15. Davis, A. M., (1988) *A Comparison of Techniques for the Specification of External System Behavior.* Communications of the ACM., 1988. **31**(9).
16. Davis, G. B., (1982) *Strategies for information requirements determination.* IBM Systems Journal, 1982. **21**(1): p. 4-30.
17. De Vor, R.; Mills, J., (1995) *Agile Manufacturing.* American Society of Mechanical Engineers, MED, 1995. **2**(2): p. 977.
18. Drucker, P., (1995) *The Information That Executives Truly Need.* Harvard Business Review, 1995. **Jan/Feb**.
19. Enguix, C. F.; Davis, J. G. (1999) *Filling the Gap: New Models for Systematic Page-based Web Application Development and Maintenance.* in *Proceedings of International Workshop on Web Engineering '99 (at WWW8).* 1999. Toronto, Canada.
20. Eppink, D., (1978) *Managing the Unforeseen: A Study of Flexibility.* 1978, Vrije Universiteit.: Amsterdam.
21. Ferguson, J.; Sheard, S., (1998) *Leveraging Your CMM Efforts for IEEE/EIA 12207.* IEEE Software, 1998. **15**(5): p. 23-28.
22. Fitzgerald, B., (1996) *Formalised systems development methodologies: a critical perspective.* Information Systems Journal, 1996. **6**(1): p. 3-23.
23. Fitzgerald, B., (1994) *The systems development dilemma: whether to adopt formalised systems development methodologies or not?*, in *Proceedings of the Second European Conference on Information Systems*, W. Baets, Editor. 1994, Nijenrode University Press: Holland. p. 691-706.
24. Fitzgerald, B.; Russo, N.; Stolterman, E., (2002) *Information Systems Development: Methods in Action.* 2002, London: McGraw-Hill.
25. Fowler, M.; Highsmith, J., (2001) *The Agile Manifesto.* Software Development, 2001. **August**.
26. Gerwin, D., (1993) *Manufacturing Flexibility: A Strategic Perspective.* Management Science, 1993. **39**(4): p. 395-410.
27. Gilb, T., (1988) *Principles of Software Engineering Management.* 1988, Wokingham: Addison-Wesley.
28. Golden, W.; Powell, P., (2000) *Towards a Definition of Flexibility: In Search of the Holy Grail?* Omega, 2000. **28**(2000): p. 373-384.
29. Goldman, S.; Nagel, R., (1993) *Management, technology and agility: the emergence of a new era in manufacturing.* International Journal of Technology Management, 1993. **8**(1/2): p. 18-38.
30. Goldman, S.; Nagel, R.; Preiss, K., (1995) *Agile Competitors and Virtual Organisations. Strategies for Enriching the Customer.* 1995, New York, NY.: Von Nostrand Reinhold.
31. Goudswaard, A.; de Nanteuil, M., (2000) *Flexibility and Working Conditions: a qualitative and comparative study in seven EU Member States.* 2000, European Foundation for Living and Working Conditions, EF0007.
32. Gunasekaran, A.; Tirtiroglou, E.; Wolstencroft, V., (2002) *An Investigation into the application of agile manufacturing in an aerospace company.* Elsevier, Technovation, 2002. **22**: p. 405-415.
33. Gustavsson, S., (1984) *Flexibility and Productivity in Complex Production Processes.* International Journal of Production Research, 1984. **22**(5): p. 801 - 808.
34. Hashimoto, T., (1980) *Robustness, Reliability, Resilience and Vulnerability Criteria for Planning.* 1980, Cornell University.
35. Hashimoto, T.; Loucks, D.; Stedinger, J., (1982) *Robustness of Water Resources Systems.* Water Resources Research, 1982. **18**(1): p. 21 - 26.
36. Hayes, R. H.; Wheelwright, S. C.; Clark, K. B., (1988) *Dynamic Manufacturing.* 1988, New York.: The Free Press.
37. Holloway, S., (1989) *Methodology Handbook for Information Managers.* 1989, Aldershot: Gower Technical.

38. Hong, M.; Payander, S.; Gruver, W., (1996) *Modelling and Analysis of flexible fixturing systems for agile manufacturing.* Proceedings of the IEEE International Conference on Systems, Man and Cybernetics, 1996. **2**: p. 1231-1236.
39. Huang, C., (1999) *An agile approach to logical network analysis in decision support systems.* Decision Support Systems, 1999. **25**(1): p. 53-70.
40. Institute, I., (1991) *21st Century Manufacturing Enterprise Strategy, An Industry-led View.* Iacocca Institute, 1991. **1**.
41. Kapoor, R., (1994) *Getting ISO 9000 for a Software Organization.* 1994, New Delhi, India: BPB Publications.
42. Katayama, H.; Bennet, D., (1999) *Agility, adaptability and leanness: a comparison of concepts and a study of practice.* International Journal of Production Economics, 1999. **62**(1/2): p. 43-51.
43. Kumar, K.; Welke, R. J., (1992) *Methodology engineering: a proposal for situation-specific methodology construction.*, in *Challenges and Strategies for Research in Systems Development*, W. Cotterman and J. Senn, Editors. 1992, John Wiley & Sons Ltd. p. 257-269.
44. Kusak, A.; He, D., (1997) *Design for agile assembly: an operational perspective.* International Journal of Production Research, 1997. **35**(1): p. 157-178.
45. Lindbergh, P., (1990) *Strategic manufacturing management: a proactive approach.* International Journal of Operations and Production Management, 1990. **10**(2): p. 94-106.
46. Lowe, D.; Hall, W., (1999) *Hypermedia & the Web / An Engineering Approach.* 1999, Chichester: Wiley.
47. Moore, G. A., (1991) *Crossing the Chasm: Marketing and Selling High-Tech Products to Mainstream Customers,.* 1991, New York: HarperCollins Publishers.
48. Murugesan, S.; Deshpande, Y. (1999) *Preface to ICSE'99 Workshop on Web Engineering.* in *Proceedings of International Conference on Software Engineering (ICSE'99).* 1999. Los Angeles, California.
49. Nagel, R.; Dove, R., (1991) *21st Century Manufacturing. Enterprise Strategy.* 1991, Iacocca Institute, Lehigh University Bethlehem, PA.
50. Naumann, J.; Davis, G.; McKeen, J., (1980) *Determining information requirements: A contingency method for selection of a requirements assurance strategy.* The Journal of Systems and Software, 1980. **1**: p. 273-281.
51. Naylor, J.; Naim, M.; Berry, D., (1999) *Leagility: Integrating the Lean and Agile Manufacturing Paradigm in the Total Supply Chain.* Engineering Costs and Production Economics, 1999. **62**: p. 107-118.
52. Ohno, T., (1988) *The Toyota Production System: Beyond Large Scale Production.* 1988, Portland, OR: Productivity Press.
53. Parnas, D. L.; Clements, P. C., (1986) *A Rational Design Process: How and Why to Fake It.* IEEE Transactions on Software Engineering., 1986. **12**(2): p. 251-257.
54. Paulk, M., (1999) *Structured Approaches to Managing Change.* Crosstalk: The Journal of Defense Software Engineering, 1999. **12**(11): p. 4-7.
55. Piore, M., (1989) *Corporate Reform in American Manufacturing and the Challenge to Economic Reform.* 1989: Mimeo, Massachusetts Institute of Technology.
56. Powell, T. A.; Jones, D. L.; Cutts, D. C., (1998) *Web Site Engineering / Beyond Web Page Design.* 1998, Upper Saddle River, NJ: Prentice-Hall.
57. Preiss, K.; Goldman, S.; Nagel, R., (1996) *Cooperate to compete: building agile business relationships.* 1996, New York: Vn Nostrand Reinhold.
58. Rockart, J.; De Long, D., (1988) *Executive Support Systems.* 1988, Homewood, Illinois.: Dow Jones-Irwin.
59. Schulmeyer, G.; McManus, J., eds. *Total Quality Management for Software.* 1993, Van Nostrand Reinhold: New York.
60. Sharafi, H.; Zhang, Z., (1999) *A method for achieving agility in manufacturing organisations: an introduction.* International Journal of Production Economics, 1999. **62**(1/2): p. 7-22.

61. Sullivan, C. H., (1985) *Systems Planning in the Information Age.* Sloan Business Review, 1985. **26**(2): p. 3-11.
62. Tan, B., (1998) *Agile Manufacturing and Management of Variability.* International Transactions on Operational Research, 1998. **5**(5): p. 375-388.
63. Towill, D.; Christopher, M., (2002) *The Supply Chain Strategy Conundrum: To Be Lean Or Agile or To Be Lean and Agile.* International Journal of Logistics: Research and Applications, 2002. **5**(3).
64. Upton, D. M., (1995) *Flexibility as Process Mobility: The Management of Plant Capabilities for Quick Response Manufacturing.* Journal of Operations Management, 1995. **12**(205-224).
65. Van Oyen, M.; Gel, E.; Hopp, W., (2001) *Performance opportunity for workforce agility in collaborative and non-collaborative work systems.* IEEE Transactions, 2001. **33**(9): p. 761-77.
66. Volberda, H., (1998) *Building the Flexible Firm: How to Remain Competitive.* 1998, New York: Oxford University Press.
67. Vonk, R., (1990) *Prototying: The Effective Use of CASE Technology.* 1990, London: Prentice-Hall.
68. Womack, J.; Jones, D.; Roos, D., (1990) *The Machine That Changed the World.* 1990, New York: Rawson Associates.
69. Young, K., et al., (2001) *Agile Control Systems.* In: Proc Instn Mech Engrs, 2001. **215**(D).
70. Yusuf, Y.; Sarhadi, M.; Gunasekaran, A., (1999) *Agile manufacturing: the drivers, concepts and attributes.* International Journal of Production Economics, 1999. **62**(1): p. 23-32.
71. Zain, M.; Kassim, N.; Mokhtar, E., (2002) *Use of IT nd IS for organisational agility in Malaysian firms.* Singapore Management Review, 2002. **25**(1).
72. Zhang, Z.; Sharifi, H., (2000) *A Methodology for Achieving Agility in Manufacturing Organisations.* International Journal of Operations and Production Management, 2000. **20**(4): p. 496-512.

Security Engineering and eXtreme Programming: An Impossible Marriage?

Jaana Wäyrynen[3], Marine Bodén[1], and Gustav Boström[2]

[1] Communications Security Lab, Ericsson Research,
Torshamnsgatan 23, SE-164 80 Stockholm, Sweden
marine.boden@ericsson.com
[2] Department of Applied IT, Electrum 213, 16440 Kista, Sweden
gusbo@kth.se
[3] Department of Computer and Systems Science,
Stockholm University/Royal Institute of Technology, Forum 100, SE-164 40 Kista, Sweden
jaana@dsv.su.se

Abstract. Agile methods, such as eXtreme Programming (XP), have been criticised for being inadequate for the development of secure software. In this paper, we analyse XP from a security engineering standpoint, to assess to what extent the method can be used for development of security critical software. This is done by analysing XP in the light of two security engineering standards; the Systems Security Engineering-Capability Maturity Model (SSE-CMM) and the Common Criteria (CC). The result is that XP is more aligned with security engineering than one might think at first. However, XP also needs to be tailored to better support and to more explicitly deal with security engineering issues. Tailoring XP for secure software development, without removing the agility that is the trademark of agile methods, may be a solution that would make XP more compatible with current security engineering practices.

1 Introduction

A question concerning Agile software development that repeatedly has been illuminated is the applicability of agile methods such as eXtreme Programming (XP). In particular, questions about the suitability of these methods to particular development environments and application domains, are often recurring in the field, addressed for example by Lindvall et al [13] and Turk et al [24].

In the security engineering community, one of the major criticisms against XP, is that it is not suitable for secure software development since the method does not explicitly specify activities for producing the documentation needed for such projects, such as design documentation and detailed interface specifications [25]. Furthermore, coupled with the lack of documentation, is the question of proof of compliance with accepted software engineering standards [23], and consequently, also XP's compliance with accepted security engineering standards. Proponents, on the other hand, claim that XP is both beneficial and compatible with security engineering.

The claims made by XP proponents and critics certainly lead to questions about the applicability of agile methods. Work has been done in the field, for example by Viega and McGraw [25] and Shore [20]. Boehm [5], Bishop [4], McBreen [14], Paulk [17] are among those, who argue that the de-emphasis on design documentation and architecture is a risky endeavour in contexts where security is important. Viega and McGraw [25], underline the importance of a solid specification. The more formal and

C. Zannier et al. (Eds.): XP/Agile Universe 2004, LNCS 3134, pp. 117–128, 2004.

clear a specification, the better the resulting system. They mean that XP does not fulfil these criteria, and even go as far as saying that XP probably has a negative impact on software security.

On the contrary, Amey and Chapman [2], Murro et al. [16] and Shore [20], have found that many of the XP practices comply with practices in building secure software. Based on the experience from two case studies, Amey and Chapman [2] report on a comparison on static and dynamic verification as control mechanisms in development. Their conclusion is that many of the XP practices are extensively known and applied in the development of secure software. Murro et al. [16], assess the introduction of XP in a company that builds complex portals with strict security requirements in the Internet development domain. They find that XP is a robust and flexible method that has improved their way of working and producing effectively. These experiences are also supported by Shore [20], who reports on the successful experiences of using XP in a security critical project, where a traditional approach previously had failed to implement the required security features.

The results presented, although only a selection of the works in the field, represent the nature of research that involves building secure software with XP. Indeed, these are all important contributions that build up the knowledge and experience base on XP's compliance with security engineering. More importantly, however, is that there is no work that has produced a structured approach to analyse XP from a strict security engineering perspective. This indicates that there is a need for a more thorough investigation. Analysing XP from a security engineering perspective, more elaborately and comprehensively than previously, would greatly enhance the understanding of XP's suitability for secure software development.

In this paper, we provide a first attempt at such an investigation by looking at security engineering standards, and by analysing how XP deals with the security engineering activities and requirements stated in these standards. The Systems Security Engineering Capability Maturity Model, SSE-CMM, [22] is taken as a starting point for analysing the XP software development process. As a complement, we also look at what the Common Criteria, CC, [7] requires from a software development process. Thus, by analysing XP from a security engineering perspective we aim to provide valuable input for a better understanding of how the two fields relate. While we do this from the standpoint of security engineering, it could also be possible to instead analyse security engineering from an agile point of view, but that would be another paper.

The paper begins with an overview of the nature of security engineering and security practices and a brief overview of XP, respectively. This is followed by a description of the problems in security engineering in general, to illuminate other relevant aspects that further motivate why this research has been undertaken. We then discuss the results of an analysis of XP from a security engineering perspective, based on the SSE-CMM and the CC. The paper concludes with a presentation of an idea for a more secure XP process, which is complemented with a short, concluding discussion and suggestions of further work.

2   The Nature of Security Engineering

In order to analyse XP from a security engineering standpoint, it is necessary to have an idea of what security engineering is. Unfortunately, a generally accepted definition does not exist. There are, however, activities that are generally included in security engineering. The Systems Security Engineering Capability Maturity Model, suggests the following list of activities to be generally accepted [22]:

1. Identify the organisational security risks
2. Define the security needs to counter identified risks
3. Transform the security needs into activities
4. Establish confidence and trustworthiness in correctness and effectiveness in a system
5. Determine that operational impacts due to residual security vulnerabilities in a system or it's operation are tolerable (acceptable risks)
6. Integrate the efforts of all engineering disciplines and specialities into a combined understanding of the trustworthiness of a system

We have chosen to group these activities in two general categories, i.e. Specify security needs and Assurance. These categories also cover the specific security activities in the two security standards that are used in the analysis.

2.1 Specifying Security Needs

The identification of risks and what is needed to prevent the risk will result in a definition of the security needs of a system. For example, the risk that anyone can login to a system over the Internet, defines the security need to have strong authentication.

The specification of security needs includes risk management, i.e. the process of assessing and quantifying risk, and establishing an acceptable level of risk for an organisation. To achieve this goal, it is important to be proactive and to identify potential security risks in the system's environment. This is to counteract the very common standard of fixing broken software today, which is the penetrate-and-patch approach, i.e. software is patched after it has been compromised [15] (To security engineers, the XP practice of refactoring can seem very similar to penetrate-and-patch). To build secure software, it is necessary to think about future threats and what effects they can have on the system. To avoid having to fix problems after the software is delivered, there is a need to get these issues right from the start.

2.2 Assurance

Assurance is defined as the degree of confidence that security needs are satisfied [19]. For a system to be classified as secure, it is necessary to present an assurance argument, i.e. a structured and supported statement of how one can be sure that security needs have been satisfied. This argument should be supported by assurance evidence, such as test results, documented code reviews and appraisals by security engineers.

In security engineering, an important part of the work consists of gathering and analysing such evidence. It is important to note here, that test results are not enough to ensure that a system is secure. Tests can only show that the system passed the test, not that it is safe against all future attacks. Consequently, testing needs to be complemented with other activities, such as code reviews, design reviews and formal verification. Even with additional techniques, hundred percent security cannot be achieved, but the level of confidence is higher.

2.3 Security Standards – The SSE-CMM and the Common Criteria

Security standards are often used to help and to certify companies developing secure systems. The Common Criteria [7] is one of the most referenced standards. The Secure Systems Engineering Capability Maturity Model [22] is another common security standard.

The Secure Systems Engineering Capability Maturity Model is designed as a tool for measuring an organisation's capability to develop secure systems. The process areas (PA) in SSE-CMM are useful as a checklist when analysing software development methods, such as XP, from a security engineering perspective. The SSE-CMM consists of a number of base practices that are organised in process areas. For example, PA05.02 Identify System Security Vulnerabilities, is a base practice defined in PA05, Assess Vulnerability. The SSE-CMM also follows other CMM's in that it provides a framework for specifying to what degree an organisation performs these PAs, i.e. the maturity level [22]. The SSE-CMM specifies twenty-two process areas for process improvement. A table that defines the PAs of immediate interest for this work is provided in the analysis section of this paper.

The Common Criteria can be described as a language for expressing security requirements on a system and its development process. These requirements represent two requirement types, i.e. functional requirements and assurance requirements, respectively.

Functional requirements in CC are used as a standard requirements repository. The requirements can be combined, adapted and may be extended to form a specification of the total security requirements of a system. These requirements together with documentation regarding threats, risks and the system's environment are gathered in a document called the security target (a security target actually contains a lot more, but will not be described in detail here). This document serves as a requirement specification for security concerns.

The assurance requirements put demands on an organisation's software development process and specify the activities that are needed to reach the CC's different Evaluation Assurance Levels (EAL). There are seven assurance levels in CC, where EAL 1 is the lowest assurance level, and EAL 7 is the highest. Table 1, presents the seven EALs and their objectives.

Table 1. An overview of the CC assurance levels and their objectives [7]

Evaluation Assurance Level	Objective
EAL 1	Functionally tested
EAL 2	Structurally tested
EAL 3	Methodically tested and checked
EAL 4	Methodically designed, tested and checked
EAL 5	Semiformally designed and tested
EAL 6	Semiformally verified design and tested
EAL 7	Formally verified design and tested

Each EAL consist of a common set of assurance classes which are the same for each assurance level, with the only difference that the requirements escalate with higher levels. The objective is to evaluate to what extent the development process involves testing, design and verification of a system or product, and whether this done in a functional, structural and/or formal manner. The EALs are therefore useful as a complement to the SSE-CMM process areas, when analysing the extent to which a development process fulfils prescribed security activities to assure that the security needs are met.

3 Agile Software Development and XP

The subject for the analysis in this paper is XP. Therefore, a brief overview of agile software development methods and XP is provided in this section.

There are a number of existing agile software development methods, where the most known methods are eXtreme Programming (XP), Feature Driven Development (FDD), Adaptive Software Development (ASD), Scrum, Crystal and Dynamic Systems Development Method (DSDM) [1]. Since XP is the agile method that is most widely used [8], we have chosen to base the analysis on XP, as a representative of the group of agile software development methods.

XP is based on a pragmatic approach, and the fundamental idea is to simplify the development of software. However, simplifying the development of software is not to be compared with a simple method. On the contrary, to get the full benefits of XP is a demanding challenge for the project team.

The cornerstones of XP are a set of tightly interconnected practices, principles and values. These depend on each other to form a whole that is greater than its parts. The individual XP practices will not be presented in detail, but we refer to Beck [3] and Jeffries et al. [12] when any specific XP concepts are used in the paper. However, in brief XP emphasizes customer involvement and promotes teamwork, which is realised through the value of constant communication with the customer and within the team. Design is simple. YAGNI (You Aren't Going to Need It) [3], a philosophy of XP, symbolizes the idea of simplicity as it emphasizes working only on known requirements and to implement only what you actually need in the present situation. The reason is to avoid overdesigning a system in a vain attempt to anticipate future requirement changes [18]. XP emphasizes rapid feedback through mechanisms, such as continuous testing of the system. Frequent deliveries are also important to enable the customer to directly evaluate and approve the results, before releasing the system [11].

XP is, in general, most effective in the context of small teams, small to middle-sized projects and chaotic development environments with rapidly changing requirements. This is accomplished by structuring the software development process into short iterations, preferably two-week iterations, where an iteration focuses on timely delivery of working code and other artefacts that provide value to the customer.

4 Why XP for Secure Software Development?

In today's competitive market, the demand on producing software in Internet time challenges the traditional ways to develop software. From a security engineering perspective, this calls for immediate attention also on the security issues, putting pressure on the prevailing ways of developing secure software.

In this respect, traditional problems within security engineering need to be considered, to better understand why this research has been initiated. Firstly, security engineering, for example the Common Criteria [7], represent time and resource consuming processes. CCs predecessors where designed mainly for military use [4] with extensive documentation requirements, which has lead to difficulties with keeping documentation up-to-date. CC inherited these requirements. Secondly, a sub-aspect of the documentation requirements is that it is often argued that (security) documentation activities should start in an early phase of the development process [25] [10]. In reality, however, it may be a waste of time and money to try to write (security) documentation when you are dealing with a "moving target", i.e. the security solution of the software is due to constant changes, and hence, keeping the documentation up-to-date will be a resource-consuming task.

These issues need to be illuminated and put in a wider perspective. As Viega and McGraw [25] argue, the demand on producing software in Internet time is the enemy of software security. The question is, how can this external business demand on speeding up software development be tackled, while at the same time satisfying software security requirements?

We believe that there is a need for agility also in secure software development. Assuming that market-driven forces will continue to put pressure on software development, XP certainly is an important alternative to take into consideration. There may be weaknesses in XP, but XP is not the only software development method that does not completely comply with the strict formalism prescribed by security engineering standards. Rather, the problems within security engineering mirror some of the inherent problems with traditional software development methods.

By shedding light on the benefits of XP together with the good practices of security engineering, such as prevention and risk management, will allow a better understanding of XP and security engineering. Therefore, we argue that a structured analysis of XP from a security engineering perspective is needed, and that it is an important effort to gain understanding of how the two fields relate, to build up a compatible process, that satisfies requirements from both camps. In the following, we will discuss the results of our first step towards this goal.

5   Analysis of XP from a Security Engineering Perspective

We have chosen to focus the analysis in this article on the SSE-CMM, since it has a clear focus on process improvement in security engineering, whereas CC is more focused on the requirements activities in security engineering. The reason why we have chosen to analyse XP from the perspective of two security standards is to get a better coverage of the security area, and to complement the SSE-CMM with CC aspects, such as assurance requirements.

Since the SSE-CMM is designed as a tool for measuring an organisation's capability to develop secure systems, it necessarily covers a larger domain than relevant for this analysis. For example, it specifies a number of PAs that describe project management and organisational practices, which are not specific to security engineering. Therefore, only ten PAs are used, as presented in Table 2. Consequently, we will focus the analysis on these topics and complement with relevant CC requirements. Furthermore, since there is no one-to-one mapping between SSE-CMM and CC, we have chosen to group relevant process areas and assurance requirements in two general security categories, i.e. Specify security needs and Assurance, that serve as the starting point for the analysis.

We analyse XP as a whole method from a security engineering perspective. However, individual XP practices are discussed when specifically addressing any of the security activities included in this presentation.

Table 2. The SSE-CMM process areas (PA), and how they are grouped with regard to the general security categories in this paper

Process Areas	Security Category
PA01 – Administer Security Controls	N/A
PA02 – Assess Impact	Specify security needs
PA03 – Assess Security Risk	Specify security needs
PA04 – Assess Threat	Specify security needs
PA05 – Assess Vulnerability	Specify security needs
PA06 – Build Assurance Argument	Assurance
PA08 – Monitor Security Posture	N/A
PA09 – Provide Security Input	Specify security needs
PA10 – Specify Security Needs	Specify security needs
PA11 – Verify and Validate Security	Assurance

5.1 Specify Security Needs

The goal of specifying security needs is to assess the security risk and to define the security features needed to establish an acceptable level of risk. Both CC and SSE-CMM require that a risk assessment is done. This is the prevailing view in the security engineering camp, and several authors argue that security is not possible to add as an afterthought [4][21][25], but has to be built in and specified from the start.

It is clear the XP does not provide out of the box process support for this area. In the XP community there is a debate around so called motherhood stories, i.e. a statement of the systems non-functional requirements [26]. However, there seems to be no consensus on whether motherhood stories are helpful or just confusing. One problem is that they cannot easily be broken down into testable and estimable tasks. This is a general problem with non-functional requirements. The CC is very useful in addressing this problem since it provides help in breaking down a general statement such as: "The system needs to protect sensitive information", into separate, more concrete requirements. The SSE-CMM also outlines process support for this area. In our point of view, without this process support security requirements could easily be forgotten, or be specified on a too abstract level to be effective. Another general problem that is especially difficult with non-functional requirements is that you need to dig for them. Users are mainly focused on functional requirements, therefore expertise is needed to help them with this task.

Recently, XP proponents are saying that the practice of an on-site customer should refer to a customer team, rather than just one person [14]. If a security engineer is present on the XP team, he or she could initiate a risk assessment activity together with the customer, and it could be his or her role to specify the security needs based on the results of the risk assessment [26].

Assessing the impact of security risks, as specified SSE-CMM's PA 02, is normally not an activity performed in standard XP either. Again, if a security engineer is present on the team, he could co-operate with the customer to do this.

5.2 Assurance

The goal of building an assurance argument is to clearly convey that security needs have been met. Traditionally, in for example the CC, this means producing large quantities of documents and performing and documenting reviews of various kinds. The higher the assurance levels, the higher the documentation requirements. This is in conflict with the de-emphasis of documentation in XP. This does not mean that documentation is eliminated in XP. If documentation is needed, i.e. such documentation that the project team deems critical for it's work, documentation is simply added as an user story and transformed to an engineering task in the iteration plan. However, from a security perspective, assurance documentation is in many respects of outmost importance, even though it may not feel important for the developers. Therefore, an XP project would either need to adapt and produce assurance evidence during development, or provide an alternative way of conveying that the security requirements have been met.

The first alternative is a possibility, but it is hard to fit with XP practices and may reduce agility. This, however, poses other problems. If security problems in the code or design are found, and refactoring is necessary it would mean that a lot of documentation has to be re-done. The second alternative, providing an alternative way of providing an assurance argument, is another possibility. In this respect, it could be argued that the emphasis on automated test suites in XP, provides an assurance argument if the tests also include security testing. Pair programming can also be seen as an assurance activity, since one of its purposes is to remove the need for code reviews. The inherent, and generally healthy, conservatism in the security industry will, however, be a big obstacle. Abandoning the reliance on documentation and reviews, often done by a third party, is a big step.

The assessment of vulnerabilities of a system is another security engineering activity that involves checking if any flaws have been introduced during the development [7], and to assure that security needs have been met. This needs to be done throughout the life cycle of the system. Although XP doesn't specify this explicitly, the purpose of this activity is in a way taken into account by the XP practices of simple design, pair programming, test-driven development, refactoring, collective ownership and coding standards.

The practice of simple design will make the software easy to evaluate from a security perspective. Complex systems with many interactions are difficult to analyse and understand, which will have an impact on other security areas. Many interactions may introduce flaws, which in turn will make the vulnerability assessment more difficult.

Extra care is needed, however, to make the other practices effective for assessing vulnerabilities. Developers need to be knowledgeable about vulnerabilities, for example, buffer overflows and SQL-injection. Otherwise, they will not notice problems when pair programming for example. If a security engineer is present in the team, he or she should be active through pair programming with developers to spread knowledge about vulnerabilities.

As a complement to the implicit code review in pair programming, automated tests could also be run at compile time, to check that developers are not inserting vulnerabilities in the code [2][25]. The construction and monitoring of these compiler modifications would be a natural role for the team's security engineer.

To a limited extent test-driven development could also help in assessing vulner-abilities, but tests are not sufficient since tests cannot assure that all problems have been removed [4].

Collective ownership and coding standards enable more people to scrutinize all parts of the system for vulnerabilities, which also is facilitated by the XP practices of simple design and refactoring that help keeping the code under control.

It is clear that providing an assurance argument will be a challenge to an XP-project. Modifications to the process are necessary, and it is unclear whether these modifications, such as more documentation, will be a good fit with the XP process [17]. This is, on the other hand, dependent on what level of assurance is required. The lower levels of assurance, such as EAL 1 and 2 in the Common Criteria, mainly rely on thorough testing which is included in XP, whereas the higher EALs require formal verification, which is not included in XP to the extent that security engineers argue for.

5.3 Summary

The SSE-CMM document suggests that a chart should be produced outlining the process areas (PA) that are covered within an organisation. Such a chart is also useful to summarise this analysis. Table 3, (although, it does not specify the maturity level) concludes if the PA is covered in XP.

Table 3. The SSE-CMM process areas (PA's) and their presence in XP

Process Areas	Performed	Comment
PA01 – Administer Security Controls	N/A	
PA02 – Assess Impact	No	
PA03 – Assess Security Risk	No	
PA04 – Assess Threat	No	
PA05 – Assess Vulnerability	No	
PA06 – Build Assurance Argument	No	
PA07 – Co-ordinate Security	Yes	Through coaching and pair programming
PA08 – Monitor Security Posture	N/A	
PA09 – Provide Security Input	Limited	Through users specifying security input
PA10 – Specify Security Needs	Limited	Developers transform specified security needs to specific engineering tasks
PA11 – Verify and Validate Security	Yes	Through testing and pair programming

The table shows that XP lacks security engineering support in many areas, especially in areas that concern Specifying security needs and Assurance. In the analysis of XP's compliance with the requirements stated in the CC, we found that XP clearly could fulfil EAL 2, although CC requires additional documentation. Although we need to be very careful in our statements about XP's compliance with the EALs in CC, it could be argued that the executable tests provide this documentation. The analysis also showed that XP covers parts of the assurance requirements stated in the EAL 3 and EAL 4. In particular, test-driven development allows both functional and structural tests. However, XP lacks both semi-formal and formal design and verification documentation as stated in the assurance requirements of EAL 5, EAL 6 and EAL 7.

6 Conclusion

The analysis of XP from a SSE-CMM and CC perspective shows that XP lacks several activities that should be present in secure software development. More specifically, the following issues need better process support:

1. Specifying security requirements
2. Proactively deal with security concerns through the assessment of security risks
3. Building an assurance argument
4. Reliance on testing for verification

The easy way to address these issues would be to add more steps to the XP process and increase the demand for documentation. This would, however, reduce the benefits of using XP. A better approach would be to modify XP in an agile way. We propose an idea for a modified XP to better deal with the requirements in the development of secure software:

1. Include a security engineer in the project team. The tasks of the security engineer would consist of:

   a) Assessing security risk together with the on-site customer
   b) On the basis of the assessed risks, propose security related user stories
   c) Pair programming with the development team to ensure correct implementation of security, and to spread security thinking in the project team

2. Document the security engineer's pair programming activities to ensure coverage, and complement with further reviews if necessary to help build an assurance argument

3. As a preparation before a security review, document the security architecture in order to provide an assurance argument

4. Complement pair programming with static verification and automatic policy enforcement if possible

   This idea is derived from the results of an analysis of how XP deals with the security activities and requirements stated in the Systems Security Engineering-Capability Maturity Model and the Common Criteria. The proposed idea combines the use of XP and the aforementioned security standards, to better ensure that the security requirements are dealt with in the development of secure software. More specifically, this idea features the role of a security engineer to be included in the project team, to spread knowledge and awareness about security issues, as well as to coach both developers and customers in the development of secure software in an XP project. The role of the security engineer could be compared to the role of testers in XP teams. For example, Rasmussen [18] discusses lessons learned from introducing XP in a software development project at a North American energy company, where the tester became a valuable team member that greatly contributed to the project's overall success. In his article, Rasmussen [18] concludes that better results will be achieved when testers are made a core part of the team, since they can aid customers in defining and automating acceptance tests, as well as play the role of an analyst and flush out hidden requirements and assumptions. This is also supported by Crispin and House [9], who have done interesting work on the role that testers play on XP projects, and which we believe also could be contributed to the role of an security engineer on XP projects.

Essentially, XP and security engineering both aim at the same thing, i.e. helping development teams to do the right things in critical development environments and should not be in conflict with each other. With this idea, we also propose that agility can be maintained, and at the same time support the goals and practices of security engineering.

7 Further Work

This paper, although based on the authors experiences is mainly a theoretical analysis. Empirical data would be of value for assessing the results and premises.

We believe that there is a need for agility in security engineering. XP is a minimalist, highly disciplined software development method, that when used appropriately, has a proven capability to produce planned results in a timely manner. Therefore, an interesting next step, would be to move towards agile security engineering. Traditional security engineering should be inspired by the agile values to constructively, efficiently and effectively deal with changing requirements and new market demands.

Secure software development is a large domain. Our effort is by no means comprehensive, nor exhaustive. What we have presented are some of the most evident concepts that we want to expose in this first round of analysis. Both the SSE-CMM and the CC specify many more requirements of how to deal with security issues, than have been illuminated in this analysis. Moreover, the analysis in this paper is limited to the development of commercial off-the-shelf software (COTS), such as ERP-systems (Enterprise Resource Planning) and e-commerce applications. Real-time software applications and safety critical applications present further challenges, and are therefore out of scope of this paper.

Acknowledgments

The authors would like to thank Bil Kleb and Erik Lundh for their useful feedback.

References

1. Agile Alliance, Agile Alliance.www.agilealliance.com. Accessed in February 2004.
2. Amey P., and Chapman R., Static Verification and Extreme Programming. Proceedings of the ACM SIGAda Annual International Conference, 2003.
3. Beck K., Extreme Programming Explained: Embrace Change. Addison-Wesley, 2000.
4. Bishop M., Computer Security: Art and Science. Addison-Wesley, 2003.
5. Boehm B., Get Ready for Agile Methods, with Care. IEEE Computer, Vol. 35 (1), 2002.
6. Boehm B. and Turner R., Balancing Agility and Discipline, Addison-Wesley, 2004.
7. CC, ISO 15408 Common Criteria for Information Technology Security Evaluation Version 2.1, August 1999.

8. Charette R., The Decision is in: Agile versus Heavy Methodologies. Agile development and Project Management, Cutter Consortium, Vol. 2 (19), www.cutter.com/freestuff/epmu0119.html. Accessed in February 2004.

9. Crispin L. and House T., Testing Extreme Programming. Addison-Wesley, 2002 .

10. Evertsson U., Örthberg U., Yngström L., Integrating Security into Systems Development. Proceedings of IFIP TC11 Eighteenth International Conference on Information Security, 2003.

11. Extreme Programming, Extreme Programming: A Gentle Introduction. www.extremeprogramming.org. Accessed in January 2004.

12. Jeffries R., Anderson A., Hendrickson C., Extreme Programming Installed. Addison-Wesley, 2001.

13. Lindvall M., et al., Empirical Findings in Agile Methods. www.cebase.org, 2002. Accessed in March 2003.

14. McBreen, P., Questioning eXtreme Programming. Addison-Wesley, 2003.

15. McGraw G., On Bricks and Walls: Why Building Secure Software is Hard. Computers & Security Vol. 21 (3), pp 229-238, 2002.

16. Murro O., Deias R., Mugheddo G., Assessing XP at a European Internet Company. IEEE Software Vol. 20 (3), 2003.

17. Paulk M., Extreme Programming from a CMM Perspective. IEEE Software, Vol. 18 (6), 2001.

18. Rasmussen J., Introducing XP into Greenfield Projects. IEEE Software Vol. 20 (3), 2003.

19. RFC 2828, Internet Security Glossary. www.ietf.org/rfc/rfc2828.txt?number=2828. Accessed in February 2004.

20. Shore J., Continuous Design. IEEE Software, Vol. 21 (1), 2004.

21. Siponen, M., An Analysis of the Recent IS Security Development Approaches: Descriptive and Prescriptive Implications. Information Security Management – Global Challenges in the Next Millennium, Idea Group, 2001.

22. SSE-CMM, Systems Security Engineering Capability Maturity Model, Model Description Document Version 3.0. www.sse-cmm.org/model/ssecmmv2final.pdf. Accessed in January 2004.

23. Theunissen Morkel W.H. et al., Standards and Agile Software Development. Proceedings of SAICSIT, pp 178-188, 2003.

24. Turk D., France R., Rumpe B., Limitations of Agile Software Development. Third International Conference on eXtreme Programming and Agile Processes in Software Engineering, 2002.

25. Viega J. and McGraw G., Building Secure Software: How to Avoid Security Problems the Right Way. Addison-Wesley, 2002

26. Yahoo Groups, Yahoo Groups/ExtremeProgramming. http://groups.yahoo.com/group/extremeprogramming/message/90285. Accessed in April 2004

An Agile CMM

Erik Bos and Christ Vriens

Philips Research,
Prof. Holstlaan 4 (WAA01), 5656 AA Eindhoven, The Netherlands
{Erik.Bos,Christ.Vriens}@philips.com
http://www.research.philips.com

Abstract. This paper describes the process for developing software in a highly volatile environment. The process is based on eXtreme Programming (XP) and Scrum, to combine engineering practices with management directives based on the Capability Maturity Model (CMM) Level 2. In December 2003 our department, Software Engineering Services (SES), was successfully certified for CMM Level 2. The assessors were especially impressed with the transparent, easily accessible and uniform project information. We describe which XP and Scrum practices we apply in the different Key Process Areas (KPA) of CMM and which activities were added. Also, the result of the assessment and recommendations of the assessors are listed.

1 Introduction

CMM [1] gives guidelines for developing quality software in the context of large projects and organizations. Following CMM involves documenting and reviewing; documenting requirements, decisions, meetings, risks, plans and effort spent on software development.

XP and Scrum [2,3] focus on a less bureaucratic way of developing quality software by focusing on good engineering practices and a human centered process.

At first glance these two approaches seem far apart.

Our department has existed since mid 2000 and currently consists of 8 permanent staff members and 20 experienced software contractors. We develop software in small teams: two to six software engineers sometimes joined by researchers and led by a team leader. The team leader acts as an XP coach/ScrumMaster, making sure the defined way of working is followed. Due to the size and the self-organizing character of the teams, the team leader also contributes by developing software. The projects (both prototypes and products[1]) are characterized by fixed time of delivery (e.g. an exhibition or a demonstration), short time frame (2-6 months), and vague, minimal and changing requirements. The projects need to quickly show whether ideas of researchers are technically and commercially feasible. If so, the results are transferred to the Philips product divisions to form the basis of a new product. This calls for quality code and adequate documentation for users of the software outside of the team. *A combination of good engineering practices and good enough documentation would be ideal.*

---

[1] Example: the Audio Fingerprinting project delivered a solution for music recognition combined with related music content delivery for mobile phones and was developed using our Agile process. See www.contentidentification.philips.com

C. Zannier et al. (Eds.): XP/Agile Universe 2004, LNCS 3134, pp. 129–138, 2004.
© Springer-Verlag Berlin Heidelberg 2004

Our approach was to take the best of CMM and the agile methodologies and combine them. We strived for CMM certification to benchmark our Software Engineering Services (SES) department and get recognition of the rest of Philips as a professional software development organization, which makes it easier to transfer our deliverables to the product divisions.

An independent CMM assessment validated the software development process in December 2003. Several references were found comparing and combining XP and CMM [4,5,6], but no references were found of actual assessments being performed on departments running Agile projects.

In the following sections the KPAs[2] are listed and we show which agile practices we've incorporated in which KPAs. We also describe the results of the assessment and the recommendations of the assessors.

2   Requirements Management

In SES, software is developed in iterations of a calendar month. For shorter projects (e.g. 3 month projects) or projects where the requirements can change within a month, an iteration length of two weeks is used. At the beginning of the iterations, an iteration meeting takes place with the whole team of developers and the (onsite) customer, usually a researcher. The customer describes the requirements. We enter them in a user story database. We developed this database to allow easy access to the user stories and to have an overview of which user stories are scheduled for which iteration (see figure 1).

Next, the team and the customer discuss Problem Reports (PR) and Change Requests (CR), which were entered in the bug database during system testing. The customer determines which PRs and CRs need to be solved in this iteration. They are then estimated and entered as user stories.

At the end of the meeting the user stories are prioritized and assigned to an iteration. The number of user stories assigned depends on the velocity[3] in the previous iteration and on the availability of the developers in the coming iteration. This makes the amount of work, which can be delivered in the iteration, repeatable (CMM Level 2: The Repeatable Level).

At the end of the iteration, the user stories are demonstrated to the customer and are either accepted or rejected.

3   Project Planning

The user stories are split-up into tasks, which are estimated by the whole team. The planning game is comparable with the Delphi method [3], which is referenced in [1, page 78] as a suitable way to determine estimates.

---

[2] For a full description of the KPAs see reference [1].
[3] Velocity is defined as: the amount of work finished in the last completed iteration. See [2] for a more elaborate explanation of its usage.

Work Breakdown Structure

General Information:

| Project Title: | Project Planning & Tracking System v3.0 (Start / End Date: 2004-04-19 / ?) |
| Switch to Iteration: | wk17/18 ▾ |

[Add Iteration] [Edit Iteration] [Delete Iteration] [Generate PDF]

User Stories for Iteration 'wk17/18':

	Description	Iteration	Estimation (hours)	Total Initial Effort (hours)	Total Used (hours)	Total Last ToGo (hours)	CA^		
☐	Solve PRs	wk17/18		14	14	0	N	✎	🗑
☐	Implement authorization	wk17/18	70	94	38	75	N	✎	🗑
☐	Add/edit user absents, including selectable rea...	wk17/18		16	22	0	N	✎	🗑
☐	Quality Assurance wk17/18	wk17/18		0	0	0	N	✎	🗑
☐	Configuration Management wk17/18	wk17/18		0	0	0	N	✎	🗑
☐	Indirect hours wk17/18	wk17/18		0	4	0	N	✎	🗑
	Total:		70	124	78	75			

[Add User Story] [Copy Selected User Stories to Iteration] wk17/18 ▾
^CA = Customer Accepted

Tasks for User Story 'Solve PRs':

	Description	Owner	Initial Effort (hours)	Total Used (hours)	Last ToGo (hours)	Used (hours)	ToGo (hours)			
☐	Assignments bugs fixed	Pascal Vogels (vogelsp)	14	14	0			✎	🗑	🔳

[Add Task]

Tasks for User Story 'Implement authorization':

	Description	Owner	Initial Effort (hours)	Total Used (hours)	Last ToGo (hours)	Used (hours)	ToGo (hours)			
☐	Change database structure (Create new, modify existing and fil...		2	8	2			✎	🗑	🔳
☐	Create "access tables" including group profiles		4	0	4			✎	🗑	🔳
☐	Create access control class		32	7	25			✎	🗑	🔳

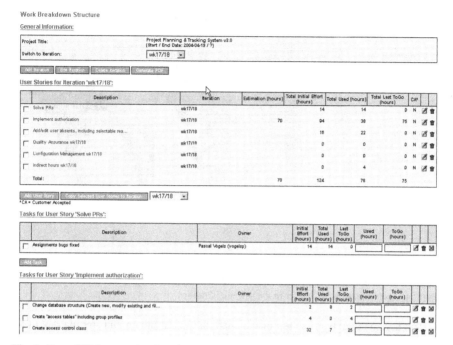

Fig. 1. Part of Web page showing the user stories and tasks for a particular iteration together with their initial and current estimations and currently spent effort

Usually there are just enough user stories provided by the customer to fill two iterations, so planning ahead for more than two months is not necessary. Some of the projects require a release planning, which is made by spreading the user stories over the next iterations, based on the velocity of the last, completed iteration and the availability of the developers. The release plan is extracted from the iteration deliverables. These deliverables are written down in the Project Management Plan (PMP), based on our only document template containing the documented procedure the CMM requires. The PMP is agreed upon by all involved persons and stored in the project archive.

4 Project Tracking

Every day the software engineers update the task(s) they worked on by entering the spent hours and a new estimation for the task. So the project planning is accurate on a day-to-day basis. Remaining tasks are discussed in the stand-up or Scrum meeting every morning.

XP and Scrum only care about the new estimates for the tasks at hand. In the CMM this is also valued, since the engineers themselves are responsible for their estimations and may update them. Project Tracking in CMM also asks for keeping track of the hours spent, so we can see if our estimates were correct and learn from the historical data we build up this way.

From the data entered we draw an inverted burn-down chart, shown in figure 2.

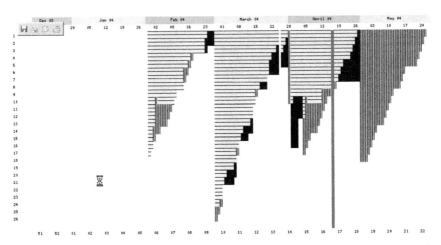

Fig. 2. Burn-down chart showing amount of planned work (in days), unallocated time and the amount of work feasible to deliver in the 4-week iterations

The horizontal axis at the top of the chart shows the month and starting day of the weeks. At the bottom of the chart the week numbers are listed. The iterations in this project are 4 weeks long. The chart shows for each day the remaining planned effort in the corresponding iteration in ideal engineering days. The following situations can be distinguished (all present in the chart in figure 2):

- The planned effort equals the possible effort as calculated from the velocity of the previous iteration, which is indicated by columns that are complete horizontally hatched
- Less effort is planned than calculated from the velocity; this difference is indicated by the vertically hatched part at the end of the column
- More effort is planned than calculated; this difference is indicated by the black areas at the end of the column

The day on which the chart is drawn is indicated by a one-day wide bar from the top to the bottom of the chart (here between week 16 and 17). In the remainder of the current iteration (week 17 and 18), the black area indicates the amount of work to be completed on each particular day in order to be able to "burn-down" the planned effort. In the future iteration ranging from week 18 to 22, no work is planned in yet, This is indicated because all columns are vertically hatched and their height indicates the amount of effort that could be planned based on the velocity of the last completed iteration.

Everybody interested in the progress of the project (customers, senior management and the engineers themselves) have access to the project information (as required by the CMM).

5 Configuration Management

Most of our projects use a CVS archive to store the source code and documentation. Bigger projects have an automatic, continuous build and test script running. Next to that, the projects have a stress test exercising the application(s) to trap e.g. multithreading issues in the code. Although we assign a configuration manager, a consistent archive is the team's responsibility. When the build fails, for any reason, it's a first priority to get it fixed again. This alleviates the burden normally put on the configuration manager: the software developers integrate only code in the archive that doesn't crash the system.

Documents (e.g. overview documents or API descriptions) have a promotion status (draft, proposal, accepted) and are also stored in the project archive. The task of the configuration manager is to tag the archive at the end of the iteration and describe, in a change log or in the iteration meeting minutes, which new functionality is contained in the tag.

6 Quality Assurance

CMM defines that Quality Assurance needs to be performed by an independent QA group. We implemented this by assigning the team leader of one project as the QA Officer for another project (lead by a colleague team leader), thereby guaranteeing independence of the QA officers. The QA group consists of all so-assigned QA officers.

Every month, the QA officer assesses the project and checks if the agreed way of working (e.g. XP practices) is followed. His report is sent to the whole team, the customer and to senior management and is stored in the project archive. Senior management is involved when major non-compliances are not resolved in time and if escalation is necessary.

The QA officer also facilitates the retrospective [7] on the projects. The results of the retrospective are stored in the project archive.

Every month the team leader writes a status report. It lists the risks identified on the project and their mitigation. It also, briefly, lists the accomplishments and difficulties encountered on the project. This report is sent to the whole team, the customer and senior management and stored in the project archive.

7 Subcontract Management

Since we don't subcontract projects, this KPA was neither implemented, nor assessed by the assessors.

8 Customer Satisfaction

The CMM, like the Agile methods, highly values the satisfaction of the customer. To measure this we ask our customers to fill in an enquiry.

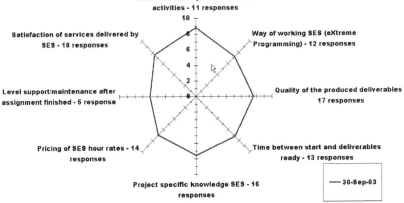

Fig. 3. Results of the latest Customer Satisfaction survey on a scale of 0 to 10 (higher is better)

The results show that most customers are highly satisfied about our way of working. In one project the customer was not satisfied. His complaint was that he couldn't see the end of the project from progress forms and wanted detailed specifications and project schedules. After escalation to senior management, it was decided not to continue our Agile way of working on this project. This is exactly the way a problem like this should be handled according to the CMM.

9 Staff Satisfaction

The CMM and the Agile methods require motivated people. To measure the motivation we have a survey filled in by SES staff to express their satisfaction about the way of working and other issues not related to the project.
Large deviations are discussed with the staff members and usually result in actions to alleviate issues[4].

10 Training

The CMM requires people to be trained. Most of the experienced software engineers have no experience working in an Agile manner. Most are trained in big processes and making large designs upfront. To get all software engineers on the same XP knowledge level, we regularly organize XP Immersions on-site. Customers are invited to join this course. This makes it very efficient to set up Agile teams. We described the way of working in a (very thin, 2 pages) 'Life Cycle Description'. It briefly describes XP and Scrum and contains references to the standard Agile books.

---

[4] One remark was that no bonding was felt by the contractors with the SES department, because most of the contacts are on a project base. This resulted in a monthly lunch meeting with a technical lecture.

Fig. 4. Results of the latest Staff Satisfaction survey on a scale of 0 to 10 (higher is better)

11 CMM Assessment Results

In December 2003, a team of two Philips Certified CMM assessors evaluated SES. They conducted 21 interviews with managers, project leaders, customers and software engineers.

The following strong points were identified:

- Good process deployment approach has led to a disciplined 'Way-of-Working'.
- The web-site is a major asset in transparency of processes and projects, and deployment of the defined 'Way-of-Working'.
- Staff expresses pride on the 'Way-of-Working'.
- Effective guidance by SES of new customers in introducing the 'Way-of-Working'.
- Good process focus! The Way-of-Working is continuously being enhanced.

Attention points are:

- The process policy is not explicitly described (e.g. do's and don'ts because of XP).
- Reviews with overall project management are not applicable in most cases. Where it is applicable it is not done.
- Reviews by senior management have little attention for the effectiveness of the process execution.
- There are few measurements on the process currently in place.
- There is a great potential in the data already collected.

11.1 Requirements Management

Observation. Acceptance criteria are sometimes not explicitly defined.
Good practice. Frequent communication with the customer about requirements and their implementation, resulting in very good mutual understanding of the requirements.

11.2 Software Project Planning

Observations. Sizes of work products are not estimated.
Good practice. Highly detailed Work Breakdown Structure (WBS). Unfortunately the estimates are not supported by use of historical data (which are largely available).
Remarks. Management of critical computer resources is generally not applicable due to the nature of the projects. Project plan review by senior management could have more attention for feasibility of the results agreed.

11.3 Software Project Tracking and Oversight

Observations. Sizes of work products are not tracked.
Good practices. Use of burn-down charts. Daily recording of effort spent. High frequent interaction on progress.
Remark. Except for effort tracking, it is difficult to see what the status of the project is (e.g. status-overview of deliverables).

11.4 Software Quality Assurance

Observations. The involvement of the QA officer in the preparation of the PMP can be improved (e.g. to share his experience). No structured independent check on the activities of the QA officers.
Remark. The QA-role can have higher impact by more presence in the project (e.g. by visiting stand-up and iteration meetings).

11.5 Software Configuration Management

Observations. No standard CM reporting in place. Baseline audits introduced only recently. Checklist used is still draft.
Good practices. Continuous builds using automated unit tests and logging of build and test results.
Remark. Planning and definition of baselines could be improved.

11.6 Conclusions of the Assessment

SES has defined and implemented an elegant way to reach the goals of Software CMM Level 2. The XP process with CMM 'flavor' is adequate, given the nature and sizes of the projects.

11.7 Recommendations

Take your right to say 'no': don't work with customers who don't play their roles as required by the process.

Upgrade PMP to ask more attention for identification and handling of dependencies and dealing with open source software.

Define an explicit approach with respect to measurements:

- Choose, do, analyze, and modify according to gained insight
- Impressive collection of historical data is excellent basis to derive and use metrics

Examine other (Philips) coding standards to upgrade the SES standards (addressing language-specific do's and don'ts).

Consider improving project status reporting (e.g., status of deliverables, earned-value charts).

Behave like a learning organization:

- Analyze retrospectives over projects to derive trends at organizational level
- Classify historical data, and use historical data in estimating future projects
- Tailor processes based on good practices encountered in projects meeting specified criteria
- Transfer what has been learned in one project to other projects

The score on the KPAs for CMM level 2 are depicted in the figure below.

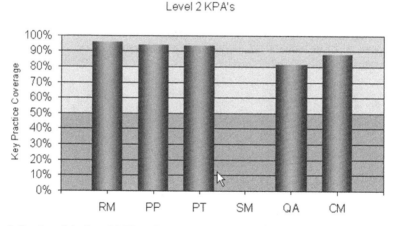

Fig. 5. Scoring of the Level 2 KPAs for the SES department. For CMM level 2 certification all KPAs must be scored higher than 80%

12 Conclusion

This paper showed that, while working Agile, with a little extra effort, also a CMM Level 2 certification could be obtained. The CMM level 2 KPAs and an Agile way of working overlap, because both focus on basic project management. The focus on people in Agile and the organizational focus of CMM are nicely complementary.

It is shown that it's not necessary to define thick procedures or write piles of documentation to 'prove' you are working on CMM Level 2. As Watts Humphrey states in the preface of [1]: you need to look at what *people* are actually doing.

Acknowledgements

Thanks to Hans Naus, Vincent Ronteltap, Wim van de Goor, Mike Cohn and Wilko van Asseldonk for reviewing this article.

References

1. M.C. Paulk et.al.: The Capability maturity Model: Guidelines for Improving the Software Process, Addison-Wesley, Reading MA (1995).
2. K. Beck: Extreme Programming Explained: Embrace Change, Addison-Wesley, Boston (2000).
3. K. Schwaber, Mike Beedle: Agile Software Development with Scrum, Prentice Hall, Upper Saddle River, NJ (2002).
4. M.C. Paulk, Extreme Programming from a CMM Perspective, in IEEE Software, vol. 18, no. 6, pp. 19-26 (2001).
5. J.R. Nawrocki et.al.: Comparison of CMM Level 2 and eXtreme Programming, in Proceedings of ECSQ 2002, pp. 288-297 (2002).
6. F. Paulisch, A. Volker, Agility – Based on a Mature Foundation, Proc. Software Engineering Process Group Conference – SEPG 2002 (2002).
7. Norman L. Kerth: Project Retrospectives, Dorset House (2001).

Adapting Extreme Programming
to Research, Development and Production Environments

Gil Broza

545 Douglas Ave.
Toronto, ON M5M 1H7 Canada
gilbroza@hotmail.com

Abstract. Affinium Pharmaceuticals engages in early-stage pharmaceutical R&D and molecular biology production processes for internal and external programs. This business requires significant informatics support in terms of small- and large-scale software, tool integration and data management. Obtaining suitable software is difficult due to customer diversity, rapidly evolving unique needs, vendor offering and high costs. Adapting the XP approach and practices for this situation, Affinium's Informatics group has successfully developed in-house software that has kept up with the science. I describe notable accomplishments, and lessons learned along the way. I propose that a small in-house group of domain-aware developers, using a customized version of XP, would achieve better results than external providers, despite limited access to resources. In closing, I suggest that this structure and methodology are generally applicable to dynamic research, development and production environments.

1 Introduction

Affinium Pharmaceuticals is a structure-guided drug company focused on the discovery of novel anti-infective medicines. Its undertakings thus encompass scientific research, development and production. The drug discovery world is navigated using high-throughput processes for protein production, structure determination, synthesis of chemical matter and myriad assays for drug viability. R&D is responsible for rapidly obtaining drug candidates via proprietary automation, workflows and protocols.

Drug discovery is an extremely expensive and time-consuming pursuit. On average, developing a novel drug costs over US$800-million and takes 15-years from initial research to marketed product [5]. To stay ahead and reach the market faster – and make the most of patent protection – companies must constantly innovate. Affinium's chosen path is that of utilizing molecular structure, through structural biology, computational chemistry, cheminformatics and bioinformatics. These pursuits are well known for the sheer volume of data they produce and manipulate. Sometimes reaching terabytes per month, this data may yield immense benefits when mined.

Affinium's line of business requires diverse software for lab and data management, maintaining and accessing scientific databases, streamlining workflow, and operating and integrating instruments. Software is purchased from vendors, outsourced to consultants, or built internally. In the next section I discuss the downsides of purchasing commercial software, and several of the difficulties around planning and engineering useful, affordable solutions, whether done internally or outsourced. I then show how the Informatics group at Affinium has adapted XP to address these problems in building our own software or integrating 3rd-party software.

C. Zannier et al. (Eds.): XP/Agile Universe 2004, LNCS 3134, pp. 139–146, 2004.

2 The Problem: Obtaining Appropriate Software

The dynamic nature of the industry poses challenges however a company acquires its software. Systems, which cost a lot of time, money and effort to obtain and integrate, often lose out to innovation and the fast pace of scientific discovery and automation advancement. New business initiatives, or changing priorities in a difficult economic landscape, may trigger obsolescence even faster. Gentler changes, such as new business collaborations or discovery programs, often introduce or modify requirements.

There exist several established vendors of informatics software for biotechnology and pharmaceuticals, but companies in these fields need to do more than choose among them. Given the highly diverse nature of activities in drug discovery, few vendors provide solutions that span the entire spectrum. Some needs are so special that no commercial product addresses them effectively. Lastly, vendors may not be quick, cheap or still around to respond to the changing nature of the business (e.g. [4]).

Data and process integration are vital to a company's scientific advancement regardless of its size or age. Data is produced and processes are developed in highly specialized departments of different disciplines, such as molecular biology, structural biology and computational chemistry. However, comprehensive data analysis and streamlined discovery operations require integration, posing serious challenges for software development. Achieving useful integration, whether between vendors' products or custom-built products, is time-consuming and expensive. Cost/benefit analyses lead many companies to opt for a mixed strategy.

A significant downside to eschewing vendors is that a desired system may take many months to enter production. Meanwhile, a lot of money is spent (and a lot more if the project is outsourced), and the requirements mutate. Unformatted or unstructured 'legacy data' piles up, which is difficult to use and later import. The scientist customers are often content getting by on their own, for instance by downloading free tools, writing Perl scripts and using Microsoft Excel. Thus, spending money to build software or database systems requires serious justification.

Developer skill-sets are another concern for companies building their own software. The subject matter is difficult to master due to its scientific breadth and specificity, so experts in both software engineering and biology or chemistry are few. Yet, successful developers must have a fairly good exposure to it in order to be conversant with their customers. In my experience, "regular" software developers often find that little of the subject matter strikes close to home for them, unlike financial or telecom systems, for instance. On the other hand, biologists and chemists with programming training often do not have enough experience in building large-scale systems.

3 Our Solution

The Informatics group at Affinium provides internal software development, bioinformatics and cheminformatics services. Unlike the biotech / pharma industry's tendency to outsource substantially [8], Affinium keeps a small contingent of full-time employees. The benefits have been lower costs and higher quality, greater user satisfaction with the group's products and availability, and overall better alignment with the company's goals. In line with industry practice [8], the group comprises 5 to 10 percent of the company's workforce.

Half of us have advanced biology degrees and programming training; the others have advanced computer science degrees, and learned basic molecular biology and chemistry on the job. The group's members have diverse software industry experience. Its manager (the author) is also the software architect; it is small enough for one person to manage this combination of roles. Overall, our makeup meets our needs.

Informatics always needs to address multiple projects, some of which have multiple customers. Affinium's ever-evolving drug discovery programs and collaborations require software of varying magnitude, which can be broken down into large-scale and small-scale development. This fuzzy distinction is made along the lines of duration, technology and maintenance. Small-scale development requires a single person for up to two months – for instance, writing scripts, software integration and small database development. Small-scale work is always done by Informatics members.

When large-scale software is needed, we compare building to buying-configuring-integrating. We take into account timelines, budgets, risk, vendor offering, and our skill-set and past experience. We have often found that scientific programs are better bought, whereas data and process management applications are better built, whether from scratch or using existing frameworks and third-party tools.

3.1 Extreme Programming at Affinium

Our methodology has crystallized slowly since the group's formation two years ago. In the first few months it combined Waterfall and XP [1] ideas: frequent releases, automated testing, no over-providing, constant communication and feedback. Later, we gravitated toward more rigorous XP through learning from the industry and our own trial and error. The present adaptation, as it applies to mid- and large-scale development, is similar to the 19 practices described by Miller [7], combined with a new one, "architect". We also apply it to small-scale development, only with much less emphasis on automated testing, pairing and continuous integration. The next section outlines our methodology, broken down using the categories presented in [7].

Joint Customer – Developer – Management Practices. As previously mentioned, we undertake a large number of projects for numerous customer groups. To be fair and agile in allocating our resources, we build our products iteratively. For new projects we use the Minimal Working Version technique: we plan iterations that culminate in a quick, good enough, usable 1.0 release, and dedicate part of our resources to its development. When the work is accepted, remaining stories and maintenance work return to the project pool. The projects are rescheduled every two to four months to keep up with business changes. At any one time, we work on three projects at most. Ideally, each developer works on a single project during an iteration, completing other obligations between iterations.

The group works in an open environment with individual stations and low partitions, which we constantly talk over. It affords minimal privacy without hampering paired work or impromptu ("stand-up") meetings of any number of people. Our customers do not sit with us: the scientists are in the lab and their managers are in cubicles or offices. Nevertheless, they are never more than a minute's walk away.

The practice of retrospectives is relatively new to us. We have held only a few so far, most of them internal to our team. They helped us to air implicit disagreements and to express reasons for actions.

Developer Practices. We design and write our code with an automated-testing mindset, although sometimes we do not actually program all the tests. Typically, we code unit tests, but verify integration and acceptance manually. When deciding between automated and manual testing we weigh considerations of maintenance, schedule, difficulty, risk and available tools against 'just enough' manual testing. We determine the coverage and depth of either kind of testing by the modules' operational profile, as well as schedule and risk. At the end of every release, we spend a couple of days on manual testing and bug-fix verifications. We delay releases when quality is at stake, e.g. data reliability, usability and severe bugs. We track all defects, fixed or not, in a central database.

The group follows an "architect" practice (not mentioned in [7]). While the developers take part in every product's entire life-cycle, some tasks are centralized in the hands of the architect. Similarly to Fowler's "Architectus Oryzus" [6], he is responsible for the vision and overall design of Informatics products, tracking design decisions, constraints and prospective development. He evaluates feature and change requests in light of existing and suggested designs. When competing alternatives are considered, he makes the final decision. He pairs with and mentors developers, reviews code, writes and enforces coding standards, and oversees high-impact refactoring (involving several modules). We find this centralization to balance collective ownership and the downsides of the "simplest thing that could possibly work" approach. For more on the thinking underlying this role, and how it scales, see [2].

We believe in collective ownership balanced by "disciplined action" [3]: one never introduces major changes without consulting first and notifying after. The reverse also holds: every necessary task will be undertaken by someone, like it or not. Anyone can improve or modify the code, but they must first consider code reuse and alternative designs with the architect, and check with the manager whether the schedule allows doing it then or later. Useful suggestions, designs and refactoring tasks, which are not undertaken immediately, are tracked for later consideration.

We work in pairs on all high-risk activities, such as product upgrades and live data manipulation. The developers often pair with the architect for requirements analysis, design and maintenance work, but only in some situations do they pair for coding and debugging. We feel that the architect and collective ownership practices, and our almost daily show-and-tell meetings, more than make up for lessened pairing.

We continuously refactor and integrate code, tests, data and documentation. We practice YAGNI ("You Aren't Going to Need It") by focusing on high-priority stories and doing just enough on them. However, being cognizant of the company's needs, we can make some educated guesses regarding their future manifestation. Therefore, we always sketch initial design ideas for suggested features, refactoring and postponed fixes for major defects. These drafts are kept in mind when designing for a given release. Some unscheduled items never get done; some take long to be implemented, and may then be redesigned. All in all, our systems have undergone minimal course corrections.

Management Practices. Given our multi-project, multi-customer situation, development projects are scheduled by a single person, the group manager. On one hand, he works with the customer groups on plans and priorities of maintenance and emerging projects; on the other, he plans iterations with the developers. The plans take into account the sustainable pace ("40-hour week") practice, which the entire group feels strongly about.

Informatics members answer only to the manager, no matter what project they work on; the group has never been part of the company's matrix structure. The manager is accountable for the group's accomplishments and performance. He keeps its members informed through collective and individual feedback, including periodic performance reviews, and he presents goals and progress updates to senior management.

Customer Practices. Software updates are rolled out typically every four to eight weeks. Each includes new and upgraded features, a planned set of bug fixes, needed refactoring and automated tests, and limited but sufficient manual testing. When a particular release targets a single customer group, they often plan it; in multiple-customer scenarios the development group plans the releases, as [9] advises. Despite their proximity, users' exposure to new features may require a few weeks, so we normally plan two or three releases ahead. Later releases are planned shallowly, and adjusted in due time.

The input to release planning includes the big-feature customers' decisions about story scope, the bug-fix and usability customers' priorities, and our assessment of performance and stability. Our analysis of cost, risk and quality shapes the final plan (for instance, known defects may remain despite acceptance.) With less-involved customers, Informatics members with biology background serve as "customer proxies".

We walk our customers through our designs, intermediate solutions and pre-release solutions. Similarly to the planning situation (and as per [9]), a single customer tests acceptance, whereas in multiple-customer situations, we do the testing.

4 How Our Methodology Has Worked for Us

Overall, Informatics customers are pleased: the software we deliver fulfils their needs. It is deployed when still useful – keeping up with new drug discovery functions – and important updates are rolled out rapidly. In this section I analyze successful aspects, problems and lessons we have learned from applying our methodology.

Many of the successes and lessons described below arose from our largest software undertaking, ProteoTrack™. It is a proteomics Lab Information Management System (LIMS), whose 1.0 alpha was developed by a consultancy using the Waterfall methodology. Two years ago the product was brought in-house, and Informatics has been applying the described methodology for its development and maintenance ever since.

4.1 Successful Aspects

The approach of providing a Minimal Working Version using iterations, and reprioritizing further work, has been very successful whether for new applications, new major features, software integration or database development. Our customers have generally enjoyed receiving a usable product early, which included the functionality they needed. Although unused to small-functionality iterations, they quickly realized the benefits. For instance, early automation of data acquisition reduced manual labor, and properly devised data repositories made reporting simpler. Rapidly developed small increments indeed promoted timely feedback and enabled us to adjust to changing priorities ([1]). They also made for a gentler learning curve for our users, facilitating training and communication.

All group members, who have previously worked in small or large 'mainstream' environments, report higher satisfaction with our approach. Specifically, not having to follow slow, rigid processes, avoiding unnecessary work, and seeing all their work in use have been terrific motivators. They also report feeling more productive despite pairing and refactoring considerably, and working little overtime. Metrics we collected confirm that per developer, we have produced more features, fixes, Java classes and lines of code while being responsible for ("collectively owning") a proportionally larger codebase. These metrics also indicate an almost constant pace.

It is worth noting that the group chose this Agile approach when the rest of the company, predominantly biologists and engineers, were set up as a matrix and following traditional goal-setting and project management practices. However, we are not at odds with anyone, as our accomplishments have justified our 'unorthodox' approach.

4.2 Difficulties and Lessons Learned

One prominent difficulty we have had is defining the actual customer. Both Informatics and the scientists needed time to shift from the "programmers vs. users" approach to XP's collaboration between providers and customers, and the shift is not complete yet. When 20 people will use a new feature, should the "customer" be just one of them? Selected four people? Their team leaders? We have tried to identify one or two representatives from each functional group, but this approach backfired several times due to disagreements or lack of participation. We have looked to leaders, people with a strong sense of product ownership, but very few felt confident enough to make decisions that affect other people. This insecurity was exacerbated when the company was formally organized in a matrix-management structure, which distanced people with otherwise similar needs (and made holding retrospectives with them more difficult.) The Informatics group is thus often left to make decisions it is not qualified to make.

With heavyweight methodologies, developers are often committed to a single project for months on end. However with a short-iterations approach, the developers can bring several projects to a partial yet useful state. One problem is managing these multiple projects, each with its frequent releases, priorities and customers. Another is saying "no" to people when the load becomes too high. Lastly, a deployed partial project requires technical support, and occasional manual tweaking for yet-unsupported behavior. With more and more projects in this state, releases stretch longer and resources are spread thin.

We have tried to develop a common vocabulary with our user base, reinforcing it at meetings and training sessions. This approach has not been entirely successful, but the weakness of our common vocabulary has not impeded progress.

Several authors have written about retrofitting software projects to XP. Having to develop and maintain a Waterfall-style, no-tests alpha version, we have observed that non-trivial feature changes often merit a complete module rewrite rather than refactoring and retrofitting automated tests. We have applied both approaches to numerous modules, and the quality and productivity achieved by rewriting, especially by pairs, were often superior.

5 In-House Development or Paid Consultants?

The benefits and disadvantages of engaging permanent employees vs. contractors are well known. This paper encourages the factoring of methodology into the equation, as more and more companies do these days. The many advantages of XP, as described above, hold whether the group is internal or external. However, our experience suggests that R&D environments, in which software needs vary and evolve rapidly, would do best to form in-house development groups who adopt or adapt XP. Significant gains include:

Agility in resource allocation. XP's short cycles allow speedier redirection of resources when priorities change. Contractors would normally tackle a single project at a time, and charge a penalty if the project was stopped.

Smoother process and data integration. An organization often undertakes several software-related projects, which mutate over time to address changing needs and priorities. It can mitigate the impact of integration, maintenance and business evolution by centralizing architectural planning in the hands of a single, internal entity.

Deeper understanding. Most R&D environments are unique. Keen knowledge of an organization's proprietary technology, various projects and processes is vital for focused, useful products. The customer can document and advise only so much; this knowledge is best found in internal groups who grow with the organization. Pair programming, collective ownership and architectural discipline help pass it on.

More architectural options. As XP encourages, we focused our efforts on the most commonly used features. We relied on manual intervention for infrequent activities, where development would give little return on investment. This approach would have been untenable had we paid someone else to write our software.

6 Conclusion

An innovative, scientific pursuit like structure-guided drug discovery has challenging needs for software whether the organization buys, outsources or builds it. Affinium uses a mixed buy-build strategy, the "build" part fully undertaken by the Informatics group, which resides outside the company's matrix structure and bases its processes on XP. By frequently reprioritizing our project pool, we have been able to deliver timely, useful products and keep up with new discovery functions and needs. Incremental delivery has proven vital for early feedback, adjustment to changing needs, and motivation. Automated testing has been a blessing in the absence of testers. Just-enough design and refactoring have been critical for quick turn-around. It has not all been roses, however; we struggle with defining customers and their involvement, and it is difficult to manage multiple short-span, frequent-release projects.

I think the Affinium environment is reflective of other small companies who have scientific, research, development or production operations. Although our software must model the business – biology, chemistry and pharmacology in our case – it is no different to produce than other software. Its design and process must still consider usability, performance, developer and user interactions, maintenance, schedules and planning, and ultimately, value to the customer. I therefore suggest that XP can be customized to suit such environments, as our two-year-old case exemplifies. I propose further that an internal, organic team is in the company's best interest, providing a more cohesive software experience than outsourced projects.

Acknowledgments

I would like to thank all members of Affinium Informatics, past and present, for taking on this adventure together. We learn something new every day!

References

1. Beck, K.: "eXtreme Programming explained", Addison-Wesley, 2000
2. Broza, G.: Position paper for the "Experience Exchange" workshop at XP2003, online at http://www.frankwestphal.de/xp2003/GilBroza.html
3. Collins, J.: "Good to Great", HarperCollins, 2001
4. Davies, K.: "The Demise of DoubleTwist", online at http://www.bio-itworld.com/archive/050702/survivor_sidebar_252.html
5. DiMasi, J.A. and related Tufts research, online at http://www.novartis.at/download/news/tufts/Tufts-PhRMA backgrounder.pdf
6. Fowler, M.: "Who Needs an Architect?", online at http://www.martinfowler.com/ieeeSoftware/whoNeedsArchitect.pdf
7. Miller, R.: "Demystifying Extreme Programming: "XP distilled" revisited", online at http://www-106.ibm.com/developerworks/java/library/j-xp0813
8. U.S. Department of Commerce, "A Survey of the Use of Biotechnology in U.S. Industry", online at http://www.technology.gov/reports/Biotechnology/CD120a_0310.pdf
9. Wallace, N., Bailey, P., Ashworth, N.: "Managing XP with Multiple or Remote Customers", online at http://www.agilealliance.org/articles/articles/Wallace-Bailey--ManagingXPwithMultipleorRemoteCustomers.pdf

Outsourcing and Offshoring with Agility: A Case Study

Clifton Kussmaul[1], Roger Jack[1], and Barry Sponsler[2]

[1]Elegance Technologies, Inc.
1721 Green Valley Rd, Havertown, PA 19083, USA
{ckussmaul,rjack}@elegancetech.com
http://www.elegancetech.com
[2]EXTOL International, Inc.
474 North Centre St, Pottsville, PA 17901, USA
bsponsler@extol.com
http://www.extol.com

Abstract. We describe techniques and lessons learned from using agile methodologies with distributed teams, specifically outsourced and offshore development teams. Such teams often need to contend with multiple organizational boundaries, differences in time zone, language, and culture, and other communication challenges. First, we present concepts and issues in outsourcing and offshoring. Second, we describe a case study involving continually changing requirements, outsourcing, offshoring, and a method inspired by SCRUM and FDD. Third, we review key lessons learned, and conclude with a summary.

1 Introduction

Agile approaches to software development share a particular set of values [6], [11]:

- Individuals and interactions over processes and tools.
- Working software over comprehensive documentation.
- Customer collaboration over contract negotiation.
- Responding to change over following a plan.

Although agile methodologies usually assume that all team members are in one location, they have also been adapted to include distributed teams [17].

This paper describes techniques and lessons learned from using agile methodologies with outsourcing and offshoring. We begin with background on outsourcing and offshoring. We then describe an ongoing relationship in which Elegance Technologies, Inc. (ET) provides software product development services to EXTOL International, Inc. Next, we present lessons we have learned that can help other projects with distributed teams. These lessons are summarized in our conclusions.

1.1 Outsourcing and Offshoring

Outsourcing is the use of external companies to perform services, rather than using internal staff. According to a 2003 survey of CIOs, 70% of companies outsource some IT function or application [5]. *Offshoring* is the use of staff in other countries, and is often associated with India, China, and the former Soviet Union. Forrester Research estimates that 277,000 computer jobs and a similar number of management and operations jobs in the United States will move offshore by 2010 [10].

C. Zannier et al. (Eds.): XP/Agile Universe 2004, LNCS 3134, pp. 147–154, 2004.

Outsourcing is done for several reasons [5]:

- To reduce costs. This is the most commonly cited (59.8%) advantage of offshoring, although 73.5% of CIOs feel it is overrated as a cost-cutting strategy [5]. Hourly rates in countries like India and China can be less than 10% of those in the US [9], but IT organizations typically save 15%-25% during the first year and up to 40% by the third year [7].
- To access specialized skills or facilities. These resources may be expensive or unavailable locally, or may only be needed occasionally.
- To be able to increase or decrease the people or other resources on a project.
- To increase development speed and reduce time to market.

A useful framework [12] analyzes outsourcing relationships along two dimensions. *Dependence* is the degree to which ownership and control is transferred to the outsourcing partner. *Strategic impact* is the degree to which the outsourcing relationship affects competitive positioning and long-term strategy. As a relationship increases in either of these dimensions, collaboration becomes more critical.

2 Case Study

EXTOL International, Inc. is a privately funded software product company based in the mid-Atlantic region, with roughly $10M in annual revenue. Most employees work in a development and operations center, or a sales and marketing office, though there are several other offices across the US. Over the last several years, EXTOL has invested significant resources to develop EXTOL Business Integrator (EBI), a powerful and flexible data processing engine, with a strong development team, and an extensive feature roadmap. Thus, EBI is a strategic asset for EXTOL and EXTOL plans to keep most core EBI activities in-house.

To allow customers to use EBI's capabilities without first becoming expert users, EXTOL plans to develop a series of user-friendly, domain-specific front ends, beginning with one for UCCnet, a global, internet-based electronic commerce service [20]. However, these front ends present several challenges:

- They are often developed in response to external market conditions which are hard to predict and difficult to coordinate, and the number and intensity of these development efforts will vary over time.
- They may require intensive domain analysis phases, and are targeted at business users, not technical users. Diverting EXTOL's existing architects and designers to work on the front ends would adversely affect EBI.
- Cash flow must be monitored closely, since EXTOL is already supporting a significant development effort.
- EBI is under active development, and new capabilities are added regularly.
- The external standards are still evolving, in some cases. For example, several months into the project the UCCnet specification migrated from DTD to XSD.
- Time to market is critical, and system requirements may change frequently in response to customers and competitors.

Thus, EXTOL decided to outsource development of the UCCnet application to Elegance Technologies, Inc. (ET), which develops software products and provides software product development services, including managing offshore teams.

The outsourcing relationship began with one ET consultant working on an hourly basis, and spending several days a week onsite at EXTOL. The consultant studied the UCCnet application domain, analyzed requirements, developed a high-level design and a list of potential features, and supported development of an in-house proof-of-concept and demo. Based on the confidence and trust developed through these initial deliverables, EXTOL decided to outsource most of the UCCnet application development to ET.

2.1 Methodology

Our methodology is inspired by SCRUM and Feature-Driven Development (FDD). In SCRUM [16], a *product backlog* contains all potential product features, including customer functionality and technology features. A *sprint* is a 30 day development period. A *sprint backlog* is a subset of the product backlog to be implemented in a given sprint. A *sprint goal* defines the business purpose of a sprint, and is used to help decide whether specific features must be deferred or changed. During a sprint, daily 15 minute meetings are used to inform and coordinate the team. In FDD [13], a team begins by developing an *overall system model*. The team then generates a list of features, and plans the features. Finally, the team bundles sets of features into packages for design and construction. Thus, SCRUM emphasizes project management, and FDD emphasizes a design process.

Early in the project, we developed an initial feature list (or product backlog) and the overall product architecture (or system model). Ongoing development involves a team of 2-3 onshore staff and 5-10 offshore staff, working in time-boxed sprints of 4-6 weeks. Before each sprint, we develop and sign a formal proposal that identifies the major milestones, the sprint feature list, and a price range. During each sprint we implement sets of features. At the end of each sprint, ET determines the final price based on actual effort and the scope of work completed. This allows us to be more responsive to uncertainty and requests for change.

During a sprint, we use several coordination techniques:

- Both teams use a shared mailing list to archive all communication.
- At the end of their respective work days, each team sends a status email to the list, describing significant changes, current problems, and any questions.
- There are also daily meetings to review status and address major problems that are preventing the project from moving forward. They are usually late afternoon in India and early morning in the US, but sometimes early morning in India and late evening in the US. These meetings are usually via instant messaging and last around 15 minutes, though they occasionally run as long as 30 minutes and sometimes involve phone and/or web conferencing.
- A CVS repository stores all requirements, designs, source code, and related documents. The code is kept in a working state at all times, with any exceptions noted in the status email, so that we can see real progress. In effect, we have daily code deliveries between the offshore and onshore teams.

Onshore staff focus on analysis, high-level design, and coordination with EXTOL, but are also involved in the low level implementation and testing. For example, onshore staff may develop GUI mockups or framework code to be completed offshore.

A top priority for the onshore staff is to resolve any open issues from the daily meeting, so that the offshore team can continue work the next day. Offshore staff focus on low-level design, implementation, and testing, but are also involved in analysis and design, and review all design documents and proposals.

Effective collaboration is probably the most important element in the success of this project, which involves customers, EXTOL's sales and marketing group, EXTOL's development team, ET's onshore team, and the offshore team. Establishing trust over these multiple boundaries takes continual effort and attention.

3 Lessons Learned

We hope that other projects involving outsourcing, offshoring, or other distributed teams can benefit from lessons we have learned, including the following:

Avoid projects that are too small to amortize the overhead required for a effective distributed team. Very small projects are best done by local teams, unless an offshore team already has direct experience. On the other hand, it is often best to start with a small offshore team and add people over time as the project grows.

Keep research, architecture, and requirements analysis close to the customer. For example, during the first few sprints the onshore team developed a core architecture and set of practices to serve as guidelines, particularly as the offshore team evolves and becomes more familiar with the project and application domain. As the project and team grew, ET's onshore staff became less involved in coding, and more involved in planning, reviews, and other coordination to serve as a bridge between the offshore team and EXTOL.

Key documents help to bootstrap the project by establishing a common framework for stakeholders spread across multiple US and foreign time zones. We depend on:

- The master feature list – every completed, scheduled, or envisioned feature.
- A detailed data model and data dictionary are key interfaces between teams and components, including the interface to the EBI software engine.
- Requirements and designs for subsystems in the current or next sprint. These documents are usually discarded (i.e. not maintained) after the corresponding features are developed and tested.
- A list of tasks and related information for the current sprint.

This supports Brooks' *documentary hypothesis*: "a small number of documents become the critical pivots around which every project's management revolves" [4]. Thus, we try to minimize the use of unnecessary or throwaway documents. For example, our GUI reviews use real screens with incomplete functionality, rather than dummy screens that might change when implemented.

Minimizing requirement changes during a sprint is even more important with a distributed team, since it can be more difficult to agree on the scope, monitor the implementation, and ensure that nothing is forgotten. Often, it is feasible to defer changes until the next sprint, which is usually just a few weeks away. If changes are necessary, we may compensate by reducing other functionality or slightly extending the schedule.

As the project matures we have allowed the sprints to become longer, in part to reduce the testing and documentation overhead for each delivery. However, we spend more time debating the scope of each sprint, so we may need to revisit these issues.

Careful coordination enables us to respond quickly to necessary changes, which can provide a competitive advantage. For example, by focusing on activities such as analysis, customer interaction, and testing, at the end of the day the onshore team can send requirements to the offshore team, and have the resulting changes implemented the next morning. This round-the-clock cycle can be very effective. Because each team is eager to start work when the other finishes for the day, this approach also discourages excessive overtime, which can lead to burnout and other problems.

Early and frequent delivery of working software is especially important, for several reasons. It gives the client frequent opportunities to review the project status and make appropriate changes, which is especially important for user interfaces. It serves to build confidence and trust among people who have not worked together previously. Furthermore, it provides an effective communication mechanism between all stakeholders. These benefits are essential in the UCCnet project environment.

Planning is still important, although it takes less time than many outsourced projects. For example, we must monitor costs, and balance short-term priorities against the need for a sustainable level of staffing. Since each sprint is a separate proposal and contract, during each sprint we spend time planning the next one.

Ease participants into relationships with remote teams, and try to arrange regular and extended visits between locations. For example, several members of the offshore team have worked in the US. ET's onshore staff have all spent time in India, and typically spend at least one day a week onsite at EXTOL. We also arrange occasional teleconferences (usually for training) between EXTOL, the onshore team, and the offshore team.

Focus on the win-win aspects of the project to minimize the potential disruption caused by contractual relationships between the distinct organizations involved. For example, the proposal for each sprint specifies a price range to accommodate incomplete and changing requirements, and to avoid having to write complete requirements before the sprint can start. We are fortunate in that many key personnel at EXTOL and ET have been both producers and consumers of software services, and thus understand the issues from both perspectives.

Effective communication and interaction are particularly important in outsourcing and offshoring, where staff can be spread across multiple locations, time zones, and cultures. It can be difficult to determine and maintain the appropriate level of communication. Working to develop effective communication early in the project makes it easier for the team to grow as needed. Synchronous communication, such as face-to-face meetings, online chats, teleconferences, and web conferences, is ideal for quick status meetings, brainstorming sessions, and reviews. Asynchronous communication, such as email, discussion forums, and shared documents, provides a persistent record of discussions and decisions, and don't require participants to be available at the same time. We employ all of these techniques regularly.

Be sensitive to cultural differences, especially between organizations and between regions or countries, including differences in how people interact with each other and resolve problems. This is especially true for outsourcing and offshoring. For example, some cultures place more value on centralized, top-down control, and may view direct questions as a challenge to authority.

Furthermore, many offshore development centers, particularly in India, have invested heavily in the Software Capability Maturity Model (SW-CMM®) [14], which defines five levels of increasing process maturity; offshore companies represent roughly 74% of CMM-4 organizations and roughly 84% of CMM-5 organizations [19]. When teams and managers are accustomed to disciplined processes and relatively static requirements, it can be quite difficult to convince them to explore other approaches. (Note that there is growing recognition that both agile and disciplined approaches have advantages, and that often a carefully designed combination of the two can be very effective [2],[3],[15].)

Concentrate on the organizational interfaces when defining processes, rather than trying to define all of the processes for everyone involved in the project. Defining processes for an outsourcing or offshoring project can be particularly challenging, since it may require coordination between different organizational cultures. It is quite feasible, and sometimes preferable, for teams to use different methodologies that reflect different cultures and requirements.

Use tools to work smarter, not harder. For example, early on we recognized that we could use a code generator for much of the access code for a database with several hundred tables. We also use JUnit and IBM Rational XDE Tester (formerly RobotJ) to support unit testing and regression testing of the user interface.

4   Conclusions

To quote DeMarco and Lister, "The major problems of our work are not so much *technological* as *sociological* in nature." [8] (original emphasis). In this paper, we have identified ways in which outsourcing and offshoring can utilize agile approaches to address these sociological problems. Key lessons learned include:

- Avoid projects that are too small to amortize overhead.
- Keep research, architecture, and requirements analysis close to the customer.
- Use a few key documents to provide a common framework.
- Minimize requirement changes during a sprint.
- Coordinate carefully to allow distributed teams to respond quickly to changes.
- Deliver working software early and often to build confidence and trust.
- Recognize that planning is still important.
- Ease participants into relationships with remote teams, and arrange face to face contact whenever feasible.
- Focus on win-win aspects to minimize potential disruptions.
- Provide appropriate tools and infrastructure for effective communication.
- Be aware of and sensitive to cultural differences.
- Focus on the interfaces between teams and organizations, and recognize the potential value of different processes in different locations.
- Work smarter, not harder, by using appropriate tools.

We expect outsourcing and offshoring to continue growing. We hope the lessons described above can help other organizations to work more effectively and efficiently.

Acknowledgements

We gratefully acknowledge the support, advice, and encouragement we have received from our customers and colleagues, both onshore and offshore.

Author Biographies

Clif Kussmaul is CTO of Elegance Technologies, Inc. He is also Assistant Professor of Computer Science at Muhlenberg College, where he delivers introductory courses through capstone projects to traditional and non-traditional students. Previously, he spent two years working with CMM5 development centers at NeST Technologies. He has a PhD in CS from the University of California, Davis, and is the author or co-author of over thirty publications and conference presentations.

Roger Jack is President of Elegance Technologies, Inc. He has experience in project management, and creating reliable and robust architectures. He is the former Vice President of U.S. Software Operations for NeST Technologies, where he managed many offshore projects. He has an MBA from Duke University's Fuqua School of Business, and an MS in Computer Science from Villanova University.

Barry Sponsler is Director of Development for EXTOL International, Inc., where he oversees development, documentation, quality assurance, and outsourcing relationships. In over 20 years in the IT industry, he has managed diverse development teams for legacy applications (e.g. AS/400), multiplatform applications using Java, a large data center with operations and programming staff, and ERP and Y2K projects for Fortune 500 companies.

References

1. Agile Alliance. Manifesto for Agile Software Development.
   http://www.agilemanifesto.org (2001)
2. Anderson, D. Agile Management for Software Engineering: Applying the Theory of Constraints for Business Results. Prentice Hall PTR (2004)
3. Boehm, B., Turner, R. Balancing Agility and Discipline: A Guide for the Perplexed. Addison Wesley (2003)
4. Brooks, F. The Mythical Man-Month. Addison Wesley (1995)
5. CIO Insight. Research: Outsourcing: How Well Are You Managing Your Partners? 1(33):75-85 (November, 2003)
6. Cockburn, A. Agile Software Development. Addison Wesley (2003)
7. Davison, D. Top 10 Risks of Offshore Outsourcing. META Group (Nov 2003)
8. DeMarco, T., Lister, T. Peopleware: Productive Projects and Teams. Dorset House (1999)
9. Dignan, L. Leaping, then Looking. Baseline 1(22):17-29 (September 2003)
10. Engardio, P., Bernstein, A., Kripalani, M. The New Global Job Shift. Business Week (February 3, 2003)
11. Highsmith, J. Agile Software Development Ecosystems. Addison Wesley (2002)

12. Kishore, R., Rao, H.R., Nam, K., Rajagopalan, S., Chaudhury, A. A Relationship Perspective on IT Outsourcing. Communication of the ACM 46(12):87-92 (2003)
13. Palmer, S. R., Felsing, J. M. A Practical Guide to Feature-Driven Development. Prentice Hall PTR (2002)
14. Paulk, M., Weber, C., Curtis, B., Chrissis, M.B., et al. The Capability Maturity Model: Guidelines for Improving the Software Process. Addison Wesley (1994)
15. Paulk, M. Extreme Programming from a CMM Perspective. IEEE Software 18(6):19-26 (2001)
16. Schwaber, K., Beedle, M. Agile Software Development with SCRUM. Prentice Hall (2001)
17. Simons, M. Internationally Agile. InformIT (March 15, 2002)
18. Software Development. Offshore by the Numbers. 12(1):39-41 (Jan 2004)
19. Software Engineering Institute. Process Maturity Profile: Software CMM® - CBA IPI and SPA Appraisal Results. (2003)
20. UCCnet. http://www.uccnet.org (2004)

User Story Methodology Adaptations for Projects Non-traditional in Scope and Customer GUI Contributions*

Denise M. Woit

School of Computer Science
Ryerson University
Toronto, Ontario Canada M5B 2K3
dwoit@scs.ryerson.ca

Abstract. Our project, which was non-traditional in scope and in customer involvement in GUI design, benefited from modification of the standard XP story development and maintenance process. We support these findings with data amassed over three years of such a project. We present the evolution of our augmented process, in accordance with the principles of XP. We present data comparing our use of the standard story process against our modified process, and identify properties of our project which render it a candidate for the alternative process. We hope our results can aid other XP planners in determining if their projects would benefit from such modified methodology, and if so, provide guidance in determining appropriate modifications.

1 Introduction

We were challenged with the task of effective management of user stories in a unique eXtreme Programming (XP) environment. We employed the simplicity rule to solve problems, as they arose, regarding user stories, and produced an on-line story environment that is web-accessible, OS-independent, easily used by programmers and non-programmers alike, with complex searching capabilities. Our story environment was influenced by several properties of our project: First, we are Linux-developers, experienced in combining existing utilities to solve problems in a divide-and-conquer strategy. Secondly, our project is large, with an extraordinary amount of dependency-laden stories. Third, our customer has exacting GUI requirements, which require explicit and precise articulation in order to provide low-risk estimations. Finally, our project's success is determined fundamentally by its GUI, and thus, the customer's view of product correctness is largely based on the correspondence of its GUI with his vision. Our stories themselves are atypical in a number of ways. They are numerous, approaching 800 over the 3 year data collection period; they naturally fall into a hierarchical organizational structure largely mirroring the product structure; they are GUI-intensive, with over 500 images currently residing in stories, as discussed in Section 2; and they exhibit a high degree of artifact-level dependence, as discussed in Section 4.

---

* Supported in part by Natural Sciences and Engineering Research Council of Canada (NSERC).

C. Zannier et al. (Eds.): XP/Agile Universe 2004, LNCS 3134, pp. 155–163, 2004.

We discuss how these properties provide challenges to management of user stories in our environment. We outline our emergent story environment, resulting from solving each challenge as it arose, employing the principles of XP to the best of our abilities. We present data collected over a three year period to support our belief that this modified story environment is instrumental in the success of our project. Finally, we compare our environment with others reported in the literature, and provide guidance to other XP planners in determining the appropriateness and usefulness of any such methodology modifications in their environments.

2   The GUI Challenges

Our project commenced in early 2000 with a newly assembled team of experienced Linux developers embarking upon our first XP project. We practiced the suggested standard process. Stories were about 3 sentences written on standard index-cards, and served as a starting point for discussions with developers [1,3,4]. We followed the sound advice: "you should try to keep stories focused on user needs and benefits as opposed to specifying GUI layouts" [9]. Thus, GUI was not precisely specified, but generally agreed upon in conversations among developers and customer during planning and implementation. The uniqueness of our project immediately posed several complications.

We experienced customer dissatisfaction with the developed GUI, and, thus, dissatisfaction with the product, as the customer appeared to rate product correctness almost exclusively by its GUI. Advice from those more experienced with XP, including our XP consultant, was that when customers are dissatisfied with the work, they may focus on the GUI because they lack the terminology and experience necessary to identify the true underlying cause of their discontent. We increased communication with the customer, and carefully explored this possibility. We discovered that this customer truly considered the GUI paramount to the success of the project. The customer's goal was to develop the product for sale/lease to third parties, and he considered the GUI a significant factor in his product's competitive edge over other products with similar functionality. Primed with this knowledge, we began to implement more extensive customer/developer collaborations during implementation. However, this approach produced unsatisfactory results because as more details about GUI became evident during development, implementation time increased significantly over that estimated; it became apparent that simple initial stories with subsequent verbal collaboration were inadequate to provide low-risk estimations of the customer's intended product. This problem was a direct result of the GUI-intensive nature of our product, its positioning in the marketplace, and our customer's GUI-oriented definitions of product correctness and project success. As the customer had very precise ideas about GUI design, often down to the pixel, and as this design significantly influenced estimations, he began including precise, detailed GUI with stories to affect more reliable estimations and project planning, creating the designs with imaging tools. GUI images were then printed and physically attached to story cards. One such customer-produced, GUI attachment is presented in Figure 1.

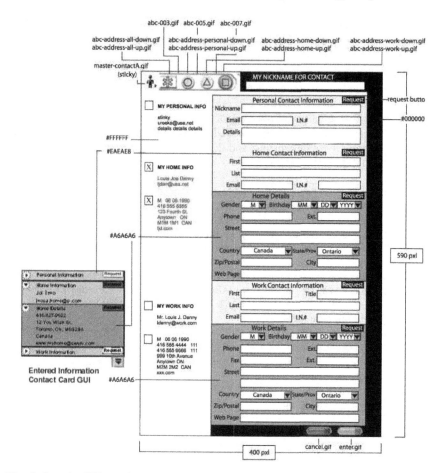

Fig. 1. Sample GUI attachment. Note that all gifs included were pre-created by customer/ graphic artist prior to meeting with developers. See Fig. 2 for story.

Our stories were relatively unchanged, except for the addition of GUI-based notes, and customer/developer conversations remained necessary before and during implementation for more precise details [4]. However, conversations between customer and developers usually resulted in modifications to the GUI. The XP values of "feedback" and "communication" allowed us to quickly ascertain the following: The extent of the GUI detail imposed by the customer made it necessary to record agreed upon modifications for developer referral, but manual modifications to the original printed image artifacts proved unsatisfactory, because iterative modifications often resulted in cards that were extremely difficult to understand, often manifesting in incorrect implementation from the customer's perspective. Also, it was challenging to keep modifications to GUI attachments consistent with story cards; necessary, as both story text and GUI were referred to during implementation. In keeping with the "simplicity" value, the customer began maintaining both stories and GUI together electronically, with editing and re-printing facilities solving our consistency and modification problems. Our process was modified to incorporate electronic stories, but this remained in keeping with standard process, as, although it is not encouraged, electronic story environments are acceptable [3]. Fig 2 contains the electronic story associated with the GUI of Fig. 1: Image and text work together to describe the customer's vision of this "contact card" functionality and its GUI.

During the first iterations of our project, maintaining stories electronically began in response to challenges relating to the GUI-intensive nature of the product, our customer's exacting GUI requirements, and the reliance of our project success upon our customer's GUI design.

- User clicks contact button on task bar, selects add or edit contact.
- New window (Detailed Contact Card (CC) GUI from Fig. 1), 400 pxl wide x 590 pxl high (fixed size with close option only), launches over SES frame set. All info entry fields are visible at launch in exact order of Fig. 1
- Field titles 8 pt Arial (bold, right justified). Field entries 9 pt Arial. User can enter/modify entries.
- Month, day, year and state/prov, country fields are pull down menus as per Fig 1.
- CC defaults into address book open in ABC frame, indicated by active/inactive status of the address icons at the top-left of Fig. 1. User may change address book(s) by selecting/de-selecting desired address icons.
- User's own details appear on bar on left-hand side of card. Information contact has permission to see is displayed in red. (permissions done in story com-a012b)
- User can press "cancel" button to abort add/edit, or "enter" button to save (see Fig. 1 for buttons.) Both close window.
- User can enter a nickname (top-right of Fig.1) If entered, this nickname is name displayed in User's address book(s) as per where User has put contact.

Fig. 2. GUI Story for Sample GUI attachment of Fig. 1. The story is at the level of detail required in order to produce low-risk GUI estimates for our particular customer. This story required 2 developer days to implement.

3   Sharing and Consistency Challenges

During release and iteration planning meetings, a single story card was shared among 15 or more individuals. The need for continual re-examination of the story card was exacerbated by the extensive amount of GUI contained therein, which, as noted above, was necessary in order to produce relatively low-risk estimations. The simple solution of multiple printouts proved unsatisfactory because of versioning and reference issues. The solution of viewing stories electronically was judged best. We maintained and referred to stories using html. This platform-independent format was necessary because stories were maintained and referenced in Linux, Windows, and Macintosh environments. The customer could employ an html editor to create and maintain stories, and could export his GUI images to gif format for story integration. By iteration 3, this scheme was implemented and used successfully. All participants preferred the electronic story environment.

4   The Scalability Challenge

The need for effective organization, display and management of stories grew proportionally with their number.

4.1   Views

Our electronic story environment evolved based on customer and developer feedback. Our final environment allowed the display of stories by hierarchical grouping, and by iteration. Story links were displayed in colors representing their status, for example, finished, pending, defunct, etc. We believe that the feedback we received during use of the on-line story environment was likely typical of other XP users, as ideas of displaying stories by iterations, and expanding stories from links, are common to other online story repositories, for example, [10,12].

4.2   Dependencies

We experience tremendous dependencies among stories, as a result of the magnitude of our project, its extreme GUI component, and our customer's exacting GUI standards. It is important to note that our notion of dependencies is not restricted to the temporal ones described in [1,3], for which the order of implementation of stories affects their estimates. Our dependencies are among the story artifacts themselves. For example, one story may describe some GUI in terms of how it differs from GUI presented in another story. One story may use terminology that was defined in another story. The dependencies are not with the code itself, they are among the story artifacts. Numerous such dependencies exist in our product--over 700 during the three years of analyzed data.

Our extant dependencies are consistent with reports of other large [6], and other GUI-intensive [7], projects. Schalliol [6] reports that the dependencies among stories necessitated the review and rewriting of story cards on a continuous basis, to the extent that a full-time analyst was assigned to developing and managing story cards with the customer. He reports an inadequacy in project testing is directly attributable to the fact that the list of story cards by itself did not include any built-in guide to interactions among past and present cards (dependencies). The dependency problem was not resolved on that project; however Schalliol suggests other large projects use a "heavier" methodology for stories, to ensure that the cards are managed, updated, and ordered well. Our story environment can be considered such a "heavier" methodology. Because our environment is in place, we, unlike Schalliol, are able to directly include dependencies among stories, using simple hyperlinking capabilities. The problem of *identifying* these dependencies, however, is more challenging, as outlined below.

The identification of dependencies is a labour-intensive undertaking which must be carried out when writing stories. Our data shows that dependencies in a story must be identified before the story is released to developer meetings, as our dependencies affect both estimates and meeting durations. If not already identified and considered, dependencies must be explored and uncovered during developer meetings; unnoticed dependencies accounted for an unexpected increase in development time of approximately 20% per dependency, according to data collected in the first iterations of the project. Meeting duration is significantly increased by dependency detection, with the same data showing that meetings in which developers detected dependencies during conversations with the customer were significantly longer than those for which dependencies were already considered pre-meeting, with the former spanning several days, on occasion, and the latter usually spanning half of one day. Our on-line story environment was invaluable in helping identify dependencies because we were able to employ complex searching. Each dependency was either found through searching, or, if identified without searching, was subsequently verified through searching. Because stories resided in plain text files, the full arsenal of Linux utilities were at our disposal, including regular expressions, grep, find, sort, etc. For our non-Linux, non-programmer customer, the simplest solution to the searching problem was to employ browser search facilities. For this, we added another story view which loaded the entire story repository as one file into the browser for global searches. Both the story view, and the Linux utilities were used successfully to identify dependencies. Had our 800 stories been available only on hard-copy story cards, it would have been impossible to identify and verify the necessary dependencies. Based on collected data relating to meeting durations, estimate increases, and dependencies, we expect that the success of our project would have been compromised had our story environment not facilitated the inclusion of dependencies, and their identification through complex searching.

5 Change-Management and Consistency

Initially, all personnel could modify stories. However, this resulted in conflict often enough that a more formal process was implemented. Conflict arose when developer and customer discussions were interpreted differently by developer than by customer. Our attempts at resolving this problem by increased communication were not entirely successful, and we began recording any story changes within the story to mitigate these misunderstandings. However, this did not resolve the problem, because when one party modified the story to reflect their understanding of the agreed upon modifications, often the other party later disagreed with this interpretation. This is obviously a problem with our attainment of the values of feedback and communication, and although we put effort into it, we were unable to make good headway without inclusion of additional process, as follows: Changes to stories could be made by anyone during a planning meeting, where both parties could view the result, but only by the customer afterward. If a developer disagreed, or if the change altered the given estimation, the developer would alert the customer, and they would continue communication. This process appeared to work well for two years. However, feedback at the start of the third year was that although developers were happy with this arrangement, they wished the opportunity to attach their own notes to the stories regarding clarifications, conversations with the customer, implementation decisions, etc. The customer also wished the opportunity to create additional notes rather than being restricted to expressing additions via modification of the original story. We facilitated this by including a "notes" hyperlink in each story which targeted another html file corresponding to that story. Developers could not edit a story, but they could edit its notes. A basic tenant of XP is that written notes may be added to story cards; therefore, regardless of how stories are maintained, it is important to include, in basic process, the facility to maintain notes. We had originally overlooked this, but discovered, by experience, its importance.

6   User Story Environment

In this section we discuss generalizations of our experiences, and related work.

6.1   Generalization

The augmentation of the XP story creation and modification process was important to the success of our project. As reported in Sections 4 and 5, our modified process mitigated issues of scalability, dependency and change management, all of which arose in our project because of its GUI intensive nature, its scope, and its intended positioning in the marketplace as a product with a "sexier" GUI than competitors. Our modified process facilitated the extensive communication between development and management required to successfully implement the required GUI.

We believe our process modifications can be generalized to other projects facing similar challenges – XP projects with any of the following properties: uncommonly great scope; a high level of artifact dependency; an unusually high level of change management; a large, complex GUI component, with project success depending on correct and complete GUI from the customer's perspective. In such projects, we expect our process modifications will be important to project success, as they were for our project, because they work to mitigate problems arising from the above properties. For example, for projects of unusually great scope, our experience agrees with other research showing that some heavier process is required to manage, update and organize stories [6], and our process is fitting in this situation. Projects exhibiting artifact dependencies, such as ours and that of [6], were found to require methods for dependency identification and cross-referencing, and again, our process is applicable. It has been our experience, and has been suggested by others [7], that projects with extensive GUI will benefit from appropriate process modification to facilitate communication, and again, our modifications are appropriate.

Our augmentations to the story creation and maintenance process can be applied to other projects with the properties mentioned above by incorporating some or all of the following guidelines into process:

- Employ an electronic story management process, to facilitate the following points.
- Use a means of managing, organizing, cross-referencing and ordering stories
- Implement a means of electronically searching stories to identify artifact dependencies, and maintain an efficient scheme for cross-referencing such dependencies.

- Allow GUI specifications to be seamlessly incorporated into stories, using an approach that facilitates change management.

It is important to note that we provide appropriate process modifications, but we do not advocate specific implementation strategies. For example, our experience shows that incorporating electronic dependency identification and cross-referencing is a vital adaptation; however, we do not advocate a specific means of implementing this, such as html, Linux search utilities and hyperlinks, because implementation should depend on the skill-set of the personnel involved and the given project environment.

6.2 Related Work

We began development in 2000, when very little tool support existed for XP development. At that time, our on-line story environment was developed in-house, of necessity. However, more recently, several XP CASE tools have emerged, for example [8,10-14], and we have evaluated a number of these to determine if they can provide additional or improved functionality in our environment.

In our situation, the CASE tools appear a weighty solution in that they incorporate extensive functionality related to planning, tracking, implementation, etc. For our needs, a simple online story environment, with complex searching capabilities, is sufficient. Additionally, it is our experience that most of the functionality included in these CASE tools would be superfluous in our environment, as feedback pertaining to our current planning and tracking processes suggest they are completely satisfactory. It would seem at odds with the "simplicity" and "you won't need it" values of XP to install and maintain a tool for which most of its functionality will go unused, and is unnecessary, in the given environment.

Some tools, such as [12,13], appear to restrict functionality to the story/planning level, thus reducing unnecessary functionality (with respect to our environment.) However, we note that complex searching capabilities are crucial in our domain, and the ability to compose existing Linux utilities invaluable. As noted above, we believe that without such facilities, our project would not have succeeded. None of these story/planning tools contain adequate searching and retrieval for our project, and this point alone renders them ineffectual in our environment.

7 Conclusions

We have described our augmentations to the story management methodology, which were derived using XP principles, in accordance with our unique project properties: non-traditional project scope, extensive and exacting customer GUI requirements, numerous artifact dependencies, and our reliance on GUI for project success. We compared our modified story process against the standard process, using data collected from our project over a three year period, and showed our modifications essential to project success. It is important to note that we are *not* presenting another story tool and advocating its wide-spread adoption. We outline a process of story management which we believe is applicable to projects with the given properties. We have reported our realization of this process, subject to our particular expertise and experience; however, we expect that if similar process were adopted for other qualifying projects, realizations or tools would emerge based on the extant skill-set of that team, and could differ from ours. We hope our results may provide guidance to other XP planners in determining if their project would benefit from similar process modification, and if so, guidance in determining the extent to which modification is necessary, and guidance relating to modification realization.

It is worth noting that the same customer and part of the team have undertaken a smaller, non-GUI-intensive, in-house project for which the standard XP process was employed successfully: stories comprising a few sentences written on cards were sufficient; acceptance tests focused on functionality, etc. The customer, while unimpressed with the GUI, was satisfied with the results, as in this case correct functionality was the goal. Having employed both the standard and our modified processes successfully, we remain confident that our modifications were essential to the success of our GUI-intensive project. Our process modifications took the form of story environment augmentation. However, is possible that the GUI, scope, and dependency issues could be addressed to some degree by augmenting the standard XP process with the addition of various other artifacts, such as use-cases, workflow diagrams, etc. We had initially rejected the use of such ancillary artifacts because we believed they were incompatible with the stated XP practices, a common belief [5]. However, in future projects we hope to explore this approach and compare it with that of our process modification.

References

1. Beck, K.: Extreme Programming Explained: Embrace Change. Addison-Wesley, 2000.
2. Beck, K.: Extreme Programming Immersion. Scotts Valley, CA. March 2000.
3. Beck, K., Fowler, M.: Planning Extreme Programming. Addison-Wesley, 2001.
4. Jeffries, R., Anderson, A., Hendrickson, C.: Extreme Programming Installed. Addison-Wesley, 2001.
5. Succi, G., Marchesi, M.: Extreme Programming Examined. Addison-Wesley, 2001.
6. Schalliol, G.: "Challenges for Analysts on a large XP Project", in Proc. XP Universe, Raleigh, North Carolina, July 23-25, 2001.
7. Wallace, D., Raggett, I., Aufgang, F.: Extreme Programming for Web Projects. Addison-Wesley, 2003.
8. Marurer, F.: "Supporting Distributed Extreme Programming", in Lecture Notes in Computer Science, Volume 2418/2002, Springer-Verlag Heidelberg, 2003. pp. 13-22.
9. User Stories: http://www.extremeprogramming.org/rules/userstories.html
10. Xplanner: http://www.xplanner.org/
11. Xpcgi: http://www.xpcgi.sourceforge.net/
12. Iterate: http://www.diamond-sky.com/products/iterate/
13. Pinna, S., Mauri, S., Lorrai, P., Corriga, C.: "PSwiki: An agile tool supporting the planning game", in Lecture Notes in Computer Science, Volume 2675/2003, Springer-Verlag Heidelberg, 2003. pp. 104-113.
14. Auer, K.: "Autotracker", in Refining the practices of XP, workshop in ACM SIGPLAN Conference on object-oriented programming systems, languages and applications (OOPSLA 2002), Seattle, Washington, Nov. 4-8, 2002.

Agile CS1 Labs: eXtreme Programming Practices in an Introductory Programming Course

Dawn McKinney, Julie Froeseth, Jason Robertson,
Leo F. Denton, and David Ensminger

School of Computer and Information Sciences,
University of South Alabama,
Mobile, AL 36688
{dmckinney,jrobertson,ldenton}@usouthal.edu,
jf301@jaguar1.usouthal.edu, densminger@sbcglobal.net

Abstract. Many students begin to form their software development habits in introductory programming courses. Although problem-solving strategies and other good practices are taught at the introductory level, early experiences in programming tend to involve small assignments and so students do not always see the benefits and value of good software engineering practices. Consequently, they develop habits which are hard to break later when faced with significant problems where good practices are essential for success. Furthermore, students report that typical CS1 lab experiences tend to be unsatisfactory and even irrelevant. In order to give the students early meaningful experiences in developing good habits using a software engineering methodology which fits the limited time-constraints of the academic environment, eXtreme Programming (XP) was employed for the lab portion of a second semester CS1 course. This paper describes how XP practices were incorporated into a semester-long project where classes met once a week in a closed lab. Specific affective objectives were also introduced which were measured quantitatively and qualitatively. This paper describes our methodology, assessment, results, and plans for improvement.

1 Introduction

This paper describes a research effort that measures the benefits of incorporating eXtreme Programming (XP) practices into an introductory programming course. We will discuss our environment, our rationale, our use of the XP practices in a semester-long closed-lab project, the results of quantitative and qualitative assessment of the approach, the benefits we found with this approach, and specifically what we intend to do to improve our efforts in Spring 2004.

1.1 The Authors

Two of the authors, Dawn McKinney and Leo Denton, have been interested in XP for a couple of years. During 2001, these two instructors had mentored a senior project team and introduced some of the XP practices to that team. After attending the XP/Agile Universe 2003 conference, McKinney decided to include XP practices in the

C. Zannier et al. (Eds.): XP/Agile Universe 2004, LNCS 3134, pp. 164–174, 2004.
© Springer-Verlag Berlin Heidelberg 2004

second semester of the CS1 lab in Fall 2003. Authors, Julie Froeseth and Jason Robertson, the lab assistants for the course, became interested in the XP aspect of the lab and led the research effort. Denton led the quantitative assessment effort and assisted in qualitative observation. The fifth author, David Ensminger, a qualitative researcher, led the qualitative assessment of the experience. After learning from the fall experience, all five are involved in an improved version of the agile CS1 labs during Spring 2004.

1.2 Our Environment

The University of South Alabama is a medium-sized state university. The School of Computer and Information Sciences offers a bachelors degree in Computer and Information Sciences (CIS) which has three choices of specializations: Computer Science, Information Systems, and Information Technology. The school also offers masters degrees in Computer Science and Information Systems. The two-semester introductory programming sequence (CS1), are foundation courses for all specializations in the undergraduate degree program. In these courses, students learn problem-solving skills and develop programs in Java. The first semester focuses on the basics of problem solving and programming. The second semester gives the students experiences solving more complex problems involving a greater degree of abstraction and the programs are object-oriented. This study was performed with the second semester course. Our CS1 courses meet for three 50-minute sessions and one 75-minute closed-lab session. Traditionally, our CS1 labs have consisted of small coding assignments that are completed by students individually and turned in at the end of the lab period or finished for homework. These assignments have ranged from simple "type-and-run" exercises to very short programming assignments. This approach is designed to reinforce course concepts and to provide hands-on practice.

1.3 Rationale for Choosing XP

According to our surveys and informal interviews, for some students the traditional lab experience is a satisfying learning environment, while for others this lab format is associated with drudgery, busy work, and is viewed as a waste of time. Other students have commented that the labs are boring or even irrelevant. Furthermore, students rarely see the value of good software development practices, such as testing, since the assignments are so small and short term. In an effort to address these concerns, to enliven the lab experience, and to make the lab a more valuable endeavor for students, we decided to use XP methodologies to guide the development of a semester-long project. During the fall semester of 2003, XP teams were formed.

Some "real world" aspects were incorporated into the lab in order to give students a sense of relevance. We also focused on affective growth in the following areas: communication, cooperation, work ethic, adaptability, and commitment. These characteristics are in the National Association of Colleges and Employers' (NACE) top-ten list of characteristics wanted in college graduates [1]. Denton and McKinney have been incorporating affective objectives into the CS1 courses over the past three years [4, 5,

17]. The affective objectives of the course included the promotion of professional practices to help students focus on good team experiences. The students had several opportunities, including exam questions, to list and briefly describe examples of these practices. At the end of the semester, students evaluated how each team member performed regarding these practices. To help the students form good habits early, they were given a brief introduction to the various models of software engineering. A software engineering model was needed for the lab that would be flexible enough to incorporate changes into the project as the students learned new concepts throughout the semester. The model also needed to give the students ample time for actual coding, encourage cooperative learning, as well as other skills, and promote the specific affective objectives of the course. An agile methodology, like XP, seemed well-suited to meet these needs.

2   CS1 Agile Labs

The lab component of the course consists of a weekly 75-minute hands-on session. Since the school has a laptop policy, students are required to have their laptops not only for the lab session, but also for the other three 50-minute lecture sessions. The closed-lab provides an environment where students can experience the synergy of the team. Other academics have reported problems with students meeting out of class to pair program and the difficulty getting the entire team together due to scheduling conflicts [18, 28]. Some of our success is likely attributable to this closed-lab aspect.

2.1   The Teams

We formed teams with the seven-plus-or-minus-two plan. This worked well since some students do not remain in the course throughout the whole semester so that even if two or three students were not present, the team still had four or five members. The teams were self-forming and chose their team names. There was a noticeable "team spirit." One problem, however, was that the strong programmers tended to end up on the same team, leaving other teams with weaker skills. These early experiences in teamwork are beneficial in that the students learn to cooperate and work with other programmers. More precisely, they incorporate "ego-less working" [24], something which is further emphasized by the collective code ownership resulting from XP practices like pair programming. The instructor, McKinney, played both the role of customer and project manager/coach. The lab assistants, Froeseth and Robertson, helped resolve programming and technical issues but were not members of the teams.

2.2   The Project

The same project was implemented by all teams. Each team was independent and had different ways of approaching the project, but being in the same room, ideas and other resources were often shared between teams. The project was an actual endeavor that the instructor of the class was interested in developing. The instructor had been using a manual system to log nutrition information. A paper database, a small notebook, and a calculator were used. The customer, who was the instructor, wanted a system developed in Java to calculate BMR (Base Metabolic Rate) and keep track of the number of calories, fat, protein, and carbohydrates allowed for each day by subtracting each time a food was recorded. One of the reasons this project was chosen is that research shows a deviation between what students are exposed to in the classroom and what is expected of them by the industry [11]. Even though students at this level may not be ready to team up with real world companies yet, we believe they will benefit from producing something they know is worthwhile for an actual customer, even if it is their instructor. Furthermore, students usually solve problems in a way that is oriented towards a static solution, but the industry needs developers who are oriented towards what customers want which is more dynamic and evolving [19]. This was further supported by XP's emphasis on the customer.

2.3 XP Practices

We made an attempt to expose students to all of the XP practices: the planning game, small releases, metaphor, simple design, testing, refactoring, pair programming, collective ownership, continuous integration, sustainable pace, on-site customer, coding standards, and stand-up meetings [3, 8, 13, 26]. The XP Practices were posted during lab sessions so that the students were reminded of the practices while working in the lab at opportune times. Hand-outs were provided and students were made aware of XP web sites. Many students became interested and communicated with the instructor about their discoveries, concerns, comments, and suggestions regarding XP practices.

Planning game. About every fourth lab session was devoted to the planning game. Because the semester is about fifteen weeks and to have time for exams and holidays, we planned for three iterations. The customer wrote user stories which were broken down into tasks and estimated by the developers. As was suggested [3], cards were used and after estimation the customer prioritized the stories. Students estimated stories in terms of minutes which were summed from the individual tasks that made up the stories. Since our unit of "ideal time" [3], was a minute, an iteration could be planned based on a total of 150 minutes, or two 75-minute lab sessions.

Small releases. Our stories were small and so the iterations could encompass two or three lab periods, and this is why the estimation had to be in minutes. We did not adhere strictly to the iteration schedule which caused some frustration and a lack of a sense of completion on the part of the students. It was planned that at the end of each iteration, the team would demonstrate the project to the customer and the other teams in the class. After the demonstration, a new planning game would start for the next iteration.

Metaphor. Communication between customer and programmers was constant since the instructor was the customer and always present. An understanding of the project was maintained by this consistent communication. The concept of our chosen project was easy to understand for all members of the team.

Simple design. Since the stories were so small, it was important to keep the students focused on the specific tasks. Sometimes students would try to incorporate features that they thought would be "cool" and the customer/project manager would step in to keep them on track.

Testing. The focus on testing and quality was a priority. In addition to being a central element in XP, it is highly valued in the industry, but often overlooked in programming courses and industry [7]. We did not have much success with this practice, because the students would test after writing the code as they did in their first semester programming experience and we did not use an automated testing program.

Refactoring. Because of the collective code ownership practice and the rotating of pairs, some design and coding improvements were made. However, due to the time limitations and the programming inexperience of the students, we were not able to focus on this. Students at this level rarely get to the level of refactoring since they are struggling to "make things work" and tend to think they are "done" once this is accomplished.

Pair programming. Students recorded on the back of task cards their pair experiences including driver, co-pilot, date, and start/stop times. This helped make sure each pair rotated between driver and co-pilot and with other members of the team which was an important goal [26]. The recording of the times helped for making comparisons between actual times on task and estimates. There were, however, a few observed occasions when the pairs were not well-matched, but since the pairs rotated, this was not a real problem.

Collective code ownership. Members of the team had access to the code at all times since the latest version was kept on a server and was available for downloading to each machine for each lab session. Pair programming contributed to the adoption of this practice.

Continuous integration. At the end of each lab, all code that was tested was uploaded to a server to be downloaded for the next lab. Students were instructed to upload code only when it was tested and working.

Sustainable pace. We did not allow the students to work on the project outside of the lab; we used the lab time as the "40-hour work week" and told them "no overtime." It was interesting how many times students asked if they could please work on the project outside of lab. We could easily see the students enjoying the experience. Occasionally a team member would "cheat," but most of the time students appreciated the freedom to do other work and to leave the project for next lab session. This practice seemed to lessen stress, but some students reported dissatisfaction with the week-long break in time between labs.

On-site customer. The instructor played both roles of customer and project manager/coach, which was an advantage since the customer was always present but a disadvantage since it was difficult for the instructor to play two roles. The instructor wore a necklace-style name-tag with "customer" written on one side and "project manager" on the other and would flip it to whatever role she was playing at the moment. We also emphasized the importance of the customer as part of the team and this concept showed up in exam questions.

Coding standards. As in most academic settings, coding standards are required in our CS1 course. Consequently, these standards were already in place and had been practiced during the first semester of the course. Still, not all students followed all standards. Individual programming assignments, which were separate from the lab, required the use of these coding standards.

Stand-up meetings. We adopted the practice of stand-up meetings. We had no idea how well these would work for students. While "standing up" students cannot easily access the keyboard of their computers and so they must pay attention. Our stand-up meetings were fun. The students seemed to like the idea and they really were an efficient way of communicating what was happening in the teams and the problems they were having [3]. Each person was required to speak. Knowing this was coming, students seemed to make sure they each were making significant contributions to the team so they could have something to say. Stand-up meetings occurred as needed, but typically were scheduled for the beginning and the ending of the lab session. These meetings rarely lasted more than a few minutes and included the entire class.

3   Assessment

Several assessment instruments, qualitative and quantitative, were used to measure the value of this agile lab approach. The authors can be contacted for more information about the instruments. For this study, data was collected from course grades, qualitative student surveys, lab observation, and Likert-based pretests and posttests that measured student interest, belonging, value, perceived competence, pressure, and effort as independent factors. We collected lots of data and found the process to be a bit tedious. The authors came up with the possibility of requiring a weekly student lab journal for the spring semester to assist in some of the evaluation and feedback.

3.1   Quantitative Measures

Our pretest and posttest data indicated that student interest, belonging, value, perceived competence, lack of pressure, effort, and belonging each correlated significantly and positively with course grade. This confirms our earlier studies [4, 17]. Though not identical to this lab's affective priorities: communication, cooperation, work ethic, adaptability, and commitment, the tested affective factors do share substantial overlap with these affective priorities (e.g. effort and work ethic). The majority of the students indicated that these factors increased for them over the course of the semester. The reasons students gave for these increases and sometimes decreases form the basis of our qualitative assessment.

3.2 Qualitative Measures

In order to gain an understanding of the students' XP lab experiences, students were asked to anonymously provide a written description of their experience during the semester. A phenomenological approach was taken to interpreting the comments and description provided by the students.

Student satisfaction. The great majority of student comments indicated satisfaction with XP lab experience. Most students described the lab experience as positive with many using the words fun and enjoyable in their comments:

"My CIS 121 lab experience was very enjoyable"

"I enjoyed lab very much because I learned from my peers more about teamwork and programming."

Student dissatisfaction. A minority of students identified several problems with their XP lab experiences:

"I had a small problem with pair programming due to a vast difference in ability (could have been desire) to write code. It seemed that a few team members actually wrote while others watched." (not balanced pairing)

"There isn't enough time in the lab to complete the assigned tasks." (sense of completion)

Real world. The student's satisfaction with the agile lab comes mostly from what is described as "real world" experience. Students reported that the software development process used in the agile lab simulated how they would work once they were employed in a computer science related field. Sixty-three percent (63%) of the students used the "real world" analogy to describe what occurred in the in the agile lab experience:

"Certainly CIS 121 reflects how I will work in real world."

"Teamwork was awesome. Everybody truly gave a great effort. The assignment was fun because it was an actual program that could be used in the real world. I learned a lot more than just programming because it was truly a team that followed real world protocol. I learned that pair programming is way better! I learned communication skills and dealing with the customer and issues you run into with what a customer wants and what you think they want."

Teamwork. The "real world" experience reported by students comes from several variables that the students were exposed to as part of the lab. The most prominently described variable was the teamwork or group work. Many students (i.e. 66 %) described teamwork as significant part of the agile lab experience:

"I think our CIS 121 lab will prepare us more for a real future. Learning how to deal with completely different people and work with them in a group."

"The lab focused on communication and cooperation with other students. The lab was very helpful because it introduced the concept of team projects. The team project concept is very important in today in computer industry. Employers in today's job market (Computer/IT) require team (group) project experience."

Cooperative learning. The teamwork environment contributed to a cooperative learning environment where students were able to share information and learn from one another. The cooperative learning included the sharing of coding skills, conceptual knowledge, and problem-solving strategies.

> "It was a ton of fun working with this team. It is hard to say what and how much was learned. When I wasn't "driving" I felt somewhat useless, but it was a good way to see how others approach a problem and help them see things they missed."

> "It is a nice experience to work with different backgrounds because they bring different views and ideas."

Professional skills. Besides the development of teamworking skills, students reported that the agile lab experience helped them develop other skills that would benefit them professionally. Students realized that to be successful in this experience they needed to become flexible and adaptable. Cooperation and communication were skills that were essential to the success of their group. Students describe the need to be committed and a good work ethic as part of the other skills developed from the experience. Some students even made leaps in their self-awareness:

> "The lab implemented many skills that are priceless. These skills included teamwork, compatibility, commitment, etc. I learned how to better work with others and use my time more wisely."

> "Not being a traditional student, I don't know the five factors were influenced greatly. However, I definitely had to change from telling someone to do something to working together to get it done."

Clear goals and objectives. Another variable contributing to the student's satisfaction came from the assignment to build the product. Students described the project and small iterations or objectives that lead to the project goal. Having clear goals and objectives for each lab and that these objectives were related to a project goal contributed to a feeling of accomplishment from students who reported the goals and objectives as part of what made the class satisfying.

> "I enjoyed the lab assignment because it was very cool trying to achieve so many goals in such a short period of time. It was a challenge."

> "The lab assignment was challenging and interesting. A clear objective could be recognized and worked toward."

Development of new skills. By emphasizing the XP process of product development the labs were able to approximate the "real world experience." In order to be successful in this environment, students had to develop more than just computer coding skills. They had to develop team skills, communication skills, organizational skills, learn to be adaptive, learn to cooperate and share information. The need to focus on these new skills and the group work enhanced the level of satisfaction that the students received from the XP lab experience:

> "It took me a few labs to start to understand how to work within the group but the skills I've started learning will stay with me. As a matter of fact, I've already used the more team oriented mind set at my job and it has made things better for me."

"Huge increase in my understanding of programming concepts. XP in labs initially seemed awkward and inefficient, but we now communicate better."

3.3 Classroom Observations

Below are comments from the observers (Denton and Ensminger) along with the corresponding affective objectives of the lab. These observations also illustrate the real-world, team-oriented, and professional character of the labs.

"Interaction among the teams and within the teams was positive; students treated each other with respect and courtesy. I also observed students laughing when they made errors. They seem to be at ease with each other and willing to accept feedback openly from their paired members and members on the team. Teams joked openly with each other and appeared to be having fun while they worked." (*communication*)

"Students congratulated each other when achievements were made."
"Pairs worked together to clean up the code." (*cooperation*)

"The class seems to work well when faced with change. They appeared to quickly size up the problems and then look for solutions. I observed this not only with the whole team but also in the working pairs. The close interaction and 'team spirit' seems to allow the groups to quickly work together to adapt to the changes they encountered." (*adaptability*)

"The most telling observation was the fact that both groups did not need to be prompted to get to work. They began to get organized as team members arrived and then immediately began discussing the project and working on tasks without any prompting from the instructor. They seemed to regulate themselves and guide their own workflow. Additionally, students worked steadily for the entire lab period." (*work-ethic*)

"The students were so 'in the flow' that they 'self-started' and barely even noticed the observers." (*commitment*)

4   Reflections and Conclusion

This paper describes the incorporation of eXtreme Programming (XP) practices into an introductory programming course. Benefits and drawbacks of this approach were identified. Anticipated improvements stemming from identified problems include: (1) the instructor should not, if possible, play the role of both project manager and customer (this has also been identified by others who have tried this approach [22, 23, 26]), (2) student journals should be used to provide a mechanism for students to monitor their progress and to receive instructor feedback, (3) stricter adherence to the iteration schedule is needed in order to give students a better sense of project completion, and (4) test-driven development needs to be automated using a tool like JUnit [10] and needs to be understood and valued by students [8, 9, 20, 23]. Progress based on these changes has already been noticed during the first several weeks of the follow-up Spring semester. Realized benefits from pair-programming and other XP practices included confidence building, "pair pressure," a sense of belonging (a key factor in retention studies [12, 25, 27]), shared euphoria (evidenced by high fives and other expressions), working code, higher course relevance, self-regulated learning, and co-operative learning. Qualitative analysis indicates that this experience helped establish a sense of satisfaction and promoted the development of professional skills, such as communication, work-ethic, commitment, cooperation, and adaptability. Course completion rates also increased though we cannot directly attribute this to the agile lab experience. In conclusion, it is clear that eXtreme Programming practices can be successfully integrated into the laboratory experience of students in their second semester of programming with beneficial effects.

References

1. ACM/IEEE Computing Curricula 2001, Computer Science Volume, Chapter 10: Professional Practice.
   Available at http://www.acm.org/sigcse/cc2001/cs-professional-practice.html
2. Beck, Kent. Test-Driven Development by Example. Addison-Wesley. 2003.
3. Beck, Kent and Fowler, Martin. Planning Extreme Programming, Addison-Wesley, 2001.
4. Denton, Leo F., Dawn McKinney, and Michael V. Doran. Promoting Student Achievement With Integrated Affective Objectives, Proceedings of the 2003 American Society for Engineering Education Annual Conference & Exposition, Nashville, Tennessee, USA (2003).
   Available at http://www.asee.org/conferences/caps/document/2003-2391_Final.pdf or at http://www.cis.usouthal.edu/~mckinney/ASEE3530.htm
5. Denton, Leo F., Michael V. Doran, and Dawn McKinney. Integrated Use of Bloom and Maslow for Instructional Success in Technical and Scientific Fields, In the Proceedings of the 2002 American Society for Engineering Education Annual Conference & Exposition, Montreal, Canada (2002).
   Available at http://www.asee.org/conferences/caps/document/2002-675_Paper.pdf
   or at http://www.cis.usouthal.edu/~mckinney/
6. Fenwick, James B., Jr. Adapting XP to an Academic Environment by Phasing –In Practices. Extreme Programming and Agile Methods – XP/Agile Universe 2003, Third XP Agile Universe Conference, New Orleans, LA.
7. Haddad, Hisham. Post-Graduate Assessment of CS Students: Experience and Position Paper. The Journal of Computing in Small Colleges, December 2002 pp 189 – 197.
8. Jeffries, Ron, Ann Anderson, and Chet Hendrickson. Extreme Programming Installed. Addison – Wesley. 2001.
9. Johnson, David H. and James Caristi. Extreme Programming and the Software Design Course. in Extreme Programming Perspectives, Addison-Wesley, 2003.
10. JUnit Testing Framework, http//JUnit.org
11. Kock, Ned, and Camille Auspitz and Brad King. Web-Supported Course Partnerships: Bringing Industry and Academia Together. Communications of the ACM, September 2003.
12. Light, Richard. Making the Most of College. Harvard University Press, 2001.
13. Martin, Robert C. Agile Software Development: Principles, Patterns, and Practices. Prentice Hall. 2003.

14. McDowell, Charlie, Brian Hanks, and Linda Werner, Experimenting with Pair Program-
    ming in the Classroom, ITiCSE'03, June 30-July 2, 2003, Thessaloniki, Greece, pp. 60-64.
15. McDowell, Charlie, Linda Werner, Heather Bullock, and Julian Fernald. The Effects of
    Pair Programming in an Introductory Programming Course. Proceedings of the 33rd
    SIGCSE technical symposium on Computer science education, 2002, Cincinnati, KY.
16. McDowell, Charlie, Linda Werner, Heather Bullock, and Julian Fernald. The impact of
    pair programming on student performance, perception and persistence. Proceedings of the
    25th international conference on Software engineering, 2003, Portland, OR.
17. McKinney, Dawn, and Denton, Leo F., Houston, we have a problem: there's a leak in the
    CS1 affective oxygen tank, Proceedings of the 35th SISCSE Technical Symposium On
    Computer Science Education, March 2004, Norfolk, VA.
18. Melnik, Grigori, and Frank Mauer. Introducing Agile Methods in Learning Environments:
    Lessons Learned. Extreme Programming and Agile Methods – XP/Agile Universe 2003,
    Third XP Agile Universe Conference, New Orleans, LA.
19. Mitchell, William. Information Technology Education, One State's Experience. Journal of
    Computing in Small Colleges (17, 4), March 2002 pp. 123-132.
20. Müller, Matthias M., and Walter F. Tichy. Case Study: Extreme Programming in a Univer-
    sity Environment. Proceedings of the 23rd international conference on Software engineer-
    ing, 2001, Toronto, Ontario, Canada.
21. Nagappan, Nachiappan, Laurie Williams, Miriam Ferzli, Eric Wiebe, Kai Yang, Carol
    Miller, and Suzanne Balik. Improving the CS1 experience with pair programming. Pro-
    ceedings of the 34th SIGCSE technical symposium on Computer science education, 2003,
    Reno, NV.
22. Noll, John and Darren C. Atkinson. Comparing Extreme Programming to Traditional De-
    velopment for Student Projects: A Case Study. Proceedings of the 4th International Con-
    ference on eXtreme Programming and Agile Processes in Software Engineering, May
    2003.
23. Noll, John. Some Observations of Extreme Programming for Student Projects. Workshop
    on Empirical Evaluation of Agile Processes (EEAP 2002). August, 2002.
24. Schneider, Jean-Guy, Lorraine Johnston. eXtreme Programming at Universities – An Edu-
    cational Perspective. Proceedings of the 25th international conference on Software
    engineering, 2003, Portland, OR.
25. Seymour, Elaine, and Nancy M. Hewitt. Talking About Leaving: Why Undergraduates
    Leave the Sciences. Westview Press, 1997.
26. Steinberg, Daniel H., and Daniel W. Palmer. Extreme Software Engineering: A Hands-on
    Approach. Prentice-Hall, Inc., 2004.
27. Tinto, Vincent. Leaving College: Rethinking the Causes and Cures of Student Attrition.
    Second Edition, The University of Chicago Press, 1993.
28. Wainer, Michael. Adaptations for Teaching Software Development with Extreme Pro-
    gramming: An Experience Report. Extreme Programming and Agile Methods – XP/Agile
    Universe 2003, Third XP Agile Universe Conference, New Orleans, LA.
29. Williams, Laurie and R.L. Upchurch. In Support of Student Pair-Programming, Proceed-
    ings of the 32nd SIGCSE Technical Symposium of Computer Science Education, Febru-
    ary, 2001, Charlotte, NC, pp. 327-331.).

A Case Study in the Use of Extreme Programming in an Academic Environment

Mary Beth Smrtic and Georges Grinstein

University of Massachusetts, Lowell
The Institute for Visualization and Perception Research
One University Avenue
Lowell, Massachusetts 01854
msmrtic@cs.uml.edu

Abstract. A group of graduate students working in a lab in a university have more distractions than a typical software development group in industry. With more distractions and fewer hours on site does it still make sense to use Extreme Programming (XP) in the development of software? Here we discuss our experience using XP in an academic environment in which the members of the development group have different schedules and other projects. We found that pair programming was an efficient and effective way to learn and share knowledge, and that unit testing and just-in-time design helped us get to an early, though scaled down release. Our interpretation of pair programming felt limited and awkward at first until we realized that we could and should spend time independently learning and researching the tasks in addition to the work we do in pairs.

1 Introduction

The environment of graduate students in a lab in a university differs from the business environment mostly in the schedules and work habits of the students. Most of the graduate students on this project are not working full time on software development; during the semesters when they have classes and other projects to focus on they are in the lab about 20 hours per week as opposed to the typical 40+ hours in business. They typically do a higher percentage of their work outside the lab since the normal behavior for a student is to go to classes, then do most of their studying and homework individually somewhere else, at home or in a quiet spot in the library, as opposed to the business environment where most of one's work is usually done in the office. Do Extreme Programming (XP) practices hinder or help the development of software in this environment? Here we discuss our experience using Extreme Programming in this environment and explore which practices worked well for us and what problems we encountered.

2 The Institute for Visualization and Perception Research at UMass Lowell

In September, 2003 a group of 6 graduate students of varying levels of experience began a new development project, with more joining in as the academic year pro-

C. Zannier et al. (Eds.): XP/Agile Universe 2004, LNCS 3134, pp. 175–182, 2004.
© Springer-Verlag Berlin Heidelberg 2004

gressed. None of us had any experience with Agile programming methodologies. We began with a description of a desired system and the goal of releasing the software to a graduate Computer Science information visualization class in the beginning of November so that the students could use it for their final projects for the class; any later than that and the students would not have enough time to use it. The class knew that they were using software under development, so its quality and scope were a bit more flexible than the time requirement. At a bare minimum the software needed a quality and scope that allowed the students to do their projects.

The name of the software toolkit we developed is the Universal Visualization Platform (UVP). The students in the visualization class would each program a different visualization which should easily plug into the framework allowing the students to focus on the programming of their visualization. We began by defining the product, choosing an IDE, learning XP, getting Java, JUnit, the IDE and source code control installed. We were all new to XP and thought that everything had to be done in pairs. Although we all have different schedules with classes and other projects, we are each in the lab for at least 20 hours a week. We each have our own desk and computer, but the lab is set up to allow us to easily share a workspace for pairing and all the developers are in the same room. With all the pairs collaborating we were able to easily get everything in place and running. By September 9, we were ready to begin writing software. We use JUnit for our unit tests. Our goal was to never check code into the repository unless all the unit tests passed. Our compile and test running was always very fast which helped meet this goal. We did, however, still think that following XP meant we were supposed to do everything in pairs. Most of us had different ways of learning the system and found it somewhat frustrating to learn as a pair. Our largest complaint about XP was that it was hard to think while pairing. At one point, we were trying to solve a simple problem, specifically; mapping points onto a scatterplot, but had different ways of thinking about the problem and couldn't jointly solve it. We took a short break to think about the problem and then came back with a solution. In October, we had the opportunity to visit some experienced XP practitioners at Hewlett Packard. They were surprised that we tried to pair all the time. They spend 4 hours a day independently and 4 hours pairing. This gives them time to fully understand a problem before they sit down and code it as a pair. Doing this earlier would have saved us some time and frustration. We now try to spend as much time on our own as we do pairing. On our own, we research the problem and do "spikes"; this is writing software independently that does not get checked into the repository and is purely for researching and exploring alternative ways to solve a problem. By the time we get together to pair, we have already considered the problem and have a better understanding of possible solutions.

3   Keep It as Simple as Possible

"Edward Tufte [1] has an exercise for graphic designers – design a graph however you want. Then erase as long as you don't remove any information. Whatever is left when you can't erase any more is the right design for the graph. Simple design is like this – take out any design element that you can." [2] To keep our design and code as simple as possible, we remove anything that is not absolutely essential.

We started work on the "simplest thing that could possibly work." We agreed that the simplest possible first internal release would have a skeleton of the framework with an abstract Tool class, a control manager, a link manager to hold the list of tools, a data manager to hold a list of datasets, and a simple data reader tool. Three of us worked on the skeleton of the framework, a control manager, a link manager. Two of us worked on the first data reader tool. We paired to create a simple Comma Separated Variable (CSV) reader. We wrote a unit test in JUnit that opened a simple data set that would not stress the abilities of the reader. We ran it and watched it fail. At this point we found pair programming to be surprisingly fun and felt productive. Each group was learning from each other and figuring things out together. In a pair, we were about twice as likely to already know the answer to each question that came up saving the time of having to look it up.

4   Low Barriers to Knowledge Sharing

Our experience with individual programming is that we would not often ask questions while working. Even if in the same room with another programmer, we would not interrupt every time we wondered if they knew the answer to the question that we were about to go in search of. While pair programming we can constantly ask any question that comes to mind, or share knowledge even when the other person does not know to ask. One of the developers at Hewlett Packard had an interesting anecdote. He had visited another HP office to teach them XP. He was not familiar with their development environment, but paired with one person in the morning and another in the afternoon. While pairing with the second person, he mentioned that there was a keyboard shortcut to what the developer had just done. The developer was surprised and asked "how did you know that?" It was because he had paired with the other developer in the morning. With no pair programming, the knowledge was effectively hoarded and not shared within the group.

5   Shared Knowledge; More Flexible Team

One day the first author was in the lab, feverishly writing a paper that was due the next day. Someone came in to discuss some software she had written. She valued his input and did not want to discourage him. Another student in the lab who had paired with her was just as familiar with the code, and easily stepped into the conversation allowing her to quietly slip back to her paper.

The lead developer on this project, one of the full time developers, is occasionally needed for other projects, distracting him from this one. We found that pairing helped the rest of us understand the software that he had written and we were able to continue in his absence. If he had gone off and written his part of the software independently, we would be stuck when he was unavailable. There was one point when we needed to add linking (highlighting related data in multiple visualizations) to the project. The students in the class, for their final project, had to analyze a dataset using multiple visualizations. They needed to be able to make selections in their visualization with the selected data highlighted in the other visualizations. The lead developer, who began the semester with the vision of how this would happen, was unavailable to make this happen in time for the students' final project. He had written the supporting structures but the actual linking code had not yet been written. We decided one Monday afternoon that this really needed to be available that day so that we could release it to the students for that evening's class, not an unusual scenario on the commercial side for demonstrations. We had been thinking about it over the weekend but had limited time to get it in. We got a simple version of it working to present in class that evening. Had the lead developer not been pairing with us all along and gone off and written the supporting structures independently, we probably could not have pulled it off so quickly without him doing it himself. By investing all along in shared knowledge, we gain extra flexibility and are not so limited by any one person's schedule. Code and design reviews do not give as intimate an understanding of the software as pair programming and continuous integration and unit tests. If he had simply told us about what he had done, or if we had critiqued it in a review, we would not have understood it as well or as quickly.

6   Code Clarity

We found it helpful to have two opinions on the clarity of the software. There were times when one of us would say "I don't understand what you're doing there." The other person would then try it a different way, "is that better?" Something that seemed very clear to one of us is not necessarily clear to the other. If we both agree that it's clear, it's much more likely to actually be understood by the next person who looks at it. Clarity can mean different things to different people and without pair programming, sometimes code gets in that is only clear to one person. With pair programming, if the vote is tied, we pull in a third as a tie breaker. That greatly increases the likelihood that the code will be clear to other developers that use it.

7   "The Ultimate in Defect Removal Efficiency" [3]

If individual programming is an individual sport, pair programming is a team sport. Pair programming has been referred to as "constant code review" [3] but in place of one or more people critiquing another person's work, we were building it together as a team. I remember pointing to the screen and saying, "Wait, we could get a null pointer exception here." If the driver is focused on the solution to the problem they may not be thinking about the surrounding issues. The person watching can catch the little things that the driver might miss.

8   Design Disagreements

Did it slow us down to have two people making every little decision? We agreed surprisingly often and when we didn't agree, the solution tended to become clear quickly. We often found ourselves handing over the keyboard and saying "show me what you mean" or "here, I'll show you what I mean." Some code is written, one of us would point to it and say, "See, that's what I meant," or "oh, you're right, that doesn't work." Abstract discussions quickly become resolved. In waterfall model design sessions, discussions are more abstract and can take a long time; code is a great way to communicate with another developer.

Two of the developers on our team had a common discussion about whether a creator function should return a reference to the object that it created. Who owns the new object, its creator, or the method that called the creator? In this case, the object that did the creation kept track of its objects, so you could argue that it should keep the object and not return a reference to it. You could also argue that the caller wanted to create it, so should be able to act on the new object. This type of discussion is typical of large design phases. Under XP, if a discussion is taking too much time, the interested parties try it to see which way works better. They eventually came to an agreement, but perhaps they could have written some code to try it both ways to see which works better instead of the long abstract discussion they had multiple times.

9   Test Driven Development

Although not all the developers like to work this way, the first author found writing the unit test before the code helped clarify the API of the class being created. We often changed the API after the code was written, and modified the test to cover what was learned during the development of that class, but this was still a helpful starting point.

Using the unit tests for testing is indispensable. Any testing done that is not covered in the unit test is nearly useless. Non-automated testing done on the software today tells you only that the bug is not there today; it says nothing about whether the bug will be there when you ship your software. Putting the tests into unit tests ensures that that bug is not there today and it won't be there when the code ships. We have no problem with coding to the test. If you write software units that are easy to test, they will also be easy to use.

10   Keep the Bar Green

In general the software that was checked into source code was working so that the other group was not slowed down. When checked in code was not working, we had no problem interrupting the other team since this is considered the highest priority. As we neared the end of October, the time of a key release, the pressure increased and some of our practices were stretched a bit. Since there was still work to be done, some of it was done from home. Being in an academic environment, working from home is something that happens often. Some code was checked in from off site that was not paired and erroneous. Two other developers had come into the lab that weekend to try to get work done for the Monday release and spent half of the day trying to get around the problem. When they reached the other developer on the phone, they were able to work with him to solve the problem, but some time and frustration was spent that may have been avoided; perhaps by pairing over the phone and making sure that all the unit tests ran successfully.

11   Continuous Integration

Past projects in the lab sometimes had integration issues. Our approach then was to do waterfall style projects with large up-front designs that led often to problems due to integration issues. It's easy in an academic setting for the programmers to go off and write a large amount of code that may not work well with the rest of the software. In this environment the developers are not in the lab full time, and long hours of work from home is the accepted work style, which makes this problem even more likely.

Our group made some mistakes, but pair programming forced a very high level of communication on us. There were moments when the code failed, but with constant integration, we quickly knew when there were miscommunications between different parts of the software and we were generally able to fix them immediately.

12 Refactoring

"If it stinks, change it" (Kent Beck's Grandma on child rearing). The developers that we talked to at Hewlett Packard hold weekly refactoring lunches. If there is a part of the code that doesn't feel right to someone or they just have a sense that it is not clear or isn't right or is difficult to change, they say it "stinks" and they change it. One person picks a section of smelly code and over lunch, they refactor. To me this was a huge departure from the days of big unmanageable legacy code. Remember Y2K? There were legacy systems that people were afraid to change. The systems were so unmanageable that no one was sure whether a date change would crash them. We can now embrace change. We have the tools and the desire to keep the code maintainable. We can study the code and "smell" it and maintain our understanding of it. We even have the confidence to make changes just so that the code can improve. A favorite quote from the developers at HP was "We never spend a whole day fixing a bug. We almost always know how to fix it as soon as we hear about it. If not, it almost always takes less than an hour." By holding refactoring lunches, they invest in the maintainability of their code as well as the shared group understanding of it. How is that different from code reviews? No one is in the position of defending what they did and why. It is more of a team effort, working together with the common goal of making improvements where possible.

13 Our First Release to the Class

On November 3, we presented our first release to the students in the class. It had all four of the minimum first release features, and one of our desired features (an application using the framework so that the students did not have to write their own application.) In class on November 24, we presented linking of visualizations. At this point, we had all four required first release features and two of the nine desired features. At each point of our development, we discussed what could be done on time and what could wait; this was the most that we could complete given the limited amount of time. There is still much that could be added to the software, but its scope, quality and time were such that the students in the class were able to use it for their projects.

14 Conclusions

In our design discussions at the beginning of the project, much time was spent discussing features such as undo/redo and session management. Had we used traditional waterfall development, we would have tried to think of everything during the design phase and the undo/redo and session management would have been an integral part of the design. Perhaps during the scheduling phase we would have seen that including it would have led to a later release, too late to use in this semester's class. But, we wouldn't have been able to do the scheduling until we had done some design, so we would have at least invested that much more time in it, including the increased amount of design complexity. Would the session management feature have ended up on the cutting room floor, or would we have guessed wrong that we could get it in this semester? If we had been off in our estimation, it would have resulted in a failure to release this semester. Since we used XP, we did just-in-time design [2]; we got in our highest priority features first and were able to have a limited scope, first release more quickly. "We are not content to imagine that everything that you can think of will be done by a given date. Neither should you be. Instead, the XP process lets the team predict, more and more accurately, how much work can be done in any given time period. Using this information, you manage project scope – choosing what to do now and what to defer until later – to ensure successful delivery." [4]

An aspect of waterfall method that we find riskier is that you may have a false sense of the current state of the project with respect to the schedule, since the integration and debugging phases are the most difficult to predict. In XP, we have frequent releases, so our integration and debugging issues are resolved early and often.

It is very tempting to check in code that has not been paired. It happened in this project. One developer commented that she didn't think that XP led to a faster release. It may feel slower, but one study [3] showed that pair programming was 14% slower than individual programming, but resulted in higher quality and fewer bugs. This study is interesting, because you would expect pair programming to be 100% slower since there are 100% more programmers per task. The knowledge sharing does speed things up and code development is faster as one becomes more knowledgeable. This study was a short term study, so perhaps on a large scale project where bug fixing and integration take much more time (more than 2/3s of the total time?) the net result may be that pair programming results in fewer bugs and fewer integration issues and thus less time. Pair programming may result in more time in the development phase but much less time in solving the less predictable integration and debugging phases.

The aspect of Extreme Programming that was most valuable to us was that pair programming was a great way to learn. We were able to generate code quickly while learning and sharing knowledge. As we learn more, we can work faster. Our tools and our unit tests give us confidence in the code, which is applicable in any environment. We had a sense of teamwork and were able to distribute work as needed which is important in our distracting environment. The development was able to continue even in the occasional absence of some of the developers and will be able to continue after graduation. The lesson to work some of the time independently researching the tasks and some in pairs writing the software, made a big difference in the effectiveness of pairing. Just-in-time design gave us a simple, easily understood design to begin with and made the difference in our ability to reach our initial release date goal. Our final release was not perfect, but we were able to prioritize time, cost, quality and scope to meet the goals of our project as we progressed.

Pair programming is not new in academia. Most faculty participating in large research projects did program in groups (second author: and it was fun). The growth of software engineering practices and the complexity of the software life cycle (beginning with the OS 360) have led to more tools, planning, design, management, and individual programming and especially individual accountability. Extreme programming is offering a more formal way to get back to those early and successful days of prototyping and developing software.

Acknowledgements

Many thanks to Kevin Yu and Asim Jalis at Hewlett Packard for their generous sharing of their Extreme Programming expertise. Thanks to Alex Gee, Howie Goodell, Hongli Li, Min Yu, Urska Cvek and the rest of the software development team.

Biographies of Authors

Mary Beth Smrtic is a graduate student studying Biomedical Engineering and Biotechnology with a Bioinformatics specialty. She is a research assistant in the Institute for Visualization and Perception Research lab in the Computer Science department at the University of Massachusetts in Lowell, Massachusetts. Her research interests include emergent properties of complex systems, scale-free networks and interactive visual data mining, particularly of biochemical pathways and gene expression data. She has a bachelor's degree in Computer Science from the State University of New York in Potsdam, New York. She has 15 years of experience as a professional software engineer. Her experience includes software development at a small pharmaceutical company, a very large software development company, a semiconductor manufacturing company and several software development startups.

Georges Grinstein is Professor of Computer Science at the University of Massachusetts Lowell, Director of its Institute for Visualization and Perception Research, and of its Center for Biomolecular and Medical Informatics. His research interests are broad and include computer graphics, visualization, data mining, virtual environments, and user interfaces with the emphasis on the modeling, visualization, and analysis of complex information systems, most often biomedical in nature. He received his Ph.D. in Mathematics from the University of Rochester in 1978.

He has over 30 years in academia with extensive private consulting, over 100 research grants, products in use nationally and internationally, several patents, numerous publications in journals and conferences, and has been the organizer or chair of national and international conferences and workshops in Computer Graphics, in Visualization, and in Data Mining (co-chair IEEE Visualization Conferences, program committee AAAI conferences in Knowledge Discovery and Databases, co-chair IEEE Workshops on the Integration of Databases and Visualization, co-chair IEEE and AAAI Workshops on the Integration of Data Mining and Visualization, co-chair ACM workshop on the Psychological and Cognitive Issues in the Visualization of Data, and co-chair SPIE Visual Data and Exploration and Analysis Conferences.)

He is on the editorial boards of several journals in Computer Graphics and Data Mining, has been a member of ANSI and ISO, a NATO Expert, and a technology consultant for various government agencies.

References

1. Tufte, E.: The Visual Display of Quantitative Information, Graphics Press (1992)
2. Beck, K.: Extreme Programming Explained. Addison-Wesley (2000)
3. Williams, L., Upchurch R.: In support of student pair-programming. In Proceedings of the thirty-second SIGCSE technical symposium on Computer Science Education. (2001)
4. Jefferies, R., Extreme Programming Installed, Addison-Wesley (2000)

Workshops: Research Close to the Action

Dave Astels[1] and Grigori Melnik[2]

[1] ThoughtWorks, Inc., Chicago, Illinois, USA
david@thoughtworks.com
[2] University of Calgary, Calgary, Alberta, Canada
melnik@cpsc.ucalgary.ca

Every year agile methods get closer to the mainstream. One of the signs of this growing maturity is the popularity of agile conferences and workshops. In particular,
workshops are considered by many as important forums to engage both researchers
and practitioners in interactive, face-to-face discussions that advance the state of agile
software development methods and practices and to coordinate future research directions. This linkage between the worlds of practice and research is not new – XP/Agile
Universe has always had workshops in its program. This year, with the greatest number of workshops at XP/Agile Universe and European XP conferences ever (8), it
seems that we have reached out to the widest range of communities yet: managers and
coaches, empiricists and economists, embedded software developers and UI designers, testers and technical writers.

The Program Committee received fifteen (15) workshop proposals, each of which
was thoroughly reviewed by at least three members and further discussed at the general acceptance meeting. Eight (8) workshops were selected based on their topic significance, merit, potential to attract attendees, and organizers' experience. All selected
workshops were facilitated by industry and research experts and drew considerable
interest and participation from conference attendees. In addition to the workshops that
have become traditional (*The Data Workshop, How to Maintain and Promote Healthy
Agile Culture*, and *Agile Development for Embedded Software Series*), several new
initiatives were launched. In particular, organizational considerations for using agile
methods and their benefits from a managerial perspective were debated in the *Getting
Leaders on Board* workshop. The community embraced the workshops on *Who
Should Write Acceptance Tests* and *Agile Tests as Documentation* which explored the
balance between the customer, the developer, and the tester in authoring acceptance
tests and leveraging tests as useful documentation. Fresh perspectives on user interface design and agile methods were given at the *UI Design as Part of an Agile Process* workshop. The *Refactoring Our Writings* initiative brought together authors to
decide on how various pieces of literature on important subjects can be consolidated
and improved.

Overall, XP/Agile Universe workshops examined a multitude of comprehensive issues and contributed to the emerging maturity of agile methods. On behalf the Program Committee, we would like to thank workshop facilitators (Carsten Behring,
Khaled El Emam, David Hussman, James Grenning, Joshua Kerievsky, Jonathan
Kohl, Mike Kuniavsky, Brian Marick, Grigori Melnik, Rick Mugridge, Johan Peeters,
William Pietri, Pollyanna Pixton, Mary Poppendieck, and Christian Sepulveda) and
all participants for their outstanding effort, energy and spirit.

C. Zannier et al. (Eds.): XP/Agile Universe 2004, LNCS 3134, p. 183, 2004.
© Springer-Verlag Berlin Heidelberg 2004

Who Should Write Acceptance Tests?

Christian Sepulveda[1], Brian Marick[2], Rick Mugridge[3], and David Hussman[4]

[1] Covexus, San Francisco, CA USA
cs@covexus.com
[2] Testing Foundations, USA
marick@testing.com
[3] University of Auckland, Auckland, New Zealand
r.mugridge@auckland.ac.nz
[4] SGF Software Co., 3010 Hennepin Ave South,Minneapolis, Minnesota 55408-2614, USA
david.hussman@sgfco.com

1 Workshop Overview

Within Extreme Programming, the customer provides acceptance tests and the developers implement the system such that it satisfies the acceptance tests. There are frameworks such as FIT that are intended to empower the customer to write and execute acceptance tests. How effective is this in practice? When and why?

Though few would dispute the customer must be involved in creating acceptance tests, should this solely be the customer's responsibility? Perhaps there are examples that the customer omitted, which once discovered by a developer, are invaluable. Therefore, shouldn't developers be encouraged to also write acceptance tests? If so, why not include testers on XP projects; they are skilled in designing tests.

We aren't trying to change XP. But testers are being integrated into many XP projects and since acceptance tests are a significant driving force in XP, the manner in which testers contribute to acceptance tests should be considered.

For the inexperienced XP customer, it can be hard to define acceptance tests. It would help many actual projects to explore guidelines to support the customer in this important activity.

2 Workshop Goals

This workshop explored the balance between the customer, the developer and the tester in authoring acceptance tests.

Specifically we discussed:

- Project examples where only the customer wrote the acceptance tests, stories where developers contributed and experiences where testers were involved
- Examples and ideas for the collaboration process among the customer, developer and tester in envisioning, defining and implementing acceptance tests
- Examples and suggestions of educating the customer regarding acceptance testing
- Limitations and risks of each role in the authoring of acceptance tests
- Guidelines and contextual factors that influence the balance among the roles for acceptance testing

C. Zannier et al. (Eds.): XP/Agile Universe 2004, LNCS 3134, pp. 184–185, 2004.
© Springer-Verlag Berlin Heidelberg 2004

3 Workshop Organizers

Christian Sepulveda was co-founder of the GaiaCom Corporation, a New York based consulting and outsourcing software development firm. He's been an independent consultant for the last four years, focusing on mentoring and leading software teams. He's worked in a diverse set of industries, from finance to fashion, on both commercial shrink-wrapped software and internal IT applications. He is a Certified Scrum Master and Extreme Programming coach that has led over thirty successful projects.

Brian Marick has been a programmer, team lead, and tester since 1981 and an independent consultant since 1992. He was one of the authors of the Manifesto for Agile Software Development, is the current vice-chair of the board of the Agile Alliance, and is an editor for Better Software magazine. His evolving approach to agile testing emphasizes using tests as examples that provoke programmers into writing the right code, a close cooperation between the overlapping roles of Tester and Programmer, and exploiting the similarities between exploratory testing and agile design.

David Hussman is co-owner of SGF Software, a U.S. based company that promotes and practices agile development. Motivated to see IT folks succeed and smile, He has evangelized agile practices as a developer, coach, customer, and manager for 4 years. He has participated and presented at agile conferences as well as contributing to the Cutter Consortium Agile Project Advisory Service and similar publications.

Rick Mugridge is in the Department of Computer Science at the University of Auckland, New Zealand. He teaches XP and TDD practices and runs XP projects. He is a regular consultant to the local software industry and is currently completing a book on FIT with Ward Cunningham.

Getting Leaders On-Board

Pollyanna Pixton[1] and Mary Poppendieck[2]

[1] Evolutionary Systems, 1115 South 900 East, Salt Lake City, Utah 84105, USA
ppixton@evolutionarysystems.com
http://evolutionarysystems.net
[2] Poppendieck.LLC, 7666 Carnelian Lane, Eden Prairie, MN 55346, USA
mary@poppendieck.com
http://www.poppendieck.com

Abstract. How can we convince managers, leaders and decision makers to use agile? This question has been asked again and again, by developers, team leads, and project managers. Together, in this interactive workshop, we discussed organizational considerations for using agile methods as well as evaluated the benefits they bring from a management perspective.

1 Summary

The first question on the table was: "How can we convince managers, leaders and decision makers to use agile?" This question has been asked again and again, by developers, team leads, and project managers. The group discussed organizational considerations for using agile methods and evaluated the benefits they bring from a management perspective.

The second question was: "Once the decision is made, what do managers, leaders and decision makers need as they begin to use agile in their organizations?"

This half-day interactive workshop first addressed how to decide if agile will provide sufficient business value and then discussed each phase of bringing agile on board and what leaders can do to assist the transition and support the agile users. Communication techniques between users and leaders, what process indicators to look for and which ones to discard, and how to understand what role leadership plays in providing agile users what they need for success are some of the topics that were covered.

2 Inside the Workshop

At the beginning of this half-day workshop, each participant was asked to make a statement about their ideas on the subject and lead a discussion around the point of view they presented. Next came a brainstorming session on how agile methods differ from traditional development methods. After this, the group discussed how corporate leaders assess and evaluate methods within their companies, the assessment criteria they use, and ways to frame how these criteria can be met in agile terms.

The group identified what the developers need from leaders when using agile for various agile methods, and how to frame the needs from leaders so they can hear them, depending on how corporate leaders assess and evaluate success within their companies.

C. Zannier et al. (Eds.): XP/Agile Universe 2004, LNCS 3134, pp. 186–187, 2004.
© Springer-Verlag Berlin Heidelberg 2004

The group identified where leadership may become uncomfortable in the process of adapting agile and how to assist them in supporting the development team. Finally, the group discussed how teams might begin to use agile without direct permission from leaders and managers.

3 Results

Results of the workshop are posted at:
http://www.evolutionarysystems.net/xp2004.html.

4 Workshop Organizers

Pollyanna Pixton has been consulting with businesses in the implementation and deployment of strategies and concepts that improve their organization since she founded Evolutionary Systems in 1996. She views a business as a system, sees the 'big picture' and analyzes how, why and where the company can be strengthened to improve productivity, increase efficiency, expand profitability and reach key corporate goals.

She brings 30 years of global executive and managerial experience for business and information technology ventures. She built the Swiss Electronic Stock Exchange, developed control systems for electrical power plants throughout the world, and converted technologies for merging financial institutions. Her background includes e-commerce, real-time applications, positioning systems, and computational research.

Ms Pixton's education includes a Master's degree in Computer Science, three years of graduate studies in Theoretical Physics and a Bachelor's degree in Mathematics. She serves on the 2004 Agile Development Conference Organizing Committee and as a guest lecturer at the university level, she discusses ethics in business, organizational development and leadership.

Mary Poppendieck is a Senior Consultant with Cutter Consortium's Agile Software Development and Project Management Practice. She has been in the information technology industry for 25 years. She has managed solutions for companies in several disciplines, including supply chain management, manufacturing systems, and digital media. As a seasoned leader in both operations and new product development, she provides a business perspective to software development problems. Lean development is just one of Poppendieck's areas of expertise. She first encountered the Toyota Production System, which later became known as Lean Production, as Information Systems Manager in a video tape manufacturing plant.

She implemented one of the first just-in-time systems in 3M, resulting in dramatic improvements in the plant's performance. Poppendieck's team leadership skills are legendary at 3M, where new product development is a core competency. One team commercialized a graphics interface controller three times faster than normal. Another team not only developed an image database system in partnership with a start-up company, but also set a new international standard for image formats. Poppendieck, a popular writer and speaker, is the author of Lean Software Development: An Agile Toolkit and Managing Director of AgileAlliance.

Third International Workshop on Empirical Evaluation of Agile Methods ("The Data Workshop")

Grigori Melnik[1] and Khaled El Emam[2]

[1] Department of Computer Science, University of Calgary
2500 University Dr. N.W., Calgary, Alberta, T2N 1N4, Canada
melnik@cpsc.ucalgary.ca
[2] National Research Council, Institute for Information Technology
M-50, Montreal Rd., Ottawa, Ontario, K1A 0R6, Canada
khaled.el-emam@nrc-cnrc.gc.ca

Abstract. The workshop brought together academics and industry practitioners to share the results of ongoing empirical research in agile software methods and to discuss the needs and prospects of future studies. It encouraged further cooperation with a view to promoting better-informed decision making.

1 Workshop Overview

This workshop builds on the success of the two previous workshops on empirical evaluation of agile methods at XP/Agile Universe conferences in 2002 and 2003. As compared to the last two years, agile methods are increasingly closer to the mainstream. However, the chasm between early successes of agile visionaries and the mainstream acceptance still exists. What is needed to cross this chasm? More organizations require support and better understanding of how agile methods affect the people, the flow and the value they deliver. This understanding must be based not only on anecdotes, hearsay or war stories but objective studies and detailed analyses.

Continuing with the last year's theme of the business value delivered by agile teams, the goals of this year workshop were:

1. to explore, through measurement, the indicators of business value;
2. to assess the achievement of quality goals of agile software development projects;
3. to determine the sweet spots – the situations when applying agile methods would be beneficial;
4. to provide input for software engineering decision support about specific aspects of agile methods and underlying practices.

Researchers and practitioners came together to discuss the current state of ongoing empirical research in agile methods: common problems, challenges, possible solutions and the options for synthesizing and disseminating the empirical results.

2 Issues

The following thematic questions were addressed:

- What key areas/aspects of agile methods should be studied empirically?
- How to measure business value delivered per unit time?

C. Zannier et al. (Eds.): XP/Agile Universe 2004, LNCS 3134, pp. 188–189, 2004.
© Springer-Verlag Berlin Heidelberg 2004

- What existing software measures and processes satisfy our data requirements?
- What kinds of experiments are necessary?
- How to obtain realistic results (students vs. developers as subjects)?
- How one remains agile while collecting data?
- Who will use the measurement results? For what purpose?

The participants discussed an initiative to create an empirical experience base of agile projects which will include both successes and failures. They provided some initial ideas on which project attributes may be useful to collect.

3 Results

Additional information, post-workshop discussions, and information about the past and future workshops are available online at: http://sern.ucalgary.ca/EEAP.

4 Workshop Organizers

Grigori Melnik is an Instructor at the University of Calgary and a Lead Instructor at the Southern Alberta Institute of Technology (SAIT) responsible for curriculum development and delivery of several key senior software engineering disciplines. Grigori is a Ph.D. candidate with the Department of Computer Science of University of Calgary. His primary research area is empirical evaluation of capability of agile methods. Other areas include e-business software development, distributed software engineering, design patterns and e-learning. Grigori has also been involved in developing Web-based enterprise systems. More recently he's served as a founding co-moderator of Calgary Agile Methods User Group (CAMUG) and a coordinator of The Canadian Agile Network (CAN) – Le Réseau Agile Canadien (RAC).

Khaled El Emam is a Senior Research Officer at the National Research Council where he is the technical lead of the Software Quality Laboratory. In another capacity, he is a Senior Consultant with Cutter Consortium's Agile Software Development & Project Management Practice and Risk Management Intelligence Network. Dr. El Emam has been involved with software quality for more than a decade, performing advanced research and consulting, and holds a number of positions in research and industry. He is a visiting professor at the Center for Global eHealth Innovation at the University of Toronto (University Health Network).

How to Maintain and Promote Healthy Agile Culture

David Hussman

SGF Software Co., 3010 Hennepin Ave South
Minneapolis, Minnesota 55408-2614
david.hussman@sgfco.com

Abstract. Though agile development often works well initially, maintaining and nurturing a healthy culture is key to the success of any agile project. As a project's culture is affected by many forces, this challenge is often quite difficult. Varying skills sets, egos, schedules, and external project dependencies are just a few issues that must be addressed by those trying to promote or maintain the cultural health of an agile project. The intent of this workshop was to use shared experiences to create a list of tools and tactics useful in managing culture on agile projects.

1 Intended Audience

The ideal candidate had lead or helped lead one or more agile projects. Candidates needed experience to write a short position paper which described their experience helping to keep an agile project healthy. Candidates were expected to be interested in sharing and learning about finding cultural smells that affected project cultures and solutions / tools that helped address the issues. Workshop attendees were asked to call out that which worked as well as that which did not work on agile projects.

1.1 Benefits for Attendance

Workshop participants had the chance to share and discuss successes and struggles as well as issues which may not have been covered by the current body of agile writings. Through discussion in large and small group discussions, the participants were to find a set of common approaches to nurturing agile culture that had been successful for more than on project, company or culture.

2 Workshop Overview

Workshop participants created a collection of cultural smells they had encountered and captured this information on posters in a story like format. Small and large group discussion of how these issues affected a project's culture as well as solutions that addressed the issues consumed a large portion of the workshop. In an effort to learn from past mistakes, the group discussed solutions that failed, and why. To further the importance of culture, as it relates to the communal nature of agile practices, the workshop tried to create some tangible output that could be used in the trenches by agile project leaders and project members.

C. Zannier et al. (Eds.): XP/Agile Universe 2004, LNCS 3134, pp. 190–191, 2004.
© Springer-Verlag Berlin Heidelberg 2004

2.1 Goals

1. Create a collection of cultural smells associated with agile projects and teams.
2. Drive out which issues have the least amount of coverage in the agile writings (as known to the participants).
3. Create simple discussion vehicles that represent the participant's experiences, which can be shared with the agile community.
4. Further the importance of culture and the way in which it relates to the success of agile projects (and the growth and adoption of agile practices).

2.2 Workshop Format

Pre Workshop. All participants read each others position papers and created a list of potential cultural smells.

First Half. Workshop participants discussed cultural smells and created a prioritized list of story titles for small group discussion. Each participant signed up for a story and took this story out into small group discussions where more detail was added to each story.

Second Half. More story detail was added as story owners took their story into a different small group discussion. Entire workshop regrouped and story owners presented their story to the group, adding or modifying the story content as per the large group discussion.

Post Workshop. The stories created during the workshop were posted somewhere at the conference. The workshop organizers created some publishable document which was posted on the workshop website and possibly published.

3 Workshop Organizers

David Hussman. A software geek for 10 years, David has developed in the following fields: medical, digital audio, digital biometrics, retail, and educational. Somewhere along the way, David moved toward an odd way of defining, communicating, and developing software. When someone organized a better version and started calling it XP / Agile, he felt right at home. Motivated to see IT folks succeed and smile, David has evangelized XP by working as developer, coach, customer, and manager on XP projects for 3.5 years. When David is not coaching, he is traveling with his family as often as possible.

Rick Mugridge. Rick Mugridge is in the Department of Computer Science at the University of Auckland, New Zeeland. He teaches XP and TDD practices and runs XP projects. He is a regular consultant to the local software industry and is currently completing a book on FIT with Ward Cunningham. Contact information: r.mugridge@auckland.ac.nz

UI Design as Part of an Agile Process

Mike Kuniavsky[1] and William Pietri[2]

[1] Adaptive Path, San Francisco, California, USA
mikek@adaptivepath.com
[2] Scissor, San Francisco, California, USA
william@scissor.com

Abstract. The workshop brought UI designers and agile developers together to discuss issues and share experiences in order to understand how agile development and UI design, both iterative processes, can work together. As part of the workshop the UI for a sample project was designed.

1 The Need

There has always been some tension between user interface designers and programmers. Whether it's caused by cultural differences (pony tails vs. black turtlenecks) or differences in procedure, comfortably working together has been difficult. It's a gulf that has created a lot of bad software and bad UIs.

This does not have to be. Good user interface design is not a linear process. As an iterative process, it consists of repeated cycles of investigation into people's abilities, expectations and needs coupled with the creation of designs. This can work well as part of an agile development process, but few teams have tried it, so it's still relatively unknown among both the designers and the coders.

2 Workshop Goals

To remedy this, this half-day workshop brought UI designers and agile developers together to discuss issues and share experiences. To focus and stimulate the discussion, most of the time was devoted to iteratively designing a user interface for a sample project, chorewheel.com. The goal was not only to produce something that would work from a technical standpoint and have a good user experience, but – more importantly – to use it as an opportunity to rapidly develop the processes by which designers and programmers can communicate and collaborate.

3 Workshop Organizers

Mike Kuniavsky is a founding partner of Adaptive Path, a San Francisco-based user experience consulting company. He is the author of "Observing the User Experience: A Practitioner's Guide to User Research" (ISBN: 1558609237) and has been designing

C. Zannier et al. (Eds.): XP/Agile Universe 2004, LNCS 3134, pp. 192–193, 2004.

user interfaces for commercial software and Web products since 1991. His clients include Wired Digital, National Public Radio, Crayola, CTB/McGraw-Hill, Scient, PacBell, Overture Services, Sony and id Software.

William Pietri is a consultant, author, and software developer. He has both used and consulted on agile development methods since 2000. His clients range from large organizations, including Bank of America, eBay, and the State of Michigan, to small internet startups, including Bianca.com, 4Charity.com, and Shopping.com.

Agile Development for Embedded Software

James Grenning[1], Johan Peeters[2], and Carsten Behring[3]

[1] Object Mentor, Inc, 501 North Riverside, Suite 206, Gurnee, IL 60031, USA
grenning@objectmentor.com
[2] Predikherenberg 35, 3010 Leuven, Belgium
yo@johanpeeters.com
[3] Am Jungbrunnen 13, 444369 Dortmund, Germany
carsten@carstenbehring.com

Abstract. This workshop brought together developers, managers and customers with experience in embedded software that had used traditional or agile approaches for specifying, testing and developing embedded software. The participants have discussed challenges that must be addressed by agile methods so they can be effectively applied in embedded software development teams.

1 Summary

Embedded software development suffers from many of the same problems of traditional non-embedded software. In addition embedded software has other difficulties and complexities over traditional software development, such as limited resources, critical timing constraints, late integration with target hardware and separate environments for development and target execution. This workshop brought together developers, managers and customers with experience in embedded software that have used traditional or agile approaches for specifying, testing and developing embedded software. Participants gained both insight into current best practices and an understanding of how the craft can be improved.

2 Goals

- Share experience and best practices used in the development of embedded software;
- Identify embedded development issues and agile approaches to dealing with those issues;
- Share experience in practices that have low overhead and contribute to successful product delivery.

3 Content Outline

Discussion topics included:

- Planning techniques
- Variable scope control
- Simulation and test

C. Zannier et al. (Eds.): XP/Agile Universe 2004, LNCS 3134, pp. 194–195, 2004.
© Springer-Verlag Berlin Heidelberg 2004

- Test driven development
- Hardware independence
- Testing for performance
- Testing for load
- On-target testing
- Off-target testing
- Concurrency patterns
- Evolutionary design
- Managing resource constraints
- Safety critical systems requirements
- Progress before hardware
- Large teams
- Small teams
- Distributed teams
- Building strategies
- Minimizing the deployment effort
- Continuous integration

4 Workshop Organizers

James Grenning is the Director of Consulting at Object Mentor, Inc. He has been professionally developing software since 1978. His is experienced in embedded and non-embedded software development, management, consulting, mentoring and training. He is currently practicing and coaching Agile software development techniques, Extreme Programming, Object Oriented Design and Programming.

Johan Peeters is an independent software architect whose main current interest is pervasive computing. He serves both large companies such as Philips and Banksys as well as small startups. In the past few years he has worked on remote controls, payment terminals, vehicle telematics and home automation.

Carsten Behring is an independent software developer who relies on agile development techniques. He has worked on several projects for major clients like Philips and Atos Origin and also for startup companies. He has a solid background in Java server technologies such as J2EE. He incorporates agile practices to facilitate his projects.

Refactoring Our Writings

Joshua Kerievsky

Industrial Logic, Inc., 2583 Cedar, Berkeley, CA, 94708-1931, USA
joshua@industriallogic.com

Abstract. Getting folks writing papers about useful information is good. However, a forest of ideas, with no organization, is bad. We would like authors and groups of authors to come together to refactor older, related papers into new, consolidated pieces of literature that communicate comprehensive ideas on an important subject. In this workshop, we began identifying agile community's most important subjects and which papers could be merged and refactored to produce excellent new pieces of literature for each subject.

1 Audience

Everyone involved with or interested in writing, teaching and learning.

2 Content

The standard "Call for Papers" that gets announced before each of the XP/Agile conferences is good. It gets folks writing papers about useful information – techniques that have worked well, experience using a process, etc. It is nice to see people from around the world contributing such papers to the various XP/Agile conferences.

However, we are now seeing something that often occurs in communities like ours: a continuous stream of conference papers, with no refactoring of the literature. This is bad. It leads to a forest of ideas, with no organization and little practical value to a broad community that has not yet joined the XP/Agile community. I would like to see authors and groups of authors come together to refactor older, related papers into new, consolidated pieces of literature that communicate comprehensive ideas on an important subject.

We need to encourage ourselves to refactor what we've written in order to produce excellent new pieces of literature.

3 Goals

- Help produce consolidated pieces of literature on important subject
- Stem the tide of duplication in our writings
- Improve on the important ideas that may now be a bit dated

C. Zannier et al. (Eds.): XP/Agile Universe 2004, LNCS 3134, pp. 196–197, 2004.
© Springer-Verlag Berlin Heidelberg 2004

4 Workshop Organizer

Joshua Kerievsky is the founder of Industrial Logic, a company that specializes in Extreme Programming. He began his career as a professional programmer at a Wall Street bank, where he programmed numerous financial systems for credit, market, and global risk departments. After a decade at the bank, he founded Industrial Logic in 1995 to help companies practice successful software development. Kerievsky has programmed and coached on small, large, and distributed XP projects since XP's emergence. He recently pioneered Industrial XP, an application of XP tailored for large organizations. Kerievsky is presently completing a book entitled Refactoring to Patterns. He can be reached at joshua@industriallogic.com.

Agile Tests as Documentation

Jonathan Kohl[1] and Brian Marick[2]

[1] Kohl Consulting Services Calgary, Canada
jonathan@kohl.ca
[2] Testing Foundations, USA
marick@testing.com

Abstract. Agile processes tend to minimize documentation. As the Agile Manifesto states, working software is preferred over comprehensive documentation. In the course of developing working software, tests are natural byproducts. What useful project documentation is already captured in these tests, and how do we leverage it? The concept of tests as documentation has been under-discussed in the community, and this workshop has attempted to facilitate that discussion.

1 Workshop Summary

It is increasingly popular to consider tests as documentation. For example, if you want to know how to use an API, you can look at its tests. If you're curious about the details of what a product feature does, you can look at its tests. But how well do tests work as documentation? Furthermore, what are the tricks of the trade? How do you make tests better documentation? What are good examples to study? We proposed to study actual tests (those developed by testers, customer tests and programmer tests).

The goals of this workshop were to identify the strengths and weaknesses of the documentation in the tests and to facilitate discussion on what tests worked well as project documentation and why. Through discussion, we attempted to answer some of these questions: How are tests like requirements, and how are they different? How can tests capture or transmit the tacit knowledge of project experts? How can tests aid the project conversation? How are they used differently by people on the project and by the people who come after?

From the answers to these questions, we suggested areas that need further study in the community and encouraged research and paper publication in related topics.

2 Workshop Organizers

Jonathan Kohl develops and applies Agile techniques on live testing projects, focusing on workable, effective techniques for tester and developer collaboration. His experience in test development spans business(acceptance), tester (manual and automated), and developer (automated unit) tests. He is a software quality professional at WestJet Airlines, and has recently published an article in Better Software magazine on Pair Testing with developers.

C. Zannier et al. (Eds.): XP/Agile Universe 2004, LNCS 3134, pp. 198–199, 2004.
© Springer-Verlag Berlin Heidelberg 2004

Brian Marick consults on Agile Testing. He was one of the authors of the Manifesto for Agile Software Development and is vice-chair of the Agile Alliance board. His experience moderating or co-moderating workshops includes a series of test patterns workshops http://www.testing.com/test-patterns/index.html, a highly successful workshop on acceptance testing at XP/Agile Universe 2002 http://www.pettichord.com/agile_workshop.html, OOPSLA workshops on software archeology http://www.visibleworkings.com/archeology/ and constructing software to outlive its creators http://visibleworkings.com/built-for-life/, and the recent University of Illinois Master of Fine Arts in Software trial run http://wiki.cs.uiuc.edu/MFA.

Fit Fest

Robert C. Martin and Micah Martin

ObjectMentor
{unclebob,micah}@objectmentor.com

1 Workshop Summary

Fit Fest 2003 was a blast. Dozens of developers participated in the development and testing of the unique SDPS project. Tests were specified, code was developed, some tests passed, and some tests failed.

Some tests failed? Yeah, but that's ok because we got to code and work with a large variety of bright people who all share the same passion.

Fit Fest 2004 should prove even more fun. Be sure to stop by. Plug your laptop in, grab a pair, and join the team.

The goals of the workshop are to have fun an learn from each other about, among other things, Acceptance Testing. Fit Fest will be held most of the week.

2 Workshop Organizers

Robert C. Martin has been a software professional since 1970. He is CEO, president, and founder of Object Mentor Inc., a firm of highly experienced software professionals that offers process improvement consulting, object-oriented software design consulting, training, and development services to major corporations around the world.

Micah Martin is a software developer from Object Mentor who has been practicing Extreme Programming since 1999. He has been involved in a variety of XP projects and teaches a range of public courses from Object Oriented Design to Extreme Programming. As lead developer of the FitNesse testing tool, it is his goal to help make Acceptance Testing a more attainable goal for the industry.

C. Zannier et al. (Eds.): XP/Agile Universe 2004, LNCS 3134, p. 200, 2004.
© Springer-Verlag Berlin Heidelberg 2004

Agile Project Management

Moderator:

Frank Maurer

University of Calgary
maurer@cpsc.ucalgary.ca

Panelists:

Mike Cohn[1], Mike Griffiths[2], Jim Highsmith[3],
Ken Schwaber[4], and Philippe Kruchten[5]

[1] Fast401k
mike.cohn@computer.org
[2] Quadrus
mikeg@quadrus.com
[3] Cutter Consortium
jim@jimhighsmith.com
[4] ADM
ken.schwaber@verizon.net
[5] University of British Columbia
kruchten@ieee.org

Abstract. Introducing agile practices into software organizations impacts how projects are planned, coordinated and tracked. In this panel, we discussed commonalities and differences between agile project management and more traditional ideas. Topics discussed included:

- What works, what doesn't in an agile context?
- What kind of company culture is required for agile project management to flourish?
- How can we transition to an agile approach?
- What obstacles will be encountered?
- How can they be overcome?
- When are more traditional approaches more appropriate?

C. Zannier et al. (Eds.): XP/Agile Universe 2004, LNCS 3134, p. 201, 2004.
© Springer-Verlag Berlin Heidelberg 2004

Agile Methods for Safety-Critical Software Development

Moderator:

Kelly Weyrauch

Medtronic, Inc.
kelly.weyrauch@medtronic.com

Panelists:

Mary Poppendieck[1], Ron Morsicato[2], Nancy Van Schooenderwoert[2], and Bill Pyritz[3]

[1] Poppendieck, LLC
mary@poppendieck.com
[2] XP-Embedded
{ronm,nancyv}@xp-embedded.com
[3] Lucent Technologies
pyritz@lucent.com

Abstract. What might have been a question of *whether* agile methods can be used in the safety-critical world is now becoming a question of *how* agile methods can be used in the safety-critical world. This panel covered some of the myths, worries, solutions, and experiences of agile development of safety-critical software. Among others, this panel addressed the following questions:

- What benefits of agile methods apply to the safety-critical world?
- What barriers must be overcome?
- What changes or additions to agile methods are needed to make agile work?
- Are there concerns from regulatory agencies?

C. Zannier et al. (Eds.): XP/Agile Universe 2004, LNCS 3134, p. 202, 2004.
© Springer-Verlag Berlin Heidelberg 2004

Is XP Still Relevant?

Moderator:

Pete McBreen

Software Craftsmanship, Inc.
pete@mcbreen.ab.ca

Panelists:

Dave Astels[1], Janet Gregory[2], Daniel H. Steinberg[3], Lisa Crispin[4],
Jim Highsmith[5], and Robert C. Martin[6]

[1] Adaption Software
david@adaptionsoft.com
[2] Wireless-Matrix
janet_gregory@shaw.ca
[3] Editor-in-Chief, Java.Net
daniel@oreilly.com
[4] Fast401k, Inc.
lisa.crispin@att.net
[5] Jim Highsmith
jim@jimhighsmith.com
[6] ObjectMentor
unclebob@objectmentor.com

Abstract. First publicized in 1998 as the new methodology that developers actually liked using, the time has come to look deeper into the XP phenomenon. At the height of the dot-com craze, the hype surrounding XP was amazing, and to judge by the publicity, everyone wanted to use XP. Now in the post dotcom era, the time has now come to ask whether XP is still relevant.

Initially it seemed that XP was widely applicable, but that was before XP had any real competition. As soon as the Agile Alliance publicized the existence of alternate agile methods, many teams that were initially attracted to XP found more appropriate alternatives.

The overall effect of all of this has been that XP has ceased to be the centre of attention and as a result the number of projects adopting XP is arguably declining. So although many projects now adopt an agile approach, few new projects are choosing to adopt XP unless there is a strong, local development community that supports XP.

This panel addressed written questions from the floor. To start the discussion, appropriate questions were planted in the audience and additional questions were taken from there. Discussion started with these two questions:

- Now that Kent, Ron and Ward have had their moment of fame, is it time to move on?
- Do we need to develop XP 2.0?

C. Zannier et al. (Eds.): XP/Agile Universe 2004, LNCS 3134, p. 203, 2004.
© Springer-Verlag Berlin Heidelberg 2004

Introduction to Tutorials

Brian Button

Principal Consultant
Agile Solutions Group
St. Louis, MO

The tutorial program at Xp/Agile Universe is privileged to bring together experts and students in software project management, development, and methodologies. About 20 different tutorials were offered where students were able to interact directly with experts in their chosen fields.

This year's conference offered tutorials aimed at different skill and experience levels. The offerings were evenly split between introductory presentations, such as overviews of agile methods, and more expert tutorials focusing on technical, hands-on, coding topics. Attendance at the introductory tutorials has consistently high each year of this conference, and this year was no exception. This bodes well for agile acceptance, as these tutorials see new faces each year.

All activities and roles in a project lifecycle were represented well this year. We had several tutorials teaching how to gather initial requirements and turn them into viable, practical user stories, and turn these user stories into customer tests. For the first year, we had everal tutorials focused exclusively on effectively managing agile teams. DBAs and developers were offered many choices, including several opportunities to write code alongside their peers, and software testers had the opportunity to learn how to use different open-source frameworks to improve their ability to lead the development effort through their customer tests.

The tutorial program this year succeeded in bringing together acknowledged experts and willing students in an environment that allowed them to work together and share information. Both student and expert learned, which is the point of any tutorial.

C. Zannier et al. (Eds.): XP/Agile Universe 2004, LNCS 3134, p. 204, 2004.
© Springer-Verlag Berlin Heidelberg 2004

Agile Requirements: Tailoring the Functional Requirements Specification Process to Improve Agility

Jennitta Andrea and Gerard Meszaros

{jennitta,Gerard}@clrstream.com

1 Tutorial Overview

Consulting led a mixed group of industrial folk and people from academia on a lively half-day romp through the world of agile requirements techniques. The session was light on slide presentation and heavy on active participatory learning. The day started off with a group project where the participants got to experience first hand some of the frustrations of typical requirements gathering techniques. During the debrief that followed, the participants shared their feelings of frustration and how the experience resembled their work place. The debrief was followed by a half-hour presentation on six techniques that can be used to make the requirements process more agile. It concluded with some brainstorming on how the process could be made agile and responsive to change.

After a break for refreshments, the participants repeated the project applying many of the agility techniques. This was followed by another debrief where the participants bubbled with the exhilaration of being able to work in an environment that was both more productive and more fun yet required fewer resources. Once again, they shared their emotions and learnings with the rest of the group. Ideas about how to apply some of the techniques to the workplace were then discussed and participants made concrete action plans for what they would do to make their workplace more agile. Everyone left re-energized about work and eager to change their workplace.

2 Tutorial Organizers

Jennitta Andrea has been a senior consultant with ClearStream Consulting since 1994 and has been a practitioner of XP and Scrum on over ten projects. Jennitta's professional experience spans a variety of roles: agile process coach, requirements analyst, developer, customer quality advocate, instructor, and retrospective facilitator. Jennitta has published and presented at a variety of venues, with an emphasis on process adaptation and automated acceptance testing (see www.agilecanada.com/wiki/Wiki.jsp?page=JennittaAndrea). Jennitta is an industrial trainer (2-day Automated Testing course; 3-day Agile Requirements course/workshop), and delivers simulation-based conference tutorials (Agile Re-quirements; Facilitating Effective Project Retrospectives).

Gerard Meszaros is Chief Scientist at ClearStream Consulting, where he leads teams applying agile software development techniques (such as eXtreme Programming) to help ClearStream's clients achieve faster and higher quality application development. He has presented successful tutorials at the past four OOPSLAs and has presented papers on automated testing and developing object oriented software frameworks at past XP and OOPSLA conferences.

C. Zannier et al. (Eds.): XP/Agile Universe 2004, LNCS 3134, p. 205, 2004.

Advanced Fit Lab

Rick Mugridge

University of Auckland, New Zealand
r.mugridge@auckland.ac.nz

1 Introduction

Fit tables are for communicating what is needed from a system as well as for automatically testing that the system performs as expected. Test tables need to clearly express such intent. *Fit* is very general purpose and open-ended, easy to extend with custom fixtures for expressing different sorts of tests.

This advanced tutorial explored the use of *Fit* in software development in some depth. Attendees learned how to make better use of *Fit* in their software development. We covered advanced topics in *Fit*, including table design and the development of custom fixtures and runners.

2 Content Outline

We covered the following topics:

- Brief summary of the three families of fixtures (*calculate*, *action* and *list*; and the initial fixtures) and how *Fit* works.
- Managing interactions between fixtures.
- Managing suites of tests with *Fitnesse*.
- New general-purpose fixtures in the three families (CalculateFixture; StepFixture and DoFixture; SubsetFixture, ArrayFixture and EntryFixture).
- Testing user interfaces.
- *Fit* table design; orthogonality, redundancy, evolution.
- *Fit* tables and legacy systems.
- The architecture of *Fit*.
- Developing custom, general-purpose fixtures using Test Driven Development.
- Developing custom runners for handling other test data formats.
- Stress and other forms of testing.
- *Fit* for Programmer Tests and non-testing tasks.

There was some time for hand-on experimentation with *Fit*, as participants brought laptops.

3 Tutorial Organizer

Rick Mugridge is a co-author of a book on Fit with Ward Cunningham, Fit for Software Development, published by Addison-Wesley.

C. Zannier et al. (Eds.): XP/Agile Universe 2004, LNCS 3134, pp. 206–207, 2004.

Rick has worked in the software industry for many years, including in embedded systems. He has considerable experience with Fit, testing, test driven development and general agile techniques. He has been consulting to industry and teaching software engineering students in Fit, testing, XP and a range of other software areas. He presented eight papers on testing, test driven development and user interfaces at various conferences in 2003.

Effective User Stories

Mike Cohn

`mike.cohn@computer.org`

1 Tutorial Overview

The technique of capturing requirements as user stories is one of the most broadly applicable techniques introduced by Extreme Programming. User Stories are an effective approach on all time-constrained projects. In this tutorial we looked at how to identify and write user stories, how to be sure we're focused on our most important users' needs, how to estimate stories, how to use stories for release and iteration planning, and the role of stories in the ongoing management of the project.

Tutorial participants, who included programmers, testers, managers and even customers and analysts on agile projects::

- learned why user stories represent a better approach to requirements than use cases, IEEE 830, or scenarios;
- learned valuable tips for writing great user stories;
- practiced user role modeling and learned how it improves the use of user stories;
- improved their estimation skills and learned new techniques for the early estimation with stories; and,
- learned how to build a sufficiently accurate release plan even with preliminary story estimates.

2 Tutorial Organizer

Mike Cohn is the VP of Engineering for Fast401k, the leading provider of online 401(k) plans. Mike has over 20 years of experience in various facets of software development, particularly C++ and Java programming and project management. Mike is the author of User Stories Applied for Agile Software Development as well as four books on Java and C++ programming. Mike is a founding member of the Agile Alliance, serves on its Board of Directors and runs the Articles program. Mike is the author of numerous articles that have appeared in IEEE Computer, Software Test and Quality Engineering, Better Software, Agile Times, and C++ Users' Journal. Mike is a Certified ScrumMaster and a member of the IEEE Computer Society and the ACM.

C. Zannier et al. (Eds.): XP/Agile Universe 2004, LNCS 3134, p. 208, 2004.
© Springer-Verlag Berlin Heidelberg 2004

Outsourcing and Offshoring with Agility

Clifton Kussmaul

ckussmaul@elegancetech.com

1 Tutorial Overview

This tutorial discussed techniques for and lessons learned from using and adapting agile methodologies with distributed teams, specifically outsourced and offshore development teams. With such teams, we are likely to encounter organizational boundaries, language and cultural differences, and other communication challenges. This tutorial was based on successful projects involving such teams.

First, we discussed participants' backgrounds and key questions, and presented an overview of recurring themes. Second, we described key ideas and issues in outsourcing and offshoring, including different project types and methodologies. Third, we presented a case study in which agile techniques were used. Fourth, we discussed a set of lessons learned, and the tradeoffs that must be considered. We concluded with a discussion of recurring themes and future trends.

Participants learned how to decide when to use agile techniques with distributed teams, and how to manage such teams more effectively. We used presentations, discussion, and small group activities, and emphasized recurring themes and a series of checklists.

2 Tutorial Organizer

Clif Kussmaul is the CTO of Elegance Technologies, Inc., which develops software products and provides software product development services, including managing offshore development teams. He has worked with distributed teams on a variety of projects including program translation, ticket tracking, business operating systems, and B2B data exchange. Clif is also an Assistant Professor of CS at Muhlenberg College, where he delivers introductory courses through capstone projects to traditional and non-traditional students. Previously, he spent two years working with CMM-5 development centers at NeST Technologies. Clif has a PhD in CS from the University of California, Davis, and is the author or co-author of over thirty publications and conference presentations. Please contact Clif at ckussmaul@elegancetech.com or www.elegancetech.com

C. Zannier et al. (Eds.): XP/Agile Universe 2004, LNCS 3134, p. 209, 2004.
© Springer-Verlag Berlin Heidelberg 2004

Traditional and Agile Project Management:
A Practical Mapping

Mike Griffiths

mikeg@quadrus.com

1 Tutorial Overview

Agile methods often appear to clash with traditional views on project management. During the tutorial, Mike guided the attendees through the practical steps of finding common ground and bridging the common opposing views.

The tutorial started by illustrating how some advocates of agile methods dismiss aspects of traditional project management as fatally flawed and not workable on today's modern software projects. Then the opposing view was explored, citing that many members of the project management community believe agile techniques are based more on speculation and an aversion to process, than established best practices.

The tutorial focused on the problem of this polarization of views and because the adoption of each approach is increasing, how conflicts are set to rise. While there is much publicity around the increased adoption of agile methods, this growth is being exceeded by the uptake of formal project management approaches as outlined by the Project Management Institute. Fueled by organizational pressures to tighten project monitoring and individual goals for project management certification, the growth of formal project management uptake exceeds 20% per annum. With the inevitability of increased interaction between agile and traditional groups, simply dismissing the opposing view as inappropriate becomes more an exercise in burying-your-head-in-the-sand than resolving the real issues arising on today's projects.

The tutorial showed how both traditional project management practices and agile techniques are based on sound management theory. It focused on recognizing the frequent areas of dispute and presented practical steps to link agile techniques to traditional project management.

2 Tutorial Organizer

Mike is a full time project manager and trainer for Quadrus Development Inc and holds PRINCE2 and PMP project management certifications, along with ScrumMaster and DSDM Practitioner agile certifications. Prior to joining to Quadrus, Mike worked for IBM Global Services in the UK, and in 1994 was involved in the creation of DSDM.

Since then, Mike has continued to be active in the agile community and co-authored the DSDM White Paper on "Combining Agile Techniques with Formal Project Management" and parts of DSDM 4.2 manual. He is an Agile Times Newsletter editor and frequent contributor to agile and project management forums.

C. Zannier et al. (Eds.): XP/Agile Universe 2004, LNCS 3134, pp. 210–211, 2004.

Having worked on DSDM, Scrum and XP projects for the last 10 years in various coach and project manager positions Mike draws from a wealth of good, and more valuably, bad project experiences to learn from. This tutorial will bring relief to both coaches struggling to integrate agile with corporate PM standards and project managers looking for order in goal seeking approaches.

The Agile/XP Team Primer:
Exploring Self-organizing Teams

Diana Larsen

1 Tutorial Overview

What does it mean when the gurus say Agile/XP development teams are self-organizing? If a team is truly self-organizing, can we layoff all the managers? How do the roles of team members and managers change when teams are Agile? What can teams and leaders of teams expect when working with Agile/XP teams on the way to self-organization?

In this session managers, team leaders, coaches and team members learned the indicators of team development, how to track a team's progress toward self-organization, how to recognize the signs that their team might be stuck and how to choose strategies to move the Agile/XP team from the impasse into higher productivity, satisfaction and success.

We all have worked on development teams where the behavior of other team members was incomprehensible, the path to effective Agile/XP self-organized teams seemed blocked or vague, or any one of a number of other problems made us feel as though being a part of the team was not worthwhile. Sometimes, we concluded the best answer might be to disband the team and start over.

During the tutorial, presenter and participants shared our stories of challenging teams and challenging situations that face teams and learned strategies and tactics for getting, and keeping, a team on track for continued development toward high performance. We learned ways for managers, coaches and team leaders to intervene with sensitivity and creativity in the team dynamics, so project teams can stay on the path to success.

2 Tutorial Organizer

Diana Larsen is an IXP coach and consultant with Industrial Logic. For more than 10 years, Diana has worked with clients in the software industry to create and maintain company culture and performance, helping to build workplaces that develop and dignify people while achieving business results. As a specialist in the "I" of Industrial XP (www.industrialxp.org), Diana serves as a coach, consultant and facilitator to senior and middle managers, development teams and others. She facilitates processes that support and sustain change initiatives, attain effective team performance and retain organizational learning. Diana is a certified Scrum Master, a frequent speaker at XP conferences and authors articles on XP management and organizational change.

C. Zannier et al. (Eds.): XP/Agile Universe 2004, LNCS 3134, p. 212, 2004.
© Springer-Verlag Berlin Heidelberg 2004

Coaching Agile Software Teams

William C. Wake and Ron Jeffries

{William.Wake,RonJeffries}@acm.org

1 Tutorial Overview

It's difficult to start a new process, but a coach can make this easier. But coaching isn't important only for those with the title "coach"; it's something the whole team can do at various times.

We discussed several aspects of coaching. Coaching can inspire, helping others down a path the coach has already visited. Coaching can act as a mirror, showing a team where it's done well and places where it hasn't lived up to its potential. Coaching can make it safe for people to practice important skills such as test-driven development, refactoring, or asking for help.

One key skill is *observing*. A coach can watch how people work together, and can model and encourage effective teamwork. We practiced through an exercise where people observed pairs folding origami.

The structure of a room affects the way people work together. We analyzed a number of rooms, assessing how well the layout supports key team interactions.

Feedback is also important. Big Visible Charts are one way to provide rich data for a team to think about. We described a number of charts, and worked through an example of their use.

Regular retrospectives also provide feedback. We described a basic "Worked Well/ Do Differently" format and several others.

The class closed with some Q&A time, where we could explore coaching issues of interest to the group.

2 Tutorial Organizers

William C. Wake is an independent software coach, consultant, and teacher. He's the author of the Refactoring Workbook and Extreme Programming Explored, and the inventor of the XP Programmer's Cube. He can be reached at William.Wake@acm. org or www.xp123.com

Ron Jeffries has been developing software since 1961, when he accidentally got a summer job at Strategic Air Command HQ, and they accidentally gave him a FORTRAN manual. He and his teams have built operating systems, language compilers, relational and set-theoretic database systems, manufacturing control, and applications software, producing about a half-billion dollars in revenue, and he wonders why he didn't get any of it. For the past few years he has been learning, applying, and teaching the Extreme Programming discipline. Ron is the author of Adventures in C#, and the senior author of Extreme Programming Installed. Ron is an independent consultant and proprietor of the www.XProgramming.com web site.

C. Zannier et al. (Eds.): XP/Agile Universe 2004, LNCS 3134, p. 213, 2004.
© Springer-Verlag Berlin Heidelberg 2004

Getting the Software You Need: A Practical Approach for Testers and the Customer Team

Lisa Crispin

lisa.crispin@att.net

1 Tutorial Overview

The tutorial brought together testers, business analysts, project managers, business managers and even a few programmers to discuss and practice skills that help an agile team deliver what its customers – the business experts, and/or the actual customers of the business – require.

Participants explored the different roles taken on by members of an agile team, and how each adds value. They discussed potential solutions to missing an important role or skill on the team. For example, what if you don't have a usability expert but application usability is key? Through group exercises, based on creating a hypothetical toy buying guide application, teams formed in the tutorial explored ways to better communicate and define requirements. They looked at ways of flushing out hidden assumptions, demonstrating priorities, and figuring out the actual progress made by the development team.

Acceptance testing was a major subject of the tutorial. The exercises helped to determine when more detail is needed in tests. One tough concept for participants was how to define the minimum success criteria. Exercises helped develop estimation and planning skills for agile projects. The tutorial looked at ways the customer team can improve its technical understanding. One of the most valuable exercises was how the development team can leverage the business domain knowledge of the "customer" team members.

The tutorial ended with a reflective retrospective, looking at how this practice helps the entire agile development team improve its effectiveness each iteration. The tutorial emphasis was on practical skills. Participants felt they had new tools they could take back to their jobs to apply.

2 Tutorial Organizer

Lisa Crispin is the co-author, with Tip House, of Testing Extreme Programming (Addison-Wesley, 2002). She has worked as a tester on agile (and not-so-agile) teams since 2000, using Extreme Programming and Scrum practices. She has more than 10 years experience in the testing and quality assurance area. She has presented tutorials and workshops on agile testing at Agile Development Conference 2003, all three XP/Agile Universe conferences, STAR West, Software Test Automation Conference, Quality Week in both the U.S. and Europe, XP Days in Zurich, and for local quality assurance user groups since 2000. Her articles on agile testing have appeared in publications such as STQE Magazine, Methods and Tools and Novatica. Her papers "Testing in the Fast Lane: Acceptance Test Automation in an Extreme Programming Environment" and "Is Quality Negotiable?" are included in Extreme Programming Perspectives (Addison-Wesley, 2002).

C. Zannier et al. (Eds.): XP/Agile Universe 2004, LNCS 3134, p. 214, 2004.
© Springer-Verlag Berlin Heidelberg 2004

First Encounter with Agile Methods

Frank Maurer and Grigori Melnik

Department of Computer Science, University of Calgary
2500 University Dr. N.W., Calgary, Alberta, T2N 1N4, Canada
{maurer,melnik}@cpsc.ucalgary.ca

Abstract. A fleet of emerging agile methods of software development (with eXtreme Programming and Scrum being the most broadly used) are both gaining popularity and generating lots of controversy. Real-world examples argue for and against agile methods. This tutorial provided an overview of agile methods, their common practices and differences, and also the reasons why they may work with some empirical evidence being presented. In order to better understand some of the practices participants were engaged into a number of interactive exercises.

1 Tutorial Overview

This high level overview tutorial provided the necessary background to understand how agile teams were trying to solve the issues in modern software development with the focus on presenting facts (with perceptions, bias, and market-speak laid aside). A concise history of agile methods was presented. A detailed comparison of agile methods vs. Tayloristic methods was given. This was followed by a brief examination of the main practices of individual methods (including eXtreme Programming, Scrum, Agile Modeling, DSDM, Crystal, FDD, Lean Programming). The facilitators' vision on where agile methods belong on the innovation adoption curve was presented. In order to highlight agile methods strengths and limitations, some existing empirical evidence was presented and analyzed. The participants were engaged in a discussion of the question of what was needed for agile methods to cross the chasm of the innovation adoption curve and move into the mainstream of software development.

Among other topics, the tutorial addressed the issues of knowledge sharing (in agile and Tayloristic teams), project management, and social aspects and implications of agile methods. The facilitators focused on value and people to help software development teams achieve higher velocity and deliver superior value to the customers.

This one-day tutorial included several engaging and thought-provoking exercises that were designed to help the participants better understand agile practices. A number of industry cases (both successes and failures) were also be presented.

Additional information and post-tutorial discussions are available online at http://ebe.cpsc.ucalgary.ca/ebe/Wiki.jsp?page=FirstEncounterWithAgileMethodsTutorial

2 Tutorial Organizers

Frank Maurer is a Professor and an Associate Head of the Department of Computer Science at the University of Calgary. His research interests are agile software meth-

C. Zannier et al. (Eds.): XP/Agile Universe 2004, LNCS 3134, pp. 215–216, 2004.
© Springer-Verlag Berlin Heidelberg 2004

odologies, e-Business software engineering, Web engineering, globally distributed software development, experience and knowledge management. He is a member of Agile Alliance and a Certified Scrum Master. He is also a founding member of The Canadian Agile Network (CAN) - Le Réseau Agile Canadien (RAC) and a founding member of the board of the Calgary Agile Methods User Group. Frank Maurer also was a Program Co-chair for XP Agile Universe 2003, Workshops Chair for XP Agile Universe 2002 and is on the Program Committee of XP Agile Universe 2004. He is also a Member of the Editorial Board of the IEEE Internet Computing magazine.

Grigori Melnik is an Instructor at the University of Calgary and a Lead Instructor at the Southern Alberta Institute of Technology (SAIT) responsible for curriculum development and delivery of several key senior software engineering disciplines. Grigori is a Ph.D. candidate with the Department of Computer Science of University of Calgary. His primary research area is empirical evaluation of capability of agile methods. Other areas include e-business software development, distributed software engineering, design patterns and e-learning. Grigori has also been involved in developing Web-based enterprise systems. More recently he's served as a founding co-moderator of Calgary Agile Methods User Group (CAMUG) and a coordinator of The Canadian Agile Network (CAN) - Le Réseau Agile Canadien (RAC).

Working Effectively with Legacy Code

Michael C. Feathers

mfeathers@objectmentor.com

1 Tutorial Overview

Test Driven Development and Refactoring are powerful tools in the XP/Agile arsenal. With them you can add new code to systems and make existing code more maintainable. However, changing systems without having tests in place can be hazardous. This tutorial presented a collection of dependency breaking and test writing techniques that can be used to get existing code safely under test for refactoring and enhancement. These techniques were used in conjunction with Test Driven Development to breathe new life into large existing code bases. Attendees did all of this and more including:

- Introduction / Testing as a Programmer's tool
- Working with and without Refactoring Tools
- Breaking Dependencies – Sensing and Separation
- Breaking Hidden/Manifest Dependencies
- Java Exercise
- Seam Identification
- UML based exercise
- Writing Characterization Tests
- Java Exercise
- Reasoning about Effects / Identifying Test Points
- Large Method Strategies
- Java Exercise
- Architectural Ramifications

2 Tutorial Organizer

Michael Feathers has been involved in the XP/Agile community since is inception. While designing biomedical instrumentation software in the late 1990s, he met several of the members of the Chrysler C3 team at a conference and was persuaded by them to try XP practices. Subsequently, he joined Object Mentor where he has spent most of his time transitioning teams to XP.

Michael first became interested in legacy code problems when he noticed he was starting to do the same things over and over again to help teams gain traction in their existing code bases when they start to transition to XP. Since then he has concentrated on discovering and refining more techniques to solve these problems.

C. Zannier et al. (Eds.): XP/Agile Universe 2004, LNCS 3134, p. 217, 2004.
© Springer-Verlag Berlin Heidelberg 2004

The Art of Acceptance Testing

Micah Martin

micah@objectmentor.com

1 Tutorial Overview

If you have never worked with Acceptance Tests (AT) before or struggled with them in the past then this tutorial would have been great for you. We covered a range of topics regarding ATs to familiarize everyone with the concept of ATs but most of the time in this tutorial was spent actually writing ATs. Acceptance Testing is not a spectator sport so anyone expecting to sit back and relax in this tutorial was in for quite an awakening. We learned the right way to write ATs; by writing them.

Becoming effective at writing ATs requires two skills. One is knowing the tools and techniques and we touched on these topics. Perhaps more important than the technical aspect is having the Acceptance Testing State of Mind. You should have learn what this means and why it is important.

FitNesse was the medium used to create ATs. All attendees brought a laptop with FitNesse installed. fitnesse.org This required that the Java Runtime Environment 1.4+ was also installed.

After taking this tutorial you were definitely prepared for Advanced FIT Lab by Rick Mugridge.

2 Tutorial Organizer

Micah Martin is a software developer from Object Mentor who has been practicing Extreme Programming since 1999. He has been involved in a variety of XP projects and teaches a range of public courses from Object Oriented Design to Extreme Programming. As lead developer of the FitNesse testing tool, it is his goal to help make Acceptance Testing a more attainable goal for the industry.

C. Zannier et al. (Eds.): XP/Agile Universe 2004, LNCS 3134, p. 218, 2004.
© Springer-Verlag Berlin Heidelberg 2004

Agile Planning, Tracking, and Project Management Boot Camp

Paul Hodgetts

phodgetts@agilelogic.com

1 Tutorial Overview

At the heart of agile processes are the iterative cycles that provide the core rhythm of every project. Effective planning, tracking, and project management strategies and practices form the essential process framework that provides the feedback, learning, and steering that drive the project forward. While much has been written on these topics, there is no substitute for actual experience with the practices.

In this intensive tutorial, attendees gained direct, hands-on experience with the iterative and incremental cycles that drive an agile project. Through carefully designed exercises simulating actual project situations, participants practiced a wide variety of planning, tracking, metric, retrospective, and project management techniques from popular agile processes including XP, Scrum, and DSDM. The attendees gained personal knowledge and insights into the crucial rhythm of an agile project, enabling them to apply these insights to their own project situations.

The exercises, arranged as a series of simulated project iterations, covered a comprehensive range of practices, including:

- Preparing releases and iterations – story development, analysis, breakdowns, and estimating.
- Conducting effective planning sessions – story prioritization, staging releases, velocity projections, task breakdowns and work sign-ups.
- Fine-grained steering using daily stand-up meetings and scrums.
- Evaluating story, iteration, and release completion using acceptance criteria and testing.
- Managing iteration and release milestones, frequent production deployments and release deliverables.
- Tracking and reporting strategies, practices, and tools.
- Using metrics and retrospectives to effectively diagnose a project and initiate evolutionary improvements.

2 Tutorial Overview

Paul Hodgetts helps teams adopt and improve their agile development processes. As CEO and principal consultant of Agile Logic, a professional services company focusing on agile processes and enterprise technologies, he provides consulting, mentoring, and training to a wide variety of clients. Paul has more than 21 years of experience in

C. Zannier et al. (Eds.): XP/Agile Universe 2004, LNCS 3134, pp. 219–220, 2004.
© Springer-Verlag Berlin Heidelberg 2004

all aspects of software development from in-the-trenches coding to technical project management, on a wide variety of projects from embedded real time control to distributed internet business applications. His recent focus has been on the integration of executive management, marketing, project management and quality assurance into an overall agile development process. Paul has served as a coach, mentor, and team member of agile development teams for more than five years. Paul is a published author (Extreme Programming Perspectives), a member of the Extreme Programming and Java/J2EE advisory boards at California State University Fullerton, and a presenter at conferences including XP Agile Universe and JavaOne.

Tutorial:
Agile Project Management – Reliable Innovation

Jim Highsmith

jim@jimhighsmith.com

1 Tutorial Overview

Symyx boasts that their process enables scientists to discover new materials at 100 times the speed and 1% of the cost of traditional research. Drug companies rapidly generate millions of compounds and then test them using ultra-speedy mass spectrometers. Alias Sketchbook Pro a graphics software package was completely planned and developed in two-week iterations.

From materials to drugs to software, companies are relentlessly driving the cost of change out of their product development processes in order foster innovation. These projects are the realm of Agile Project Management (APM) which operates under a philosophy of Envision and Explore rather than Plan and Do.

The APM tutorial focused on quick starts, iterative exploration, delivering customer value, low-cost change, frequent feedback, and intense collaboration. The tutorial discussed projects in which: new, risky technologies are incorporated; requirements are volatile and evolve; time-to-market is critical; and high quality must be maintained.

The APM presentation included core agile principles, a project management framework, and specific practices. The framework phases were: Envision – determining the product vision and project scope; Speculate – developing a feature-based release, milestone, and iteration plan; Explore – delivering tested features; Adapt – reviewing the delivered results and adapting; Close – concluding the project.

2 Tutorial Organizer

Jim Highsmith is Director, Agile Project Management Practice at Cutter Consortium. He is the author of "Agile Project Management: Creating Innovative Products", Addison Wesley 2004; "Adaptive Software Development: A Collaborative Approach to Managing Complex Systems", Dorset House 2000, and, "Agile Software Development Ecosystems", Addison Wesley 2002. Jim is a recognized leader in the agile project management and software development movement. He has published dozens of articles including "The Agile Manifesto," co-authored with Martin Fowler, in the August 2001 issue of Software Development). Jim has worked with organizations worldwide to help them adapt to the accelerated pace of development in increasingly complex, uncertain environments.

C. Zannier et al. (Eds.): XP/Agile Universe 2004, LNCS 3134, p. 221, 2004.
© Springer-Verlag Berlin Heidelberg 2004

XP for a Day

James Grenning and Micah Martin

{grenning,micah}@objectmentor.com

1 Tutorial Overview

The day starts amidst the buzz of attendees hooking their laptops up to their team's network and showing that they have the installed and completed the preparation work. To make XP for a day run smoothly, attendees were required to download an initial exercise and get the green bar from JUnit. Once their unit tests were running, attendees would run the FitNesse acceptance tests and note that one of the test pages for Hunt the Wumpus was reporting an acceptance test error. Prior to the first iteration, attendees made the test failing tests pass marking the beginning of an enjoyable day of XP.

All gathered around the planning table to review the stories for the latest release of Hunt the Wumpus. Teams made a guess at their velocity and an iteration was planned. The teams began work on their deliverables.

There was some chaos as people got to know each other and divide up the work. Programmers were writing unit tests and acceptance tests. The coaches found some non test driven code and had to delete it. That was a popular move. Half way through the first iteration teams had not yet completed half their work. The instructors, with their coach's hats on, suggested the teams talk to their customer and renegotiate the scope. They were all bullish and decided to press on and not bother their customer. "We'll catch up." they said, or "We're 80% done". The room became more animated as the clock ran down. A few that had their work done sat smugly waiting for the final bell. When the iteration ended there were a lot of 85% done stories. Unfortunately, 85% done is 100% not done. The instructors, now with their customer hats in place, were disappointed.

After lunch we reflected on the experience and discussed how the teams should have handled some of the situation encountered.

Our second planning game broadened the scope and looked out a few iterations. This time the team was a bit more realistic and chooses less work. This iteration went more smoothly. The teams already knew better how to work together. One team was finishing early, the other negotiated mid-way through the iteration for less work. Teams proudly delivered almost all their stories with acceptance tests.

After the final iteration we shared success stories and lessons learned.

2 Tutorial Organizers

James Grenning is the Director of Consulting at Object Mentor, Inc. He has been professionally developing software since 1978. His is experienced in embedded and

C. Zannier et al. (Eds.): XP/Agile Universe 2004, LNCS 3134, pp. 222–223, 2004.

non-embedded software development, management, consulting, mentoring and training. He is currently practicing and coaching Agile software development techniques, Extreme Programming, Object Oriented Design and Programming. James has been published in IEEE software and the C++ report. He participated in the creation of the Manifesto for Agile Software Development.

Micah Martin is a software developer from Object Mentor who has been practicing Extreme Programming since 1999. He has been involved in a variety of XP projects and teaches a range of public courses from Object Oriented Design to Extreme Programming. As lead developer of the FitNesse testing tool, it is his goal to help make Acceptance Testing a more attainable goal for the industry.

Scripting Web Tests

Brett Pettichord, Brian Marick, Paul Rogers, and Jonathan Kohl

`bret@pettichord.com, marick@testing.com,`
`paul.rogers@shaw.ca, jkohl@telusplanet.net`

1 Tutorial Overview

Students in this tutorial learned how to write automated customer tests for a web-based application. They used an open-source tool kit to create tests that drive a web browser. Most completed a suite of multiple tests by the conclusion of the tutorial. This hands-on tutorial used open-source software installed on student-provided laptops. Students learned to write these tests using the Ruby scripting language and the Web Testing with Ruby toolkit, available at http://rubyforge.org/projects/wtr/. A timeclock application was used as the target of the tests.

The tool kit consists of a library to make it convenient to access the COM interface to Internet Explorer, including it's document object mode. Similar methods could be used by any language the provides access to COM (which is to say: most languages). Students also made extensive use of the interactive Ruby interface, which facilitates learning and exploration. (Similar interactive features are also part of the Python and Tcl languages.)

The hands-on learning experience allowed students to focus on the issues of greatest personal interest. Many appreciated being able to continue to experiment with and review the class exercises after the completion of the tutorial. The tutorial instructors are contributors to the tool kit and have used it in testing commercial software developed by agile teams.

2 Tutorial Organizers

Bret Pettichord helps teams improve their software testing and test automation. His software testing philosophy is context-driven, focusing on good relations with developers and agile methods that get results with a minimum of overhead. Bret co-authored, with Cem Kaner and James Bach, Lessons Learned in Software Testing, a Jolt Award finalist. He is host and founder of the Austin Workshop on Test Automation. He also writes for Software Testing and Quality Engineering magazine and Stickyminds.com. His ideas about homebrew automation, agile testing and testability have been featured in Application Development Trends and The Rational Edge. Based in Austin, Texas, Bret is principal of Pettichord Consulting LLC, and consults for leading software companies across North America and speaks at conferences world-wide.

Brian Marick is an independent consultant specializing in testing on agile projects (www.testing.com). He is an author of the Manifesto for Agile Software Development and has been a programmer, team lead, and tester since 1981. His evolving approach

C. Zannier et al. (Eds.): XP/Agile Universe 2004, LNCS 3134, pp. 224–225, 2004.
© Springer-Verlag Berlin Heidelberg 2004

to agile testing emphasizes using tests as examples that motivate programmers before the code is written, a close cooperation (and overlap) between testers and programmers, and exploiting the similarities between exploratory testing and agile design. For more about his approach, see his blog; in particular, scan down the right side for "Agile Testing Directions".

Paul Rogers is a professional software tester specializing in test automation in a variety of languages. He uses Ruby extensively as a testing tool in various testing projects, from embedded firmware applications to web applications. He has written a controller in Ruby for testing applications with Internet Explorer, and contributes to the open source WTR project for testing web applications. He is a software tester at Wireless Matrix in Calgary, Alberta.

Jonathan Kohl develops and applies Agile techniques on live testing projects, focusing on workable, effective techniques for tester and developer collaboration. He uses Web Testing with Ruby as an automated testing tool for web application projects. He is a software testing consultant with Kohl Consulting Services in Calgary, Alberta, and has written about pair testing with developers in Better Software magazine.

Interaction Design Meets Agility:
Practicing Usage Centered Design
on Agile Development Projects

Jeff Patton

jpatton@acm.org

1 Tutorial Overview

This tutorial discussed using interaction design techniques, specifically Constantine & Lockwood's Usage-Centered Design, throughout an agile software development process. Tutorial participants learned by participating in a process miniature: a time compressed agile project design and planning session.

After introducing and discussing the business problem, participants divided into teams and began by building a user role model from user roles brainstormed onto 3x5 cards. The role model gives visual representation of the people using the software and their goals. Participants annotated the model describing clusters of user roles, relationships roles have with each other, and marking highest priority, or "focal" roles.

Using the role model as reference, tasks users might perform to meet their goals are easily brainstormed. Using already written task cards, participants constructed and annotated a task model. Annotations on the task model indicate task dependencies, process flow, and focal tasks. Clusters of tasks were annotated to indicate the existence of an interaction context: a distinct place in the software where like-tasks are performed.

Finally, task cards were again used to create a model of the business process from which a release plan is easily derived. The release plan focuses on delivering, as early as possible, the simplest complete working system – a *system span*.

During this tutorial, participants moved a software project from an idea, through design, to an incremental development plan. The tutorial gave further guidelines on using the created models throughout the remainder of the project as well as applying other interaction design techniques during agile style development.

2 Tutorial Organizer

Jeff Patton has, for nearly ten years coached and developed software with top-notch teams on a wide variety of projects from on-line aircraft parts ordering to rules-based pricing engines. He has successfully helped to design, develop, and deploy software now in use by thousands. Although he prides himself in specializing in nothing, Jeff has placed emphasis on the study and practice of OO design and development, agile development methodologies and Extreme Programming, user-interface design, and interaction design.

C. Zannier et al. (Eds.): XP/Agile Universe 2004, LNCS 3134, p. 226, 2004.
© Springer-Verlag Berlin Heidelberg 2004

Agile Implementations, Agile Impediments, and Agile Management

Ken Schwaber

ken.schwaber@verizon.net

1 Tutorial Overview

We can read about Agile processes in books and articles. However, the management of projects using an Agile process represents a significant shift for both the project team and the organization as a whole. The shift internal to the team occurs as the project manager teaches the customer how to drive the project iteration by iteration to maximize ROI. The other internal shift as the team realizes that self-management means exactly that - the team has to figure out how to manage its own work cross-functionally. Even more difficult is helping the team and organization overcome the bad habits they had acquired prior to implementing the agile process - waterfall thinking, command-and-control management, and abusive, opaque relationships.

I wanted for attendees of this session was how to:

- Understand the Agile approach to managing projects and products, including
- complex, mission critical, large projects
- Bid and contract for systems development work in a fixed price, fixed date
- environment using Agile project management processes;
- Use Extreme Programming wrapped by Scrum to scale to multi-team projects or enterprise wide-implementation for multiple projects;
- Solve the customer involvement problem by having customer drive the project to maximize ROI;
- Solve the morale issue within engineering organizations by letting them, the
- people who do the work, manage themselves while they work cross-
- functionally;
- Solve issue of product quality incrementally;
- Generate more frequent and focused product releases;
- Enjoy developing software.

2 Tutorial Organizer

Ken Schwaber will teach the course. He is one of developers of Scrum and has formalized it into an Agile process. He implemented and used Scrum extensively to help projects succeed and organizations compete over the last ten years, from small to large, from software products to networking products, from commercial to internal software projects. He employs Scrum for project management practices and Extreme Programming for engineering practices. He is active in the AgileAlliance. He can be reached at ken.schwaber@verizon.net. The Scrum web site maintained by his company is at www.controlchaos.com. He is currently co-Chairman of the Board of the Agile Alliance.

C. Zannier et al. (Eds.): XP/Agile Universe 2004, LNCS 3134, p. 227, 2004.
© Springer-Verlag Berlin Heidelberg 2004

The Lean Maturity Measure Assessment and Implementation

Mary Poppendieck

mary@poppendieck.com

1 Tutorial Overview

This tutorial started out by proposing a new measurement for gauging the maturity of a software organization: the average cycle time from customer request to filling that request. This measurement was supported by examples from many industries, and then a discussion ensued about when, exactly, the measurement should start, when it should stop. Whenever the start and stop point are, it is important that the measurement encourage rapid, repeatable, reliable delivery of real customer value.

The tutorial went on to present assessment techniques for the current state of a software development organization. The first assessment tool was a map of current value stream and the current decision-making process in an organization. The second assessment tool was an evaluation of disciplines such as coding standards, code control, build processes, automated testing, etc. Groups were formed, and each group worked on the assessments.

A final assessment tool was used to evaluate team membership and representation of various functions on typical software development teams. Various approaches to team composition and leadership were discussed in the groups.

The tutorial went on to present the idea of a Kaizen event, which is frequently used in lean manufacturing. It discussed how such an event could be modified to address software development problems at the organizational level. Groups developed a list of "do's" and "don'ts" for Kaizen events.

2 Tutorial Organizers

Mary Poppendieck, a Cutter Consortium Consultant and Managing Director of the Agile Alliance, is a seasoned leader in both operations and new product development with more than 25 years' of IT experience. She has led teams implementing solutions ranging from enterprise supply chain management to digital media, and built one of 3M's first Just-in-Time lean production systems. Mary is the President of Poppendieck LLC. And co-author of the book Lean Software Development: An Agile Toolkit, which brings lean production techniques to software development.

C. Zannier et al. (Eds.): XP/Agile Universe 2004, LNCS 3134, p. 228, 2004.
© Springer-Verlag Berlin Heidelberg 2004

Agile Databases

Pramod Sadalage

pramod@thoughtworks.net

1 Tutorial Overview

The past few years we have seen the rise of agile methodologies. One of the most important aspects of agile methodologies is iterative design. Many people have questioned whether iterative design can be applied to applications with a large database component, it is always considered that application developers can work in iterative fashion while database design cannot be done in iterative fashion, hence the database is the bottleneck for the team and the database cannot be agile.

At ThoughtWorks we have developed a number of techniques to integrate the database world into the application world and provide a seamless way for developers, QA, analysts, client and dba's to work in an iterative fashion so that the team can be more productive. These techniques include making database part of the Continuous Integration cycle, allowing everyone to have their own database. Deploying any build anywhere anytime, having automated tests for the database, make db build an ANT task, using code generation etc.

These techniques not only worked during development, but also helped us to deploy into existing production systems with automated migration effort. For years the norm for object developers was to work in an evolutionary manner but for database developers to work in a more serial manner, now the two groups can work in the same manner and thus be more productive as a team.

2 Tutorial Organizer

Pramod Sadalage works as a Data Architect and Lead DBA at ThoughtWorks, Inc, a leading custom e-business application and platform development firm. He works on large J2EE custom dev applications, which use XP, an agile methodology that has not been sufficiently discussed in the context of databases. While on these projects, he pioneered the practices and processes of Agility in the database.

C. Zannier et al. (Eds.): XP/Agile Universe 2004, LNCS 3134, p. 229, 2004.
© Springer-Verlag Berlin Heidelberg 2004

Transitioning to XP

Michael Hill

uly@mindspring.com

1 Tutorial Overview

The primary target in this session was the transitioner, those folks from management and/or development who have been anticipating the challenge of bringing their teams into eXtreme Programming. If you are/were currently seeking to be a catalyst for change in your group, then you were ready for this tutorial.

Here's a recap of the activities that took place:

- Basic Transition Concepts
    - Transition is Flipping The Cube
    - Who is a transitioner?
    - Where are we going?
- II. Preparing For Transition
    - Closing The XP Sale
    - Rigging The Environment
    - Preparing The People
- III. Surviving the Chaos of Transition
    - How Far Have We Come?
    - Mastering The Cooperation Challenge
    - Mastering The Technical Challenge
- IV. Imperfect Worlds
    - Sneaking XP under the Door
    - Working w/Heavy-Process Partners
    - Partial Adoptions That Really Work
    - Verticalizing Requirements Documents
- V. Open Season On XP Transitions

The final hour of this session was devoted to the questions and answers that the attendees offered. Real challenges from real teams was the order of the day.

2 Tutorial Organizer

Michael Hill has been transitioning teams to XP for six years, against a background of twenty+ years as an independent contractor. He has worked with dozens of different projects and platforms. He is presently at work on a book on Transitioning to XP.

C. Zannier et al. (Eds.): XP/Agile Universe 2004, LNCS 3134, p. 230, 2004.
© Springer-Verlag Berlin Heidelberg 2004

Large Scale Agile Software Development

Ron Crocker

ron@roncrocker.com

1 Tutorial Overview

All of this XP and Agile Methods hype is wonderful, but how can people who work on large-scale projects (where large-scale means projects are those with more than 100 people and are longer than 1 year duration) take advantage of the benefits in quality, efficiency, and time promised by the hype? That question was answered in this tutorial. We had the chance to discuss a proven approach enabling agile collaboration among teams on large projects. This tutorial covered:

- Why large projects ARE indeed different
- Why existing agile methods (XP, Scrum, ...) are insufficient to deal with large projects
- A set of agile practices enabling agile multi-team collaboration
- My experiences using the practices

The ideal attendee was the practitioner, a software or process engineer in development leadership role or with influence on such a person. They were familiar with developing large systems and the attendant difficulties.

The goals were to:

- Convince you that agile practices can apply to large-scale software projects.
- Describe a set of practices that allow large-scale software projects to be agile.
- Enable you to convince your management and peers that agile can work for these projects, using my experiences and the materials from this presentation.

2 Tutorial Organizer

Ron Crocker is a Fellow of the Technical Staff in the Network and Advanced Technologies group of Motorola's Global Telecom Solutions Sector, where he has pioneered the application of advanced software technologies and processes in the development of next-generation cellular telecommunications systems. Ron was the lead architect and developerof a 3rd generation cellular system implementation, developed using >150 engineers from >5 countries, all done in an agile way and achieving outstanding results. He is the author of the forthcoming Addison-Wesley book Large-Scale Agile Software Development, which may be available by the conference. This presentation forms the basis for the book, and serves as a guide for convincing the skeptical that wonderful successes can occur in large-scale projects.

C. Zannier et al. (Eds.): XP/Agile Universe 2004, LNCS 3134, p. 231, 2004.
© Springer-Verlag Berlin Heidelberg 2004

Refactoring to Patterns

Joshua Kerievsky

Joshua@industriallogic.com

1 Tutorial Overview

This tutorial, which has been steadily maturing at conferences since 2000, examined how to combine the art of refactoring with the practice of designing with patterns. Attendees learned how to do pattern-based refactoring by combining low-level refactorings. They also learned which code smells indicate the need for pattern-based refactorings, which patterns are commonly refactored to, towards or away from, and how automated tools help us refactor. The tutorial concluded with an overview of the 27 refactorings from the book, Refactoring to Patterns.

What I wanted for attendees was the following:

- Understand how refactoring and patterns go together
- Learn when to refactor to, towards or away from a pattern
- Learn how to combine low-level refactorings into higher-level refactorings
- Study the smells that often indicate the need for a pattern-based refactoring

Here are some of the goals that were met:

- The principles and practices of patterns-based refactoring
- Common smells that suggest patterns-based refactorings
- When we refactor to, towards or away from patterns
- Examination of several real-world pattern-based refactorings
- How automated tools help us refactor

This session was intended for the experienced object-oriented developers. Some experience with refactoring, patterns and test-driven development was encouraged. Examples were in Java.

2 Tutorial Organizer

Joshua Kerievsky is the founder of Industrial Logic, a company that specializes in Extreme Programming. He began his career as a professional programmer at a Wall Street bank, where he programmed numerous financial systems for credit, market, and global risk departments. After a decade at the bank, he founded Industrial Logic in 1995 to help companies practice successful software development. Kerievsky has programmed and coached on small, large, and distributed XP projects since XP's emergence. He recently pioneered Industrial XP, an application of XP tailored for large organizations. Kerievsky has written XP articles in Extreme Programming Examined and Extreme Programming Perspectives, and has recently authored the book Refactoring to Patterns.

C. Zannier et al. (Eds.): XP/Agile Universe 2004, LNCS 3134, p. 232, 2004.
© Springer-Verlag Berlin Heidelberg 2004

Author Index

Lecture Notes in Computer Science

For information about Vols. 1–3053

please contact your bookseller or Springer-Verlag